From Russia with Hope

Russian Women's Journeys to the West

By

Elizabeth Stewart

To Angus, who always believed in this project, and Amy, Berenice, Daniel, Jonathan, Marcus and Zara who kept up the pressure to publish these stories

Table of Contents

Preface

The initial impetus for this book came directly out of a Russian journey. A few years ago I joined a group of students who were visiting St Petersburg and Moscow for the first time. I wanted to 'see' Russia through their eyes and to learn what insights they had into this - to them unknown - culture.

The highlight of the trip took place in St Petersburg where the group attended four or five days of lectures given by academics and other important figures including a trade unionist and a politician. What particularly impressed me were the lectures given by women, women whose lives had been and continued to be affected by the changes which occurred in and stemmed from the demise of the Soviet Union in 1991. The women were strikingly more open than their male colleagues about both their own lives and the lives of their children. One woman in particular talked about the changes in perception of both her own society and the West brought about through travel.

Upon returning to the UK I began to formulate a book which would focus on the life experiences of Russian women, pre- and post-1991. Here I must emphasize why Russian *women*. The majority of media coverage about Russians is about men, whether as media moguls (Lebedev), football team owners (Abramovich), or so-called 'oligarchs' (Berezovsky). Even where women are discussed, the focus is overwhelmingly on a certain restricted world. We can learn much about the wives of oligarchs (or those whose husbands will allow such coverage), the very rich women who come to the UK to stock up on luxury goods, various ways of dating Russian women or the Russian women who are earning great sums as models (such as Natalia Vodianova). The lives of 'ordinary' women are seldom discussed.*

In developing a project of this kind, I focused on two questions: what do I want to find out and how will I present my findings? I considered a variety of possible ways of organising and presenting the interviews which were to form the basis of the project. My decision was to focus on Russian women who for a number of different reasons had emigrated to the United

Kingdom. Within that framework, the most promising strategy was to identify women of different ages whose formative experiences within Russia might be expected to offer some points of comparison. As far back as the earliest years of Bolshevik rule in Russia, the specific situation of women -- the 'woman question' (as it was universally called) -- had been the focus of heated debate, debate which continued up until the collapse of the Soviet Union. With that collapse, two questions arose: What had been the realities of women's lives in the final years of Soviet rule? And how was the collapse of the Soviet regime reflected in any changes in their lives and attitudes?

All of the interviews are in two parts, the first part about life experiences in the Soviet Union and Russia, and the second about their lives as immigrants in the UK. The intention is to let each woman speak for herself so that her individual voice can be heard rather than being interpreted. It is vital to listen closely to how each woman describes her own life and her own experiences, in her own words. The life-stories are from both Russia and the UK, allowing the women to tell their own experiences of childhood, of childbirth and abortion, of religion and marriage, of hopes fulfilled and dashed, of the longing for one home and the creation of another. What they do in effect is to describe the first and second acts of their lives.

Their stories are those of women who grew up in one country and for one reason or another left that country and came to settle in Britain. Some came alone; some came with partners; some came willingly; some less so. All but one are still here, some happily, some not so enthusiastically. The country some of them left years ago is no longer the same country today. For some, that is a bonus; others, however, do mourn some aspects of life in the former Soviet Union. What they share in common is the fact that they originate from that landmass that is currently Russia. And they share the processes they all went -- or are going -- through, that of being an immigrant in Britain.

There are some omissions to this study. Russian women living here who don't speak English are not included. I did attempt to interview some trafficked women but my contacts assured me that that particular path would not be encouraged, could be dangerous and would possibly distort the intended focus of the book. It is true that this study is biased towards educated Russian women, but it must be remembered that they came from a country which deeply values education. These women are also fairly established in their familial relationships. Many are currently married; many are second or even third wives; some are divorced. Most are pretty settled in this respect.

Adapting in different ways to their changed circumstances, these women's stories stand as vital keys to a more general immigrant experience in the twentieth and twenty-first centuries. The book examines issues that dominate the social landscape of the UK and the world and will do for generations to come. The insights into these women's lives address the gap in our understanding of the lives of Russian women, while at the same time cast light on the deep seated realities of a nation whose character and place in the global order is very much in flux.

This book presents a community of immigrants at a time of ever-increasing global movements of people. The question facing societies such as the UK over how to integrate and respect these groups cannot be answered while the lives of the immigrants themselves remain so little understood. Some of the women answer questions as to what immigrants seek in coming to these shores as well as indicate which values in British society are indeed prized. These stories represent inspiring tales of twenty-one amazing women who, in sharing their past, their feelings, their thoughts, their families and their laughter, challenge us to understand the immigrant experience of this century and beyond.

I am very grateful to these women who have shared their lives with me. I thank them for their time, their honesty and their thoughtfulness, answering some very difficult, let alone, personal questions.

* Another important impetus for this project came from a book published in 1983 entitled *Moscow Women: Thirteen Interviews* by Carola Hansson and Karin Liden. The authors went incognito to Moscow to attempt to learn

how Russian women were dealing with the specific problems they faced as women in the USSR.

A Word on Method

The participants took part in the knowledge that the interviews would be published. The twenty-one women were chosen on the basis of a 'snow ball' technique. The assumption behind snow ball research is that an interviewee recommends another interviewee who subsequently agrees to be interviewed. This doesn't mean that everyone knew everyone else. In fact, there were several small 'snow balls' which grew and grew. Everyone was offered the ability to remain anonymous. While only three did not , all the names (with the exception of the mother and daughter interviewees) have been changed and any really significant information which might identify anyone has also been altered, e.g., husband's name or children's names changed, some schools not identified, actual homes not specified, etc.

All of the interviews were recorded and saved so that they could each be transcribed verbatim. This was done through the combined efforts of my secretary, Tia Exelby, and myself. In any event, the tapes were listened to many, many times. Every effort has been made to accurately transcribe each and every tape. The only omissions are the banter between interviewee and myself, the humour expressed in a variety of ways, and my sharing of my own personal history as an immigrant to this country.

After transcription, I attempted to 'transform' each interviewee's participation into recognizable English. This process inevitably somewhat diminished the idiosyncrasies and nuances of the spoken language as well as omitting some of the characteristics common to those speaking English (e.g., the almost universal misuse of the verbs 'to go' and 'to come'). While one of the prerequisites for the book was that the interviewee must speak English, there was a *very wide difference* in the women's spoken English. As one would expect, on the whole those women who came to this country in the 1960s, 1970s and 1980s spoke somewhat better English than some who came later; however, this is not a hard and fast rule. In fact the

9

younger women, those in their thirties, spoke very well. The role that the English language has played in all of these women's lives is vital, as the texts reveal. (The parallels with the experience of successive waves of immigrants are obvious.)

I have divided and grouped the texts by age and have introduced each of the four sections with some notes about the women in each age group. The youngest women who came to this country, namely the women in their thirties, arrived in the 1990s and 2000s. Six of the seven women in their forties came to the UK in the 1990s, some of whom came before the demise of the Soviet Union. Only one woman in this age group came in 2000. Almost all of the women in their fifties came during the perestroika period, roughly since 1988. One woman in this age group left the USSR in 1975 when she married a British man. Three women in their sixties and seventies left in the late 1950s and 1960s, whereas two arrived in 2000 and 2001.

Each age group -- no matter when they came to the UK -- shares certain characteristics in common. For example, they experienced their respective childhoods in roughly the same time period and had similar as well as distinct experiences living in the Soviet context. The oldest group also lived under Stalin and Khrushchev, whereas the youngest remember times just before Gorbachev. Their experiences here were somewhat coloured by when they actually arrived in Britain and under what circumstances they left their native land. As is evident from the interviews, they all adapted in different ways. Their observations about their childhoods, their experiences in Russia, childbirth, husbands, role of women, religion, etc., as well as their views about life in Britain then and today make fascinating reading. To really understand each woman -- as well as to form a general view of their collective experience -- both parts of the interviews must be seen as forming a collective whole.

Points of Departure

We live in a world on the move. Whether fleeing persecution, seeking economic improvement or just expressing an age-old wanderlust, thousands (indeed millions) of people make up the statistics of vast population movements. But these statistics are made up of ordinary - and sometimes extraordinary - women and men. This book contains the personal accounts of twenty one such migrants. In fact, its central purpose is to record their experiences which should be seen as representative first of the many other women who have followed the same path and secondly of the many millions who have had to and continue to move from one society to another.

Such experiences are of course significantly moulded by the contexts in which they occur. Russia and the UK, the points of departure and arrival for the twenty one women, have undergone enormous social change in recent decades. The following chapters show a range of responses to the changing social landscape of Russia as it moved from the Soviet to the contemporary era. Within that diversity, however, one can identify a variety of topics which illuminate what life was like during the Soviet period and its immediate aftermath. While we can think of these responses as a map of prominent aspects of Soviet life as experienced by women, no two travellers are exactly the same. Experiences differ according to age, locale, social status or other factors; in the case of these women, Communist Party membership - or not - emerges as a key issue. The main purpose of this first chapter is to offer a guide to what to look out for as we travel with the twenty one.

Timing

The first question all the women were asked was *When did you leave Russia?* The question of timing is highly significant as it determined different experiences of living in Russia as well as influencing how each woman was able to leave. In the 1960s and 1970s, for example, the women who emigrated did so mainly by (unacceptably) marrying 'foreigners'. These women mostly went through very hard times in order to be able to leave the country. They were followed by the KGB (the security services) and sometimes deprived of livelihood and chosen jobs, with knock-on effects on wider families and their respective jobs. For this group also, the subsequent journeys were frequently highly tortuous with one woman, for example, going first to Poland with her parents and her brother before emigrating to Israel, then to Germany, finally coming alone to the UK.

Things were more straightforward for the women who came during the perestroika period in the late 1980s. They accompanied husbands who had been posted to London, usually as international civil servants. The expectation was that they would return home after the posting but with the demise of the Soviet Union, they remained in London. In contrast, those who left post 1991 often arrived in order to better their lives, some because their husbands found jobs required in British businesses, some for research and development, some on exchanges, or some just wanted to leave Russia having experienced great hardships in the 1990s. Two of the youngest women came to further their education, while one came to seek employment and hopefully remain to study, thus continuing the trend over time from 'freedom seekers' to economic migrants.

Family

Over many centuries, for all migrants the decision to move has been not merely individual but more broadly familial. For each of the women here their decision to leave Russia has to be seen against the background of generational history, of parental and grandparental struggle and achievement. Points of departure concern not only country but also kin and so we learn of parental backgrounds, where parents spent their respective childhoods, their education and occupations, their current ages and where they live if they are still alive.

One link between the individual families of the twenty one and larger social forces is expressed in the absence of any large families of origin. Just over a third of the women, eight actually, were only children. Ten had only one sibling, one had two brothers while the two remaining women were in families with step children. These personal realities vividly express a matter which was a constant source of concern for Soviet demographers and planners: a declining birth rate, the nadir of which occurred in the 1960s. [In fact they hardly reached the 2.4 children mark!]

Almost all the women had fascinating stories to tell of one or other of their grandparents, most of whom were remembered with a great deal of affection. Many of the women either spent their childhoods with grandparents who were living in communal flats with their parents, or spent their summers with their grandparents at the *dacha* [summer cottage]. In some cases grandmothers effectively raised them while their parent(s) were working in some distant part of the USSR or even in the same city. Thus 'family' for many of my interviewees often consisted of grandparents, especially grandmother [the *babushka*], parents and children, a reality which makes these families similar to all others in Russia. In a commonplace if not nearly universal expression of the difficult movement between a more traditional and a more modern society, many of the women continue to miss the intimate connection they had with their grandparents and regret that their children are being denied that cherished relationship of child and grandparent.

The history of Russia in the twentieth century is one of enormous human loss and, in a way typical of migrants from many countries, many of the women carry memories of family loss. Several told of how their grandparents dealt with World War II or, more precisely, how World War II dealt with them. Vera and Kira lost their respective grandparents, all of whom perished during and due to the war. Others tell of the death of their grandfathers while fighting in the war. Galina discusses how the capture of her grandfather for one week determined the rest of his life. Some were evacuated from the cities they lived in to other places more remote from the war, e.g. from Leningrad to Kazakhstan and Uzbekistan. The realities of Russian suffering are brought alive in Helena's chilling discussion about how her father and her grandmother were on the last boat to leave Leningrad before Lake Lagoda froze over, leaving her grandfather in Leningrad to be a victim of the siege of Leningrad, resulting in his death by starvation.

The not so Wonder Years: teenage experiences, interests and living conditions

Whatever the freedoms and constraints of a particular culture – ethnic, national, political –the physiological and psychological changes involved in adolescence are universal. Memories of this life phase are doubly revealing of individuals and societies. This is no less true of the twenty one than of any other group. Capturing a time of great change, the reality of which is nevertheless only retrospectively clear to them and us, the oldest women remember times in the 1950s, both prior to Stalin's death in 1953 and during Khrushchev's subsequent more lenient thaw. The difference between lived experience and an informed judgement upon individuals and events is evidenced in Vera's recollection of crying when she heard that Stalin had died. Perhaps even more revealingly, in a mirror image of a generation's fears in the West, she shares her anxiety that America was going to attack the Soviet Union 'because we were completely without any information, absolutely like a planet completely isolated from the rest of the world.' But in the mix of humanity, where there is isolation and consequent fear, there is also curiosity and ambition. So, Nadia in Kiev listened to Voice of America and the BBC, especially to the cultural programmes like the latter's jazz programme while Anna listened to Voice of America and the BBC, thinking they were part of her education, part of her language learning as an interpreter and translator (from Russian to English).

Demonstrating both human resilience and the everyday reality of developing lives in a society seen from outside as simply abnormal and suffused in terror, many of the women emphasise the importance to them of cultural interests and activities. Some discuss how difficult it was to get tickets to different cultural events. Others, like Maya, indicate a reality that will be instantly recognisable to young night-clubbers throughout the Western world. Being young and pretty, 'we never had trouble getting spare tickets.' Masha in Leningrad indicated that tickets (to theatre, ballet, concerts) were very cheap and readily accessible. 'I went almost every weekend.' Instead of culture or complementing it, there was sport. Yevgenia did lots of sport, including figure skating ('very Russian!' she

14

exclaims), but had a concussion so had to stop. Larissa did sport throughout her school years. Others were interested in art, especially Helena and Marina (an artist herself who married an artist), and many, if not most, in reading books.Victoria's lengthy discussion underscores the point that she doesn't think people in the West 'realize how rich the cultural life was in the Soviet Union and how much we read.' Highlighting the destructive role frequently played by uninformed fantasies about apparently alien societies, Victoria relates this judgment to her view that the West had no idea how they really lived.

Moving On – or not? Ceilings, glass or otherwise

Like women in all societies, the twenty one encountered various obstacles in their journey to desired and necessary qualifications. How one got into a specific university is indicative of many aspects of Soviet society, both positive and negative. On the positive side, acceptance to a university was supposed to be by exam results, results which were stringent in the case of the very best universities such as Moscow or Leningrad. Many of the interviewees did have such high qualifications. Some, however, compared their required degree of preparedness to that of boys, indicating that girls had to be better prepared (Galina) and implicitly saying that boys had 'preferential treatment'.

Apart from such gender considerations, a different obstacle concerned *blat*. The Russian word *blat* means 'fixing; string-pulling; influence; contact, etc.. .', [1] or use of personal networks for obtaining goods and services in short supply and for circumventing formal procedures.[2] By means of *blat*, some of the women were able to attend universities or courses that perhaps they wouldn't have been able to so do otherwise. This doesn't mean that they were any less qualified, but simply that admission depended on *blat*, was arranged by *blat* or was helped by *blat*. One

---

[1] R.E.F. Smith, (1962) *A Russian-English Dictionary of Social Science Terms*. London: Butterworths, p. 39.
[2] A.V. Ledeneva (2006) *How Russia Really Works: The Informal Practices that Shaped post-Soviet Politics and Business*. Ithaca, New York: Cornell Press, p. 1 etc..

respondent noted that she was told not to apply to a specific university 'unless you have friends in very high places', which some of the respondents did have.

Another obstacle was that of anti-Semitism. In the case of university entrance, several of the women 'knew' that they would be unable to attend -- or even to apply to -- some universities either because places were allocated in such a way that only one or two Jewish women could/would be accepted or because any application was worthless. Their knowledge concerning this shaped not only where they eventually applied but also what careers they chose.

Rushing toward the Tender Trap

Russian women generally marry at an early age and the twenty one certainly followed this path. Almost all of the first marriages took place when the women were between the ages of twenty (four) and twenty four (two women), with age twenty two having the greatest number (six). Irina states that 'lots of other girls started getting married in year three when they were nineteen or twenty, so at age twenty two I was quite old!' Victoria explains this as follows: 'At that time an unmarried woman at twenty five would be considered a spinster, so you had to kind of rush into marriage and make sure that you have a husband and kids by the time you are twenty five.' This situation holds true today as thirty one year old Yevgenia, the only respondent not as yet to have married, explains, 'Overall people get married younger in Moscow and start families younger; it's not normal if you don't get married! If you're not married by the age of thirty, there's something wrong. If you're divorced with a child, that's fine.' Another reason for early marriage in Soviet times was the very real fear of being separated. Upon graduating from university, many young people were supposed to be sent throughout the country for a two, sometimes three, year placement and, as often as not, couples would or could be separated; but not if they were married.

Terra incognita or 'don't ask what's south of the border': Sex, sex education and birth control

One thing that was largely shared across the different generations represented in the twenty one was a lack of youthful knowledge about sex. In response to a question regarding their learning anything about sex from their mothers, the answers were a resounding no!. With one or two exceptions (usually the younger women and those whose mothers were in the medical profession), none of the Russian mothers shared any of their knowledge of sex with their daughters. This lack even and often included explanations about periods or puberty (Vera). While there were exceptions, even these involve very real limits. Nadia, for example, agrees that with her mother it was mainly 'a hygienic education' as well as a discussion of the consequences of sexual activity. Masha (in her fifties) indicates that talking about sex wasn't appropriate because 'it wasn't considered intellectual enough, a low subject which wasn't worth discussing.' Nor did the school system provide any sex education classes or any answers on the subject.

So how did they learn about sex? They said that either they had a sister or most often their girlfriends or classmates told them. One woman answered that she learned 'Naturally!' while another spoke about 'natural curiosity.' One or two mothers employed tactics in a more indirect way. Helena was told by her mother not to read the English novels she had placed in Helena's room until she got married, so of course Helena read them immediately (a wise mother?). Other women described how they learned some facts about sex by reading Western literature (Liza), whereas Maya also learned from books 'but Russian literature was never that explicit nor was the foreign literature.' Anna's husband took her to the public library where they read books together.

Where age did emerge as an important factor was in the matter of contraception. Some of the oldest women talk about contraceptives as being 'an absolute taboo', describing the condom as being very badly designed and of poor quality. The Russian word for condoms was 'galoshes' because the rubber was thick and they didn't fit very well. The later generation was more familiar with condoms, although some still expressed the view that in Soviet times contraception was a dirty subject. Obtaining contraceptives seems to have depended on where you lived and your background. For some, contraceptives were readily available by making an appointment with a doctor. Others were too shy to go to a shop to buy condoms because they weren't married, some of whom no doubt followed the practice of another of the women who speaks of using the calendar as her only contraceptive. Generally the pill was not popular for women in their forties xx(even 50s???) because it was considered to interfere with hormones and to be harmful to the body. The coil and the diaphragm were available for some, but again you had to be married. The youngest women have had no such problems obtaining a variety of contraceptives, many free of charge as well as those being able to be purchased.

Consequences: Abortion as a contraceptive

Any discussion of contraception in Soviet times necessarily leads to a discussion of abortion. For a large part of the female population, abortions were the common form of contraception. Before 1955, abortions were illegal and typically the consequences from these operations were such that afterwards women either couldn't have children or they themselves died. With the decline in the population, abortions were legalized in 1955 on the dual grounds that many more women would subsequently be able to have children and more women were needed in order to have children.

In the 1970's, something like 7 million abortions a year were performed in the Soviet Union so obviously the operation wasn't something unusual. Multiple abortions were common, often as a means of controlling when to get pregnant. In some cases the women (and their husbands) were definitely limiting their family size due to economic circumstances. If some of the twenty one did not themselves have an abortion, they certainly knew of girls or women who did. Stories were often told to frighten girls into not having sex altogether, as sex led to abortions. One interviewee indicates that one mother put her daughter through an abortion without any anesthetic to teach her to never have sex.

Many of the twenty one who had actually had abortions said the word 'horrendous' (frequently used in Western commentaries) should be changed to 'barbaric'. The main problem was lack of any form of anesthetic. But there was also a subjective element involved which concerned the staff who performed the operations. Some of the women in charge were described as 'very dominating and negative'. The ethos was one in which 'they had to subjugate you,' an attitude characteristic of a medical environment in which you had to be obedient and go by their word. There was an additional judgmental attitude summed up by Anna: 'it was very unpleasant because they looked at you as if you were dirt, as an offender.'

As with education, the possibility of getting an abortion depended on where you lived, who you knew and/or your ability to pay for care. Once again, *blat* was important but seems to have played an additional role here, determining not only access but also quality of treatment. Those who could pay or knew someone went to better hospitals, better clinics and had better treatment. The most important variable, however, was whether or not any form of anesthetic was available. With *blat*, women would be taken care of. Thus, Larissa says: 'I knew I would be given an anesthetic or something like that, so it was not as scary and I was hoping that I wouldn't feel anything. I didn't feel anything but [even with this *blat* derived support] the whole scenario and the whole attitude of the doctors and this kind of conveyer belt industry (which

it was) were still very horrific and it was very traumatizing nonetheless.' The disturbing image of a conveyor belt reoccurs.

As to the consequences of an abortion, responses among the twenty one are mixed. Some described the emotional shock as incomparably greater than the physical difficulties they went through but others took the abortion in their stride as a means of controlling the presence or absence of offspring at a specific time in their lives. The consequences could be practically and therefore emotionally disastrous. For one woman, her second abortion proved to be the one that 'ruined my life'. As it turned out, her tubes were 'blocked' with the result that when she wanted children in a second marriage, this was impossible.

Giving birth

Although the realities of life in Soviet Russia meant that fear of pregnancy was a pervasive aspect of the lives of many of the twenty one, others, when married, accepted the pregnancies when they happened. But as with abortions, giving birth often depended on *blat*, on knowing the right person, on payment. Those who came from families who had connections via their occupations or their membership in the Communist Party had a much easier time, whereas those in more public hospitals could have a rougher time. These realities emerge graphically in the twenty one in the contrast between Galina's story at a very specific Moscow clinic (thanks to her father being in the *nomenklatura* – a list of appointments reserved for the Communist Party) and Liza's story of barely reaching the public hospital when, after the birth, she was told that 'they couldn't be expected to assist babies around the clock' (as the baby was born in the lunch hour!)

In many of the maternity units, up to fifteen women in one large room would be giving birth at the same time. What they also shared in common, however, was the Russian practice whereby husbands were not allowed to participate at the birth of their children. In fact, many of the fathers (who weren't even allowed into the hospitals) only saw their children when the child was held up to a window, the father standing somewhere in the grounds of the hospital; the maternity floor could be anywhere from the third floor upwards, so the first viewing of the progeny wouldn't have been spectacular!

As described above, many of the women originally lived with either parents or in-laws. When their child was born, the grandparents were then involved with the newest member of the extended family, helping in a wide variety of ways. Many of these grandparents were themselves employed but most seemed especially to help their daughters with childcare. For some of the women the help was very welcome, but others were very interested in trying to find living accommodation separate from their parents.

A Familiar Story? Gender issues and Equality

When asked if there were any problems specific to women, the twenty one spoke about several areas that concerned them. Two of the oldest discussed difficulties in getting jobs, saying that factories preferred male workers. Vera specifically notes that 'women in Russia were treated like dirt' and did awful or menial jobs, especially hard physical work. At the other end of the age scale, Irina says that employers think twice about employing women because they assume they will get married, get pregnant, have children, take sick leave, etc.. Helena describes how she has only been able to pursue her career as a interpreter/translator outside of the country, her specific job being closed to women in the Soviet Union

All the women share the view that rising to the top of a profession and promotion within a profession are more difficult for Russian women than for Russian men, a proposition supported by Western research. Some of the women do argue that there is no discrimination in the workplace, but more suggest that Russia is a very male dominated society. Nadezhda speaks about the lack of equality in her job as she and her husband were equally qualified but he earned more and unlike her, was immediately offered a flat. [Soviet statistics indicate that Soviet women at that time were paid about 70% of what men were paid.] Natalia suggests that the mentality of the society is against women, or as she puts it, it is like an 'Asian society where the man is everything and the women follow'. Irina (in her thirties) phrases it differently: 'I think men probably think they have more advantages just because they are men.'

Of course there is another approach to this. Several women expressed the view that there were no problems specific to women because in their view that '... was just my normal life.' (Anna) Putting it another way, Maya describes life as work (fulltime), children, cooking, etc... Masha suggests that women worked as soon as they get home. Marina says women work at home, at work, deal with problems with the children, with the house,

21

whereas men have problems with themselves! Sophia feels that there were no specific gender problems; the only problem was Communist ideology!

This range of views about the existence and acceptability of gender differences in social roles is accompanied by a high level of agreement about a lack of choice surrounding participation in the workforce. Equality meant that women could work just like the men and that this was not a matter of choice: men and women were equal in the sense that as a woman you 'had to go out and earn your living - that was your privilege as an emancipated woman, whether or not you wanted it.' (Liza) Tanya sheds light on another aspect of equality when she says, 'Equality, I tell you what, it makes me laugh a lot. When I came here [to the UK] and was really learning about feminism, I thought crikey we had all that! We had that much equality in the Soviet Union and in Russia subsequently. I remember when my mum had my sister, her dream was to be at home, to stay at home. Well one thing was she couldn't financially afford it, and the second thing was that it wasn't in the culture. The culture was to work, so is that equality? Women worked.'

Party Time

All Soviet children became members of youth groups organized through the school system. These were communist organizations for children of different ages: the young Octobrists were for children aged seven to eleven; the Pioneers were for children aged ten to sixteen; and the Komsomol (the Communist League of Youth) for young people between sixteen and twenty eight [ages differ according to different authors]. Membership in these organizations started with the youngest children enrolled on a mass scale and ended up with a more select group entering full membership in the Communist Party itself. Significantly, entrance to university usually required a student to be a member of the Komsomol. With the exception of those now in their thirties, the Komsomol was omnipresent in the lives of the twenty one in ways both commonplace and, as we shall see, of fundamental impact on their lives. Most of the women were members but individuality asserted itself and consequences

22

followed. Maya was thrown out of the organization when she married a foreigner; Liza 'forgot' to renew her membership and thus exited. Larissa was the head Pioneer of her entire school and was very involved in school activities until she was eighteen. But when she chose to leave the Komsomol ('I was becoming a bit of a rebel'), she was refused permission to participate in an exchange at a university in the UK on the grounds that 'I had not been politically educated.'

What is clear is that instrumental rather than ideological considerations determined the actions of the twenty one. Being a member of the Komsomol and perhaps the Communist Party was in most cases a means to an end. Galina frankly describes how she would have joined the Party if she had remained in Moscow, saying 'I should have joined the Party before I was allowed to start my doctorate [in economics] because ... economics was considered to be a political science. To be a professor in political science you must be a member of the Communist Party. ... with political sciences you would never have been allowed to start your research.' Victoria explains how most of the people who joined the Party just had to do it. 'It's just like getting a higher education or getting promotion. It was the same thing. If you were not part of the Communist Party then you would not get promoted, no matter where you were.' Victoria thinks of party membership like a trade union card, a card which allowed her and her husband as a member of the party to travel outside of the USSR. The negative side of party control and consequence advantage is evident in Kira's account of the way in which her Jewish husband's lack of position at Moscow State University was determined by the party.

Several of the women had parents who were members of the Communist Party. This enabled them to have a more comfortable lifestyle in terms of housing, consumer goods, education, transport or travel. These positive factors are, however, countered by Masha's description of her grandmother's funeral. Her paternal grandmother, a religious woman, who died in 1958 asked in her will for a ceremony at the Russian Orthodox Church. The problem for her father was that as a member of the navy it was more or less compulsory for him to join the party and as such, he was forbidden by formal command to attend the funeral.

23

Belief and Identity

This clash of ideology and religion easily leads one to ask about the role played by religion in other families. The oldest of the twenty one had grandparents who were religious in the sense that several belonged to the Russian Orthodox Church, especially those who grew up in small provincial towns where the churches were destroyed after the 1917 Revolution. Others were in mixed marriages; others say no religion was evident in their lives. Kira feels she was discriminated against because her last name, that is, her father's name, was considered to be Jewish, whereas her mother's last name was strictly Russian. When she applied for some jobs, her last name was the negative determining factor. She also describes her husband's discrimination due to his Jewishness. Vera points to the policy discussed in Stalin's time of sending Jews to their own 'homeland', to Birobidzhan in the Far East, something not desired at all by her relatives.

The accounts of the twenty one make clear the way in which religion has the potential to unite and divide in both families and countries, regardless of personal belief. Several of the women in their fifties said that religion played no role in their own lives but was important and relevant to their grandparents. This was a reality which greatly concerned the authorities anxious as they were to suppress different religions and fearful that grandmothers would instill religion in their grandchildren. Victoria expresses the view that suppressing religion was both good and bad: 'the bad thing was that it was suppressed and the good thing was that it was not promoted as it is now. Now I just can see that it is being imposed on people and I don't like that at all. It's just again another extreme, … some good came out of it because religion divides people a lot and in a multinational country as the Soviet Union was, we were not divided.' Families could also be divided by religion. Galina speaks about her maternal grandmother as a sort of religious person, but her grandfather 'who was the Lenin of his community was so against religion that he was like a fighting atheist. She [her grandmother] had to hide all the small icons not because of officials but because of her husband and he was always mocking all the stories about the resurrection of Lazarus.'

24

In the next age group several said religion played no role in their lives, although again some of their grandparents were religious. Larissa said her grandmother taught her how to pray, although religion was not relevant, especially since the churches had been destroyed and she was living in an atheistic society. Helena indicates that for the authorities and her fellow citizens being Jewish is not a religion: 'It's ethnic origin for the Russians. The fact that we were Jewish did not just play a part; it made us who we are and shaped our lives in a way that our lives have become.' She returns to this topic several times.

For the generation of women in their thirties religion, especially the Russian Orthodox religion, has emerged from the shadows and has played a more active role in their lives. In their grandparents' time, 'religion didn't have a chance' and many grandparents were antireligious. But some of the women were christened in the Russian Orthodox Church (in Russia) and some went to church prior to the 1990s. In the 1990s with the loosening up of the restrictions on the Russian Orthodox Church, Tanya's and Yevgenia's mothers went to church more often. In fact, Yevgenia's eighty year old grandfather has now been baptized for his daughter's sake, although Yevgenia adds that religion isn't for him. Luba is a Christian coming from a Moslem region of the country and is very aware of the perceived cultural differences these religious distinctions have made and are making within that society.

The 'Ideal Woman' and the 'Problem' of Femininity

Each of the women was asked what she thought was the 'ideal' woman at the time she lived in the Soviet Union. Asked to consider the images portrayed in the Moscow metro of peasant women, sturdy and hardworking, and their more industrial counterparts, again hard working, smiling, strong working women, none of them agreed with these stylized statues. Liza said she would laugh her head off if these were the ideal women. The only one who answered that the ideal woman - as well as being a mother - would be a member of the party and serve the state was one of the oldest group.

Across the generations, some of the women mentioned the Russian stereotypes of being either a glamorous ballerina, a beautiful figure skater, or a healthy sports person, all able to travel outside the borders of the country and lead privileged lives. Some mentioned women who were role models for them, such as an aunt ('a very fair, brave woman') or a doctor who combined caring for her patients with her family life (the mother of one of the participants). One woman admired businesswomen who would own their own business while realizing their education. Another participant admired an educated and cultured woman. Most striking in the range of responses is the overwhelming suggestion that the ideal woman is one who successfully combines the role of worker with being a mother and a wife. This ideal woman is described as being hard working and very busy with her (interesting) job or career, her family and children, her home, her friends. Galina goes so far as to say this woman is not ideal but lucky, lucky to have a career, a good education, an admirable husband, children, a separate flat.

Several women link the ideal woman with looking smart, looking good, being well dressed, making an effort in both appearance and in being pleasant. The majority of women indicated that femininity to them was above all a matter of appearance. Russian women 'must be beautiful, attractive and make themselves as pretty as possible.' In the words of Victoria, 'Russian women always looked (and look) after themselves'. This could include having manicures, eyelash tints, visiting the hairdresser, etc... And of course they needed makeup before being seen out of the house! Many wore full makeup, some makeup obtained from their mothers who travelled abroad. There are however two dissenting voices from women in their forties. Nadezhda says that 'if you are feminine, if you wear feminine clothes and have a feminine hair style, everyone thinks that you are a prostitute. It was not in fashion to be feminine'. This difference of perspective may be accounted for by the fact that Nadezhda grew up in Siberia. The second dissenting voice expresses the view that a femininity which emphasized appearance was in conflict with the need to assert female equality. In Sophia's judgment the importance of showing yourself as equal, meaning equal to men, meant that showing 'something feminine wasn't popular.'

The majority who did place a high value on appearance were confronted by practical difficulties. Finding fashionable, sometimes even wearable, clothing was always a problem. Some hunted for stylish clothing, visiting 'toilets' in Moscow where black market things were being sold. Natalia from the seaport of Odessa found lots of Western imports. Others sewed or knitted articles of clothing, sometimes using patterns from the West. The majority knew someone who would make up clothes for them, usually a tailor or dressmaker that their mothers employed. Kira was lucky in that her aunt was the head planner in a (spring and winter) clothing atelier. Galina was fortunate in that her two friends would buy something acceptable, one for each of them and one for her, so they shared the pickings amongst themselves. Public holidays, like International Women's Day on the 8th of March or New Years were/are the occasion to give material in order to make up dresses. The biggest problem was in finding footwear, something which some now have addressed in London by purchasing a considerable number of shoes and boots! The spirit of Carrie Bradshaw, if not Imelda Marcos, is alive and well among Russian women!

For a couple of women femininity was linked to either career oriented women, that is, women who only had a career and were not interested in having children, or to Western discussions of femininity or more precisely, feminism. 'The opposite of femininity was feminism: we loathed it because we thought that feminists are women who don't like men giving them a hand when they get out of a car or out of a bus!'(Tanya)

Images of Womanhood

All societies contain competing images of the characteristics which embody desirable social values such as good citizens, nuclear families, enterprising entrepreneurs and so on. The twenty one's discussion of their individual understandings of the meaning of a 'strong woman' in Russian culture reveals the tensions and even contradictions between social images and personal values. With regard to social images, several of the women suggested that a strong woman is literally physically strong, a massive, huge woman in orange overalls, whether peasant or worker, as portrayed in the statues which appear in the Moscow metro. 'Probably in Soviet times the peasant woman holding grain or working on tractors ... was the female figurehead of the woman who is capable of anything and everything.' (Victoria) But others added the fact of a publically engaged career woman, a person who would become a party member, who would be happy to be elected to different positions -- a strong woman in Soviet times. So the ideas of a strong woman were related to the Revolution and to Soviet ideas about what it means to be strong, ideas which include women who wanted to be equal to the men, who lost their lives to their ideals and/or sacrificed their lives to the community, to their work. The way in which social change brings confusion and contradiction - and probable demands for further change - is precisely indicated by Nadia. Now in her sixties she recalls the period of de-Stalinization and indicates that women were strong in character but also had to be feminine at the same time. Her generation was brought up after World War II with images of very sophisticated ladies from Hollywood. This was a contradiction for them. On the one hand there were the images of the peasantry and the working class and on the other hand there were the role models offered by all of these movies. So, she says, if you look at girls of her generation they were pretty confused.

Interestingly some of the women used examples from Russian culture, people such as Tchaikovsky's patron (Nadezhda von Meck) and Russian poetesses such as Tsvetaeva, Akhmatova, and Mandelstam. Chekhov in the 19th century is cited for writing about the aristocracy, decadence and women wanting to be strong even though they never were. Tanya feels that a strong woman in Russian literature is someone who is very feminine on the outside and tough on the inside, someone who's able to face all sorts of challenges.

Juxtaposed with these cultural role models - whether individual or symbolic - were more personal ideals. Many of the twenty one saw a really strong woman as one who kept the family together, was the leading core of family life. She's the breadwinner, she looks after children, she looks after her husband, she has good relations with family members, with children, and she is content with herself. Two of the women mentioned specific women whom they consider to be strong: Nadezhda thinks of Raisa Gorbachev as a very strong woman (whereas Anna Karenina is not!) and Larissa cites her former junior class teacher, a woman who didn't really have anything else in her life but the school. So to be 'strong' is somebody who is strong in spite of all the shortcomings, of all the disadvantages, of all the problems she has to face.

Masha and Liza on the other hand point out the difficulty of actually revealing strength. Masha speaks about strength in terms of being a wise character, but adds that 'the main thing is not to show that you are strong. Not to show off. This doesn't mean playing dumb or being meek. Men should perceive you as you are, otherwise it would be a great deception afterwards.' Liza agrees that the woman is supposed to be wise, but 'as a girl in Russia I think you are not expected to show your brains, but as a woman, yes you are.' Galina suggests that this was demonstrated during the perestroika and post-perestroika period where she says women coped with the hardships better than men. Speaking of Russian society in general, Marina says it is mostly masculine. 'Men will be at the top of society. It's really a difficult style for women, this patriarchy. Maybe this is an influence from the East because we are in the middle between the East and the West. We're like a Turkish country.' Maya echoes this, saying that, while women are strong, Russian men are quite macho: there are certain things they wouldn't allow their wives to do, that's in the culture. 'So we have macho men and strong women!' Vera quips that Russian men often 'sit there the whole day thinking about the Russian soul while women really work.' Women are very strong because they have to put up with a lot.

The Point of Departure as seen by others

Many migrants over time consider the degree to which what matters in their adopted society applied or not to and within their point of departure. To what extent did the twenty one see Western held views about balancing work and family, degree of closeness to one's parents and the prime emphasis on children as applying to their lived experience of Russia? Of those who commented on these issues, many expressed the view that they never thought about 'balancing work and family'. This was the life they knew, says Tamara, and they never complained about it. Victoria says she never thought that the balancing was difficult because 'it was just a fact of life that you had to cope with.' Masha replies that the teaching profession gave her flexibility, while a more assertive answer comes from Anna who indicates that balancing was not a problem for her because she liked her career and had a 'certain freedom from housekeeping.' That 'certain freedom' surely must have come from the fact that the grandparents helped out with looking after the children, with the children's education, with the cooking and cleaning, and with financial help in some circumstances. Many of these women were close to their parents because, as Galina asserts, you didn't have any other place to live! Broadly speaking, there was agreement that the child was the center of the universe. One view was that this involved a lifelong commitment in which children remained infants and the parents had to look after them until the latter were pensioners! An alternative view was there were limits to the child-centeredness because children grew up with the idea that everybody works.

So, there we have them, snapshots of the continuing and novel aspects of the different Russia(s) that provided the formative experiences of our twenty one. Hopefully, these snapshots provide a useful map or aide-memoire. But the broader the map, the less clear the human detail. So now let's hear from the twenty one in their own voice

Women in their sixties and seventies

Of the five women in the group currently in their sixties and seventies, three were the first to leave Russia or the Soviet Union as it was at that time. Two of them married 'foreigners', a British man and a South African, respectively. The third went with her nuclear family to Warsaw where she began a new life. Of the remaining two women, the oldest came in 2001 whereas the fifth was one of the last to arrive in 2004.

The accounts they offer of their living conditions in the Soviet Union are very illuminating about accommodation in that period. One lived with three other people in a small 60 meter square room, another shared a communal flat which was divided between her family and another, and a third unusually lived in a house. While their childhoods were spent in Leningrad, Kiev, Vilna and Sverdlovsk, they obtained their higher educations in Leningrad, Warsaw and Moscow, degrees ranging from an undergraduate degree, several masters degrees to a PhD.

Their memories of their youth and university days are filled with anecdotes which paint vivid pictures of life in Stalin's time. **Nadia**'s description of listening to Radio Free Europe, the BBC and the Voice of America, the last specifically for its jazz, evokes the excitement of this activity. In contrast, there is **Vera**'s account of how she cried when Stalin died, thinking that America was going to attack. **Vera** also tells of the role that anti-Semitism played, both in her own life and also as it affected both Soviet and Polish society. Anti-Semitism also appears in **Kira**'s account when she speaks of the Party's discrimination against her husband in his attempt to gain an academic position for which he was by far and away the top candidate. The power of the Party and individual efforts to maintain autonomy strikingly emerge in the story of her father's 'replacement'. In a similar way discrimination is central to **Anna**'s account of her life in the Soviet Union: discrimination because of anti-Semitism but in addition because their daughter married a foreigner and left the country, she and her husband were not allowed to do so for many years. **Tamara** also relates the sacrifices she had to go through during those years before she was allowed to leave the Soviet Union to live with -- or not live with, as

31

the case turns out -- her British husband; for a year and a half she was followed by the KGB.

Of course, some aspects of their stories contradict each other. **Nadia** describes listening to jazz whereas **Vera** says you couldn't listen to jazz, let alone dance any foreign dance (except classical dances such as the waltz, the foxtrot, the tango, but no 'boogie woogie'). But they do not contradict each other when they answer the question as to whether or not they thought there were any problems specifically related to women. The same could be said about their answers on sex education, contraceptives and abortions. The last topic has specific poignancy for **Tamara**.

The second part of the interviews dealt with their arrival in and adjustment to the UK. **Vera** came alone and lived alone until she met and married her husband, a Soviet dissident who sought and was granted political asylum in London. **Kira**, the most recent immigrant, arrived with her husband in 2004. **Nadia** emigrated with her South African husband in 1965. **Tamara** came as described above, ostensibly to be with her Scottish husband. **Anna** and her husband

had to wait to leave the USSR until he was 'cleared' of his so-called classified information. She also had to wait until the British allowed them to join their daughter in London, that is, when the couple was 65 and no longer able to claim benefits in the UK. With the exception of **Kira**, English wasn't a problem as they had all studied English either in school or at university. In fact, **Anna** had been an interpreter of English [for the Russians] all her working life.

The husbands who are Russian are described as typical Russian men, that is, not all that helpful with domestic tasks -- and that's putting it mildly. As **Vera** says, 'Involved or helpful around the house with cooking, cleaning, childcare, shopping? Russians? Never, good Lord, never.' But **Anna**'s husband has always shared the tasks with her and is currently looking after his mother who is soon to be 101 years old.

Like all of the other women interviewed, if these women miss anything it is their family and their friends. This is especially true for the latest to emigrate, **Kira**. But as **Tamara** wistfully says, 'I don't miss anything specifically. But [perhaps] my youth, it's nostalgia but not for the place … maybe the friends, not specific friends but what friendship meant.' **Vera** on the other hand indicates that since she has been here so long she probably doesn't miss anything. And **Nadia** says that after a period of integration she said to herself, 'I'm here and I'm going to live here. End of story.' Perhaps **Anna** is best placed to miss the least because she is now living so close to her only daughter.

These women have created successful and productive lives for themselves in this country. They have adapted to the climate, both literally and figuratively, and are glad to have come here, leaving behind various aspects of Russian life which they now see as oppressive, such as the entwined friendship patterns so characteristic of Russians past and present. In other words, they have indeed made their lives here with characteristic 'positiveness' towards British society. This generalization doesn't include the most recent immigrant, but perhaps that is to be expected given **Kira**'s recent emigration at an advanced age. Yet she too is trying new strategies and ways of living in the UK.

Anna (73)

Life in Russia

I wouldn't call it [a double burden] a burden. I would say that women had double duties or chores but I never considered it a burden. I just took it as it should be done. What was typical of most of the families was that the woman would come home from work and do the cooking, cleaning and take care of the children, while the husband sat in front of the television set.

Anna is the oldest person interviewed. She is also the mother of Helena, one of the other interviewees. As such their responses to the interview overlap and intertwine but also diverge as they came to this country at different times in their lives and under different circumstances. Anna's daughter Helena, who married an Englishman and emigrated to the UK in the 1980s, influenced Anna's life and was the reason that she came here in 2001. Anna graduated from a pedagogical institute in Leningrad and for most of her life has earned her living as an interpreter and translator. Her mother was educated as a professional chemical technician and worked in a research institute. Her father had a higher education as well and all his life worked for the government in the Department of Finance. She has no siblings as after World War II started in 1941, her parents weren't 'comfortable to have another child'. Her maternal grandparents, especially her maternal grandmother who helped to bring her up, are remembered but not those on her father's side because they were killed in Kharkov when the Germans came in World War II. Her husband trained as a radio engineer and worked at a classified research institute in Leningrad. Her mother-in-law is alive at the age of 100, living in London.

Childhood

My childhood was first spent in the Ukraine. During World War II we were evacuated to Kazakhstan, then to Uzbekistan, and after the war we moved to Leningrad. My father returned about 1946 when I was eleven years old. After the war my mother never worked again as a chemist but worked in a library, so I was reading all the time.

University

How did I choose what to read at university? I was not really a good pupil. I took English lessons when I was about eight or nine and decided then that I would read English. I had a private tutor. All of the family--my aunts, my uncles, my father-- were in finance and I hated that. There was a family meeting and they decided that I should go to a financial institute. But because I wasn't a very good pupil, to become a teacher seemed easier so I went to this pedagogical institute. I graduated in Khrushchev's time, and with the Thaw various research institutes set up various scientific information departments and I found my first job as a translator/interpreter in one such institute. And I was there for 30 years. I loved it! The Arctic and Antarctic Research Institute is a world-famous Institute in the polar community, really a unique organization. This allowed me to travel, that is, to go to meetings abroad. (I was almost the only Jew travelling.) The whole Institute was like one big family; people would spend a year on these expeditions and become like a family. Our director was a very decent person and he liked me, that is, he liked how I worked. ... I was very lucky; I had a good protector and I liked what I was doing.

Daily routine

Even when my daughter was born, that didn't interfere with my career. I was very involved. My parents took care of Helena. Every morning I got up and listened to the BBC or Voice of America for twenty minutes. I thought that was part of my education, part of my language learning. Once I was listening to the radio and I said,' Papa, papa, Kennedy was killed in a taxi,' and he said, 'Kennedy might have been killed, but not in a taxi.' You can understand the level of knowledge at that time; it was just appalling. My father had connections and he helped me with my career. First of all he found the place for me at the Institute. Then he introduced me to a publishing house and I translated books in my spare time. At eight o'clock

35

in the morning I left home -- we started working at nine -- and I returned home at five. At first, when my mother was still in good health, she took care of the house. After work I translated those books. My mother did the cooking. As for queuing, we all shared that. When my father retired it was his duty to buy things. Once my mother was ill, I started to cook myself.

Marriage

After my mother worked in the library, she worked in a theatre ticket office in Nevskii Prospect [the main avenue in Leningrad/St. Petersburg]. Once two ladies came in and they were our neighbors in Kharkov before the war. One of them came to visit the one who lived in Leningrad, and the latter invited my mother to come and visit her. (My dad hated going anywhere; he just loved to be at home.) So I went with my mother and a son my age was there. When we were married in the registrar's office, the same question was asked. 'Who introduced you, was it a matchmaker?' My future husband was a student at a technical university and when he graduated, he started working in a classified research institute. He was trained as a radio engineer; he was lucky, he liked his job and he defended his thesis and continued to do various research projects. He suffered because of anti-Semitism. I didn't but he did, and that prevented him from defending his thesis at the next stage, the Doctorate. So he got a Candidate degree. We were married in 1959.

Experiencing birth in Leningrad

The Soviet atmosphere was such that you did everything with the help of your friends, *blat* [fixing; string-pulling; influence; contact or use of personal networks] or you paid. My mother was given the name of a midwife and we went to her, but she said that she couldn't promise anything but if, when we came to the hospital, we ask the midwife on duty to come down to us, then she would take care of me. So my mother did that and the midwife knew that she would be paid. They were very attentive, never left me alone when the actual labor started. I think it took me about four hours; it was not bad. But it was horrendous but because it was natural [there was no medication]. But you keep forgetting those things.

I was more worried about returning to the communal flat where we lived in one room, that is, my mother, my father, myself, my husband. I remember I was feeding my daughter Helena in hospital and I was crying and the woman next to me in the bed said, 'What do you have? Is it a girl? You're right to be crying - she's so ugly!' and I thought she was so beautiful! [Aren't women awful!!] The most important thing was that she was born healthy.

Discussion of sex, sex education and birth control

No, I didn't learn about sex from my mother. When I was going to get married, my husband took me to the public library, took some books from the shelves and we read together. That was my sex education! I was 24 when I got married.

Contraceptives and abortions

Maybe I heard something about contraceptives but we didn't use anything; actually sometimes we used condoms but I didn't get pregnant for two years. After my daughter was born, I had and wanted to have two abortions. One of the abortions was very bad because I didn't use any acquaintances or any connections, no *blat*. The next one was done by the wife of a friend and everything was okay. It wasn't hard to arrange an abortion. The only thing was it was very unpleasant because they looked at you as if you were dirt, as an offender, and that was not very good. For some of the older women it was forbidden or impossible. But by my time everything was okay.

Living accommodation

We lived in this communal flat, the five of us, but at night time my husband went back to his mother who also lived in one room. And then when Helena was three months old, my father got a flat for all of us and that was like paradise because it had three rooms and it was our personal flat. Because of personal connections, dad got a telephone. We were very very happy. But as was the [Soviet] system we then exchanged flats. And then we had a big 100 meter square flat, four big rooms in the center of the city. It was in very poor condition so we repaired it. An American scientist passing through Leningrad visited our flat (as well as others of his friends who lived in the new modern flats) and said to my father, 'You should have been a big boss' [on account of the size of the flat]. When we left seven years ago, the situation was very bad so we sold that flat for not much money, whereas today it would have been worth much more. But we sold it as soon as we were allowed to leave in 2001. In fact, we left it to be sold by someone else; we didn't want to waste any time.

Definition of a good mother

First of all, a mother should take good care of the child(ren), in the physical sense. And I think good mothers should give some freedom to a child and give very light, almost unnoticed, direction. A mother should be interested in the child's life, but not oppressive. My mother was like that.

Were there any problems specific to women? What does equality mean?

I did not perceive anything as specific [specific problems for women] because I thought that it was my normal life, particularly when my mother was ill (she was paralyzed), and so I had to take care of everything. I was very busy but when there was a possibility for me to go abroad or even travel within the Soviet Union, again with the help of friends I found an old lady who came to us and prepared food. So I could leave home for ten days, maybe. Mostly it was three, four or five days. And my father took very good care of my mother when she was ill.

When they were both healthy, I left my daughter with my parents without thinking that anything could happen to her. My parents were very reliable. My husband is also a very good father. He was more involved in Helena's physical education, taking her to the skating rink, when she returned late from the art school he picked her up, etc.. He didn't cook but he cleaned. Even now we have sort of divided responsibilities; I'm cooking and he's buying and cleaning.

Was there a 'double burden' in the USSR?

I wouldn't call it a burden. I would say that women had double duties or chores but I never considered it a burden. I just took it as it should be done. What was typical of most of the families was that the woman would come home from work and do the cooking, cleaning and take care of the children, while the husband sat in front of the television set. When we were

younger, my husband had the double burden because he had to work and he had to study. When he finished his dissertation and defended it and had a lot more time, he had a lot of responsibilities at home. We always shared.

Did religion play any role for you?

We were not a religious family at all. We were not religious, I think, because my parents were not brought up in that spirit and I was not interested in it at all. Through my daughter's friends, maybe she was more interested but we didn't allow her to be involved. That's why she's more involved with art and music. We knew when the different holidays were, like Passover, and it was my duty (because everyone else was afraid) to go to the synagogue to buy matzo [unleavened bread]. But we ate matzo because we love it!

Were you a Party member?

Neither I nor my husband were members of the Party.

Were you able to travel?

I started to travel in 1969 and I was allowed out not more than two times a year. On my second trip I was so naïve that I was teaching Russian to the KGB man who was in the group, but I didn't know he was a KGB man. He wanted to correct my translations and I just argued with him. At the same time when we were staying in Tokyo, the Leningrad Philharmonic Orchestra also stayed there. There were two young men from my student years and we were not allowed to talk to them, to associate even with Soviet Russian people abroad. But these young men came to my room and left a lot of porcelain which they had bought while they were travelling around Japan. That was not allowed! After that, I did not travel for three years which I thought was my punishment! But then I was returned to the list [to travel] and I continued to travel once or twice a year until Helena married [a foreigner]. And that was it. People around me said, 'Poor you, poor you, Helena left you' and I said, 'No, I'm not poor, I'm happy for Helena.'

How do you picture the ideal woman in the Soviet Union?

I don't know, all women are different. This doesn't exist! I think my aunt was the person whom I would relate to intellectually. She was a very fair person; she always fought for people who were in any way wronged. She was very brave.

What did femininity mean?

Femininity meant nothing to me. I think it's just typical for women to have this interest in makeup and clothing. I remember my grandmother -- I thought she was very old at the time -- and she was always interested in new things, new shoes, new dresses. I had a tailor and always a good tailor, maybe not very good, but expensive.

Does the idea of a strong woman in Russian culture mean anything?

If you mean Soviet Russia, then a strong woman would be a career woman, a person who would become a Party member, who would be happy to be elected to different positions. But that was a Soviet stronghold. In normal terms, a strong woman would be the woman who has a good family, good relations with family members, with children, and a person who was content with herself.

Pensions

At that time it was the law that if you worked in one place for thirty years, you got the biggest pension. So as soon as I worked for thirty years I left the Institute. I got my pension aged fifty five. But I continued to work freelance. Now I transfer my Russian pension to the UK.

What were the consequences of your daughter marrying a British man?

I was not allowed to leave the Soviet Union while I was working at the Institute. When I left it, I was allowed to come immediately but my husband was not allowed. As soon as Helena married, my husband was thrown out, not simply sacked, but thrown out from his job at the research institute.... Eight years had passed since he was forced to leave that job, but he was still refused permission to leave the country. But then it was perestroika and he wrote a very long letter to the authorities, proving that they should let him go. (A famous Academician, of course he was classified, who married Eisenhower's daughter was let out of the country. So my husband said,' Do you think I know more than this Academician?') The idea of the letter was to prove that although my husband dealt in developing some strategic things, he dealt only with some very small pieces of that equipment. He was never a leading designer or a scientist; he was always doing his little bit. When he was fired originally, he suffered a lot. But he never complained. He worked at different jobs that were way below his education and knowledge. And finally he started to work as a translator and he continues doing that. So we're all doing it now and we help each other. We work as a family!

Validating some Western views about the past: Balancing work and family

Balancing work and family was never a problem for me. I liked it [my career] and I had that certain freedom from housekeeping. For me, my career (though it wasn't a very important career) made my life interesting. I met people … and I was not only a housekeeper.

Prime emphasis on children

I think that I was very much influenced by my parents. My parents believed that to have one child was quite enough. [You did have two abortions.] My parents were against more children because they thought life was difficult anyway. My husband still grudges me that, but if we had had another child it would have been different, or maybe not.

Degree of closeness to parents

Yes, that's true; we were very close. Helena grew up in that atmosphere and she sort of inherited that. When she left, we wrote a letter to her every day and she answered us every other day. We were in very close contact and of course we called her because she had no money to call us.

Life in London

Why did you leave Russia? Why did you come to London?

We left Russia in 2001 because my daughter was married and living in London. It was very difficult in Russia. We were [originally] allowed to go to Israel but we didn't want to and we knew we couldn't go to England. We even got refugee status to go to the States but we never used it. When we were interviewed in the US Embassy in Moscow, the lady asked various questions about my husband's scientific degrees and about my travels abroad. She said that we were not oppressed like other people were. We said we weren't, but still it was very difficult for my husband to become a postgraduate student, because he had to get all A's and different other things. He was not promoted, but we had a sort of normal life and she said, ' I will grant you that status because you are so honest.'

How difficult did you find it to adjust to:

No difficulties at all!

Climate

Much better than Leningrad.

People

We don't mix a lot with British people. We live in a very close family circle and that's why this aspect doesn't affect us.

Language

No difficulty to adjust. The fact that we both could speak English when we came here was a great help. Now there is Russian TV and we watch it a lot but even without it I would be quite happy watching English TV.

Property

My daughter found our flat so we didn't have to go through the process. The most important thing was that we were near her. When my daughter said the flat was on the third floor, my mother-in-law [who is now almost 101] said, 'If I can walk at all, I can walk the steps. If I can't, I can't.' It's only this December that she has stopped going out.

Transport

Sometimes we complain about trains. We complain about trains because we really are spoiled. My cousin came to visit two years ago. He was fascinated with everything he saw and he said we live on another planet. We never complain about the National Health Service.

Shopping

I wasn't shocked or overwhelmed by shopping when I came here. Maybe it's in my nature that when I returned from my trips abroad I was more impressed -- well, I've seen it and my friends would say to me, 'How can you not get mad at things here, compared with there?' And I would say I would never compare; there are two different worlds and that's that.

Russian food

In the beginning we did miss Russian food. But now there are Lithuanian shops all around; there are three within easy reach. More and more we're using their products. At first everything you could buy here was good and looked perfect. Then we'd say this isn't like we used to have. The only thing that it is better are English potatoes.

Role of husband

It's not that his role has changed; it's that his life has changed since his mother became so ill. He thinks that it is his sole responsibility to take care of her. He's even reluctant to leave her with me. He doesn't want to burden me. My daughter and I were persuading him to have someone to help us, to allow us to travel together. He knows that we disagree with him, but we can't change him. His health is not very good and that worries me. He's 73 this year; the same as me.

What are your ideas now about femininity? What does equality mean here?

I haven't changed my views about femininity or equality or the role that women play. I never thought about that. For us, for me, for my friends, it was like a joke. I remember we had an American delegation visiting and we had a dinner where the director and the other scientists proposed a toast to women. I was interpreting and I said, 'It was a toast to ladies' health,' and they said, 'It's not ladies, it's women'. I was very surprised. When you return from work, you have your bag, you have another bag with food that you bought in the middle of the day, and sometimes people brought you flowers (I had no hands to carry the flowers). So if they [the

Americans] want our lives, we could give it to them because we didn't understand this search for femininity. We were not allowed to get presents from foreigners but we could get books. So in the 1980s I read some of these feminist novels; I also received records for my daughter. An important delegation brought me some perfume; it was always by Worth.

Does religion play any role now?

No.

Would you go back to Russia to live?

Never, never, never.

What do you miss the most?

I wouldn't say I miss anything. Now with cheap telephones I can talk to my friends for hours and they write letters. When I first came here I used to go to Russia regularly, twice a year. My first impression when you get there is that people are so angry. They look at you as if you are an enemy. Things that you are used to here and don't notice that you have already changed, like if you knocked into somebody here, you would say 'Sorry' or 'Excuse me', whereas there they just look at you as if you're mad. Everybody bumps into each other. I think it's even worse in St. Petersburg than in Moscow because people are poorer. If you use the car all the time, you don't see the people and you don't need them.

How would you characterize British society?

Judging by the people that I know, it is a very friendly society. People around us are very friendly, always ready to help. But otherwise I have no relationship with this society at large. And I guess I'm not typical because I'm living so near to my daughter; she's sort of a buffer between me and the wider world. She helps a lot.

What do you value most and least about living in London?

45

What I value most is my daughter and my family! I really don't know what I value least.

Inflation!

Tamara (70)

Life in Russia

Women's problems were hard work, hard physical work, terrible physical work and practically spending your life working hard: physically hard, mentally hard throughout your youth and a very very unglamorous life. As for equality, well we were equal…. We were equal because we didn't think about it; it didn't come up at all.

Tamara is one of the oldest respondents of the group. She has a university degree in English literature as well as a degree from the Leningrad Institute of Theatre, Music and Cinematography. Before she retired, she taught Russian at an English university. She met her first British husband in Leningrad and left the Soviet Union in 1969 after their marriage. Due to medical procedures performed in Leningrad, she has no children with either her first or her second husband. Her mother taught German in the Soviet school system and her father was a naval engineer. She is an only child. Her maternal grandmother played an important role in her life as they lived together in a very small room.

Childhood

During the war, we were all evacuated from Leningrad at different times. My mother was evacuated because she was a teacher; her school was evacuated two weeks after the war started. My grandmother stayed and had to be evacuated over Lake Ladoga which was then frozen in the winter of 1941. She travelled with my aunt and they were bombed but because of the ice they were saved (some say it was a miracle). My father was at the front throughout the war. When he came back from the war, he never came back to my mother but they were never officially divorced. He never wanted to remarry, but he always had girlfriends. His last girlfriend when he died was my age then, about twenty two.

University

My mother wanted me to study languages. I wanted to study literature and because some of my friends were journalists, writers or poets, I wanted vaguely to go into journalism. But in 1956 (when I was going to university) it was practically impossible because apart from the exams, you had to submit your publications. They could be, for example, just rather amateurish newspapers but I didn't have any so, although I passed exams very well, I was told to choose anything else in the faculty of philological studies. I chose English language and literature. Books were then not available in English. Why did I choose English? Because I (as well as my mother) didn't want German. She herself was a German teacher; my aunt was teaching German at the university; and my uncle was a professor of English phonetics. It was a road chosen for me! I liked the sound of English, even more American English. I read Dickens, Jack London and Thackeray which were then only available in Russian. They were all very well translated. We read quite a lot and throughout the university course we studied European literature. That was five years of studying very intensely from the ancients to the modern, but there were certainly very blank spots.

After university

It was sort of preordained that I would become a teacher with the sort of course I was taking. You were given a diploma which stated that you are suitable to be a school or university teacher. I didn't really want to be a teacher. My mother was a teacher and it was horrible, horrible work and I never liked teaching, looking at her. The vagueness of the children sort of irritated me because of the lack of discipline, the noise and so on. I didn't know what I wanted to be. I just wanted to be in some literary profession, maybe a critic, maybe a script writer, maybe something to do with films and theater and literature.

And that's what I did after I graduated. But it was an absolute accident. A year after I graduated from university I had a job at a school; I was teaching at the school where my mother was which she had arranged. I was teaching English and really disliked it. Then one day I was walking along some street and I met my friend who was in Leningrad just for a

48

week. She came from Novosibirsk [Siberia]. She was trying to get into the Institute of Theater, Music and Cinematography because by then she had married a man who was an actor and she wanted to learn something about the theater. She suggested we get together because maybe it would be interesting for me. I went to take my photograph and get some documents and the next day I submitted my documents. Three days later I was going through the exams and I passed all of them.

So I got into the Institute of Theater, Music and Cinematography and then my life just made a sort of sharp turn. I enjoyed it tremendously and I thought I was in the right place. At the end of the first year, my supervisor said, 'You know, you better stop doing what you are doing and go to the postgraduate course straightaway because a lot of subjects are parallel to what you have already done during your first five years.' So I went to the postgraduate course and started writing. My subject was the American theater. I had a choice of what to study, but you can imagine it was extremely difficult to choose exactly what it should be about because there are a lot of names that couldn't be mentioned. This was 1962/1963, so there were people like Tennessee Williams who were just not studied. What we could write about were people like Arthur Miller, some friends of the Soviet Union, some political friends. So that's what I was doing. The postgraduate degree involved three big exams as well as a dissertation. I had just done exams and at some point I met my future husband.

Accommodation

Until about 1961 we lived in a small 60 meter square room, that is, the three of us, my grandmother, my mother and myself. Then with the help of my uncle, who was not a very high placed bureaucrat but he did have some connections, we managed to get a self-contained flat which was at the very edge of the city. It seemed to be miles away, of course; now it's right in the middle. It consisted of two tiny rooms again for the three of us. None of us had privacy or a room of one's own, but we had a bathroom, a kitchen, and that was luxury. That was from 1961 to 1969 when I left.

Marriage

My future husband was from Scotland. He was a Russian scholar and a specialist in Russian grammar; he was my uncle's friend. They met in Edinburgh where my uncle was teaching for two years at the beginning of the 1960s. One day my uncle said to me, 'My very dear friend is coming to Leningrad to do some more research. Would you get him some tickets for some play?' By then I worked in the theater as well as studying so I could get tickets. That's how we met. He was eleven years older than I was. He was married, he had a daughter and he was an established academic in the UK. We married at the very end of 1968 which means that we were sort of together for three and one half years although our meetings were very infrequent. We lived together in Leningrad only at those times when he came for a few weeks.

Discussion of sex, sex education and birth control

I learned absolutely nothing from my mother about sex, except that her sex life was going on in front of me. She never discussed it or told me what was going on. Nor did she ever discuss birth control with me. And my girlfriends never talked about it either.

Abortions

I had two abortions and my friends were certainly having abortions as well. My first abortion was very difficult and the second one ruined my life. Having an abortion was like being on a conveyor belt; it was a total 'coming and going' and I think that then the statistics were that every woman had to have or had had seven abortions. Abortions were a form of birth control. Of course I became pregnant but not because I wanted to. The second one ruined my life. As it turned out, my fallopian tubes were blocked; it was a total mess inside me. All that came to the surface years later when I married for the second time and wanted to have children. The children were not coming and I went to have a test where it was discovered that both tubes were blocked. That was in 1974. Then the British surgeon said, 'You have to decide whether to perform some sort of operation and make one tube, you know the artificial thing, but then there would be a chance of....[details supplied]. The chances of this were very high in my case because I was thirty seven (which was very old in 1974). The doctors asked me what had happened and whether I had had any abortions. I said, 'Yes, I have had two.' So they assumed it was because of that. I married my second husband in 1973 and I probably went for the tests in 1975. My second husband had had no children.

Infidelity

As for infidelity in the Soviet Union, all women slept around, but we were young and unmarried then. But we were always, always afraid of being pregnant. If you were pregnant, then it was an abortion. Practically everyone I knew had an abortion.

Women's problems

Women's problems were hard work, hard physical work, terrible physical work and practically spending your life working hard: physically hard, mentally hard throughout your youth and a very unglamorous life. As for equality, well we were equal. The question of equality was never a question that occupied much time. We were equal because we didn't think about it; it didn't come up at all. I never felt being submerged in a sort of man's world; I never felt that I was locked into my intentions by men. Maybe we were all what's called the intelligentsia, you know we were quite self-sufficient. We never had any problematic sort of things except we didn't have enough freedom, enough books to read, enough possibility to talk or to go and see things.

Was religion any relevance?

Religion played almost no role for me. My mother was a Christian, a Russian Orthodox, as was my grandmother. In their stories it [religion] was always cropping up. First of all, in the schools religion was an obligatory subject, particularly what my grandmother went through. As for my mother, she grew up in a small provincial town, a lovely town where there was a church, where there was a congregation as it was everywhere until the Revolution. Then everything was destroyed, not just the churches. But although the Soviets were worried that the *babushkas* would implant religion in young children or hide icons under the bed, we didn't have any.

Were you a Party member?

I was never a member of the Party. I was a Pioneer and I was a Komsomol member but never a member of the Party. I was never pressed by any authorities to join the Party. I suppose if I were pressed I would have, but that was conforming enough. I was never in a sort of cornered situation.

Ability to travel

I never left the Soviet Union before 1969 but I did travel within the country. Unfortunately it wasn't as much as I would've liked to now.

How do you picture the ideal woman in the Soviet Union?

The ideal woman would probably be some kind of ballerina, who was glamorous, beautiful and travelled. But I didn't have any image like that. An idealized image of femininity was not that of the peasant women in the Moscow metro. We laughed at that and I don't know any peasants!

What did femininity mean?

Femininity meant a lot. I remember I had a teacher at school who was a bit better dressed and better looking than the rest. Probably that was why I chose English because she taught the English language and she was very feminine. She was a very nice person and spoke very good Russian; even then I appreciated a good turn of phrase and a good style of language because others were just horrendous. So I liked her very much and femininity was very important. As for clothing, my mother didn't sew but it was the 'done' thing then to have a dressmaker who would do everything for you because there was nothing in the shops.

Problems with balancing work and family?

You could stress balancing work and family life. My mother didn't have family life because she was a single mother who had a lover throughout all her days until the day she died, the same man. My grandmother was widowed very early so she spent her life helping her daughters, but not my mother. She helped her two other daughters, bringing up their children. Also she did everything in the dacha which belonged to all of the family. My aunt, who worked as well as having a family, was very harmonious. I wouldn't say she was suffering, but everyone was tired and spending their lives in the queues, getting this and getting that but also they had to work. They never complained about it. That's the only life they knew.

Life in London

Why did you leave the Soviet Union?

I left the Soviet Union because I got married in Leningrad in December 1968. I would never have been allowed to leave if I hadn't got married. I came to the UK in July of 1969. Between December 1968 and July 1969 I was preparing to go to England. To do that I had to be sacked from my job. I lost my living permit (my *propiska*) - the most valuable thing for non-residents. I went through lots and lots of family discussions about what would happen to me when I was in Britain. I worried how difficult life would be because my husband lived in Aberdeen and it was very remote. I had always lived in the capital city so I was a bit apprehensive. He spent three and a half years of his life just to get me to go [to the UK] and he divorced his wife for me. It was terrible really.

Then in May, two months before I left, I got a telegram from him saying, 'Don't come; I love another woman.' This just floored me. I had a nervous breakdown, and so did my mother. In the following weeks we were just lying on the sofa, side by side, in a state of total shock. But that was not the end because after that telegram, I got probably ten or twelve other telegrams and telephone calls saying, 'Please come, I love you and we will talk about everything here.' The third telegram said, 'Don't come, this is final, I'm not going to meet you'. Then a telephone call would come and there would be sort of embarrassed silences and so on and so forth. Of course everything at that time was bugged; every telegram was a very public affair. So my family, my mother's sisters, their husbands -- they were all involved because I was out of it, I was unwell. I was just not discussing anything. They were just deciding what to do. At one point I told him, 'Come here and we'll get divorced.' He said he didn't want to come and that I should come to England.

My mother said to me immediately that this new woman is probably making his life hell. When I think about it now, we actually didn't know each other at all. Although I really loved him and he loved me, the way we went through this three and one half years, the sacrifices we made (including the abortions, which he didn't know about but I told him later on) were just immense. I was followed by the KGB for a year and a half (just bodily); somebody was behind me for a year and a half of my life because I was marrying a foreigner from a capitalist country which was unheard of. I thought I was the only one in the whole Soviet Union! Of course when I later came to England, it turned out that I wasn't and there were other wives like me, not many, but probably five. It was decided that I had to go to England because I had lost everything. I was just a nonperson. And I had to see what was happening -- maybe divorce him, maybe return, maybe not, maybe try to stay for a few months. And that's how I came to England.

I came by boat to Tilbury. I was met by a woman who turned out to be his new girlfriend which I didn't know at the time. She was very sorry for me and said she had rented a flat for me in Hampstead [north London]. I didn't know anything about Hampstead; it was all the same to me. She herself lived in Bristol and was a scholar of Russian language and literature. She said he would come to visit me which he did. The only thing I could tell them was to just leave me alone. You know when he told me who this woman was, I was absolutely horrified. Not that I was

54

disgusted. I was really kind of a piece of cabbage as I was in such a state; I couldn't think of anything but I started living in Hampstead. In about three days I had a few friends such as my landlady and her husband who were very nice to me. When my husband met me he brought a file and said, 'Do you want to work in Oxford, do you want to work for the BBC, do you want to translate, do you want to do this or that?' They were just papers, papers, papers, all about working; I could do anything! I said maybe later; you know I just wanted to see what London was like. For about a month I lived in London, maybe a bit longer. He came again and he probably came three or four other times. But it was absolutely clear to me that I didn't ever want to live with him. He wanted me to come to Aberdeen because he had bought a house for us, he had decorated it, and all his friends were expecting me. It's an absolutely incredible story. I said I wasn't going to Aberdeen; please just leave me alone. Then at some point I thought I have to work; he was giving me money of course but I thought it would be better if I were to work. So I decided to go to Oxford because by then I found out that there were two or three Russian wives like myself there. Two of them were in fact people I vaguely wanted to meet and of course my husband knew their husbands through teaching. So I went to Oxford and my husband helped me rent a flat and paid for it. It was 'ballooning from that' -- I had new friends in about three months and I was living almost a normal life. My husband was kind of very peripheral to this. About five or six months after that, he came to Oxford and we met again. He came to me and said, 'You know I'm in love with you, please come and live in Aberdeen.' And I said never, just never. He was very impressed at how quickly I had gone from zero to some kind of life, some sort of established interesting life.

How difficult did you find it to adjust to:

Climate

The climate was wonderful!

People

I found it very easy to adjust to being in the UK. I never had a problem. And I never had a problem adjusting myself to England, but I suppose it's not because England is such an easy country to adjust to, but my character is to root myself very easily. I never thought that I was a laughing stock or that it was a peculiar situation or anything about myself that seemed to be strange to the English. Maybe it was; I had lots of encounters but I was open to these encounters. I'm not like those people who always say that they went through all kinds of troubles and are still in a sort of unsatisfactory situation as far as England is concerned. My second husband is English, a Londoner. He's a scholar who specializes in Italian Renaissance. He's retired now and we live in the house where he was born.

Language

The language was not a problem, although my spoken language was, I suppose, very peculiar and very accented. I never had any sort of problem of not understanding or of not being understood.

Property

Unlike some of the other women, I didn't have to look for property because my second husband owned our house. This is the house where he was born. But sitting tenants practically destroyed our lives. I mean they destroyed his life; they were vampires. One of them, after forty three years, finally went to Spain in 2003. The other one finally went into a nursing home and she thinks she still has the right to the house....

Transport

I was going from London to Oxford almost every weekend, staying with some friends in London. I was using the train and this cost.

Lack of family and problems for my mother

I did miss my mother but she was not allowed to come to see me for about three years. She applied for a visa but she was always rejected. There was no explanation. The authorities said that I, her daughter, should come and see her which of course was a trap and I knew that because everything was. They knew what happened; they knew that the marriage was busted but officially I was not divorced. My first husband never wanted to divorce me because he had just divorced his first wife and he didn't want to go through that again. Until three or four months after the day I met my second husband, I wanted a divorce myself, and then in 1974 we started the procedure.

Shopping

I was both thirsty and hungry for shopping and I still am. I enjoy it! I live in a very normal way, I'm not a sort of maniac or fanatic. But yes, I love clothes and I'm aware of men and women who are dressed well. I guess I spend a lot of money on this. In Moscow, they are all dressed as if they were going to a party, to banquets and receptions. I think the reason is the same as I said--hunger; they want to be dressed well because even if it is sort of not in their own memory but the memory of their parents in some sort of way, they are just very keen on presenting themselves as stylish. I mean they go over the top, it's laughable, but I understand it! As far as **Russian food** is concerned, I don't miss it.

Role of husband

My second husband isn't Russian and so he wasn't brought up in Russia. So of course he hasn't changed his role. But he did start to study Russian as soon as we met and he is still doing this. But he's not like a Russian husband who would have left me to do everything. We share our burdens, without discussing it, without quarrelling about it. It's sort of like this: he goes shopping, I go shopping, we drive the car, you know, alternatively. We are not saying it's your turn, it's my turn; it all comes in sort of a natural way.

Concepts of femininity and equality

You know this isn't anything I think about. It was always very remote for me. I think we are all equal, that is, I've never thought that women have to fight for their rights because their rights are all equal. The whole feminist sort of issues--it's not that they bore me, I don't know who invented them. You know there was a reason for feminism to go forth and evolve but I never understood it. I never thought it was really justified because I think men and women are absolutely different beings. The difference is just as important as the similarity, and that's it.

Religion

I became a Russian Orthodox Christian about seven years ago and so did my husband. He went from Anglicanism to Russian orthodoxy and I don't think it was because of me. He went to the Ennismore Gardens Russian Orthodox Church long before we met, just out of curiosity and because he loved the liturgy. He loves singing, maybe because his professional life had very much to do with the church. He was writing all of his life about popes, cardinals, papal Curia and the history of the Renaissance which of course is the history of the church. So he was interested in the Russian Church as well and I suppose his interest was mainly because it's a very static church. It is based on dogmas. It never changed and never capitulated to this and that; it's very severe and I suppose it attracted him as a sort of counterpoint to the Anglican Church. I think the Anglican Church is probably very opportunistic but I don't know.

Are you going back to Russia?

No, I don't want to go back to Russia to live. Never, but I go there nearly every year.

What do you miss the most?

My youth, it's nostalgia but not for the place. I don't miss anything specifically-- not food, maybe not the climate, but maybe the friends, not specific friends but what friendship meant. We had a close circle of friends and we were close. You know maybe we were too close, very intimate.

Now I've learned that to be remote and aloof in relationships is good. I like it but sometimes I miss it; I have a few friends here but it's not like it was. I think sometimes that, thank God, it's not like this here. I don't hear confessions and I don't confess myself. It's just not needed and I don't need it.

How would you characterize British society?

It's very confused for many reasons. When I met my second husband's family, his father was dead and his mother was 75. What I observed was quite a terrible thing to me now. They were mother and son but they behaved as if they were remote friends, seeing each other probably once a week. They were having drinks together, they were discussing general things, never private things. I thought it was so cold and so remote and so insufficient. But now I like it. I think this is what in Russia we had in spades, this sort of closeness and being in each other's pockets. I'm glad that nothing like this happened to me. At the moment actually I have a Russian neighbor (you know I am surrounded by Russians in my street) who just wants to be friends with me. She phones and asks if she could come and look at my books; she asks if I'm going to church and could I give her a lift. I told her recently to use the library because I don't want to be her librarian. She's an interesting person but not all the time! She would just cross the road and she probably thinks it's normal, but I don't.

Going back to British society, I don't know what I really think. I love England, I absolutely adore everything in England. I came to this sort of very, very passionate feeling probably straight away when I came here, but I think England has done so many things just to betray itself. You know it just went as far as possible away from everything which we admired. You know I admire this sort of pride, the sort of feeling of being the best. I always loved it: I always thought it was wonderful to feel that you can afford your democracy and your very wide feeling about the world. Now England is sort of getting smaller and smaller in a sort of mental way, apologizing all the time for itself, being always third-best, fourth best and talking about it all the time and doing everything to be even worse. I feel that it is awful. I think it is getting simply compromised in my eyes and in the eyes probably of foreigners who had a kind of preconceived idea through literature, through history and not seeing it anymore.

What do you value most about living in London?

What I value most is my husband! It's having a home at last although I've been living here now for thirty three years. You know it's having a simple quiet life and having everything in my life that I need, except it is disrupted all the time.

Vera (68)

Life in Russia

Anti-Semitism was always there and one felt that one was Jewish. I remember the panic in the 1950s when Stalin had a plan to send the Jews to Siberia and one of the Russian writers advised him not to do it because foreign communist parties would be very angry about it. So one knew one was different, but concrete religion didn't come into it.

Vera left Khrushchev's Soviet Union in 1958 because her parents, who were Polish citizens before World War II, were allowed to return to Poland. So she, her brother and her parents moved from Vilna to Warsaw where she studied English at Warsaw State University. In Warsaw her father studied tailoring and her mother worked in an office. All of her grandparents perished during the war. After Poland, she has lived in Germany, Israel and then the UK where she has taught English and Russian. In London she met her Russian husband who sought and was granted political asylum. They have one son. As one of the older interviewees, she shares experiences going back to Stalin's times.

Childhood

My childhood was spent in Vilna. If we had stayed I would probably have tried to go to university either in Vilna or in Minsk because education was very important. Otherwise you would have been considered not quite *comme il faut*, of the same status, because this idea of everybody having a higher education is very strong; you always need a piece of paper for everything. If you don't have a diploma or certificate of sorts you actually can't get anywhere at all. I don't know whether this has changed now a bit, because in the West (to be honest), you make it, you make it! Nobody is going to go into all these nooks and crannies of whether you went to university or not, although it all depends on which university you go to. I went to university in Warsaw when I was 18

What was your home like in Vilna?

It was a flat that belonged to some famous lawyer before the war. Because it was a phenomenal flat, it was a communal flat which was divided between two families. We shared a kitchen and a loo; there was only one loo and one bathroom. It was really not very nice. We found in the morning that the soap was eaten by mice. It was and is still not very clean there.

What was your life like in Russia?

I was at school from 9am until 3pm and then you would come home and do your homework. But I finished school when I was seventeen and for a year I worked in a factory to get work experience. I didn't work there, I just worked a bit. I didn't exert myself. I would start at 8am at the factory and then come home around three or four o'clock, so that was a normal day.

My mother worked at that time; they all worked. When I came home we had a nanny. She looked after us when we came back from school, but I cannot remember particular extracurricular activities in those days. I was a young Pioneer and Octobrist. We all were very devoted and then when Stalin died, we were all crying and thinking now America is going to attack us because we were completely without any information, absolutely like a planet completely isolated from the rest of the world. My parents were never ardent communists or anything like that, but it would never occur to them to listen to the BBC.

Why did they want to go to Poland?

Basically I wanted to go to Poland. I just found Russia boring; that's all, I didn't have any idea about politics. Of course my parents came with me; they couldn't let me go at eighteen on my own, but I was pestering them. My brother is four years younger; he didn't have a voice in the whole thing. He was only fourteen but he didn't object in any way. He didn't find it a very happy experience to start with, but he didn't take it so hard. I felt

62

very well there because university days are usually care free, basically. We came to Warsaw on the seventeenth of October and on the nineteenth I went straight to university, I didn't wait. I lived in a hostel for a while.

When you went to Poland you must have had Polish in your passport?

No we all had Jewish [in the passport]; it's only by blood, not where you were born. But in Poland you didn't have anything and nobody quite knew who you were if you didn't want them to know. But on a human level you could hear a lot, but not at the state level. You could have any position you wanted, relatively it really wasn't bad. There were trials, show trials in Poland, but never show trials like in Russia. So they were a bit more liberal. The Poles had a sense of humor. It was fun when we came in 1958 because it was not so communist then. It was a bit freer and people were joking about the government a bit, not a lot, but a bit. In the late 1960's it was different. Gomulka was there and anti-Semitism had started again and that was why my parents left. They were almost forced to leave in 1968; they were the victims of this 1967 campaign; before that it wasn't too bad, it was okay. Basically there was Jewish theatre, you know relatively speaking, considering it's a communist system, it was not too bad, nothing compared with Russia; much better. There was no nationality in the passport.

So you're happy that you made the jump from Warsaw...?

Yes, I think it was wise. I think it is also my view that Jews shouldn't live behind the Iron Curtain. So you see I am probably not one of your typical interviewees. There is this dimension that is a bit of a problem, it muddies the water. When you are young of course there are some things that you don't notice, so my university years were quite nice in Poland. I heard and saw a lot of anti-Semitism, only not at the state level. There was no state anti-Semitism in Poland, but it was on an everyday level. In Russia it was also on an everyday level and it was also on a state level; it was double. In Poland it wasn't in your passport. Poles never put nationality in your passport, not even the communists.

63

University

I went to university in Warsaw when I was eighteen. I always wanted to study languages. I am a complete idiot as far as maths and science go. My technology abilities, to say 'zero' are to overstate it; it's minus zero! So I was better at humanities, nothing brilliant, but better than maths. Why did I choose to study English? I think it's always somehow subconscious to move, particularly from those very 'lovely' parts of the world, of course. I think subconsciously it probably matters, and besides England was considered, is considered, the pinnacle of civilization, to be honest, behind the Iron Curtain. The English always try to denigrate themselves and they don't realize that there are parts of the world who really think very seriously that England is the last place where, except of course the United States, where civilization is really high.

What kind of English literature did you study? Thank God, in Poland they were a bit more liberal; we didn't have this rubbish [Jack London was mentioned]. We had classical English literature, starting with Beowulf and Chaucer and going all the way through modern things. We didn't have certain modern authors; we couldn't have Orwell, for instance. That was out of bounds. Otherwise it was a bit milder, it wasn't so severe.

Marriage

My husband is sixteen years older than me. He was a journalist and he asked for political asylum in the UK in 1966. He was a political defector. He worked in all sorts of journalistic institutions and now he has retired at the very young age of 82. He took early retirement at 82 from the BBC's Russian service and he is Russian. We got married here in March 1968.

Discussion of sex, sex education and birth control

I had no sex education in school. My mother never talked to me about sex -- not a word, it was the generation. People found it awkward there; people did not even explain about periods and puberty or anything. You had to learn it from friends, from your class mates. Contraceptives were also an absolute taboo. In Poland I knew women who used abortions as contraceptives, but in Russia I hadn't heard anything. Don't forget I lived in a small provincial place; things would get out too quickly. It's intimidating to live in a small place; you do behave a bit differently. As for infidelity it was never discussed, nothing of the sort. An absolute taboo.

Abortions

I don't know anybody who had one to be honest; in Poland, yes, but not then in the Soviet Union.

Definition of a good mother

Probably a good mother should get more involved in a way with the children but I happen to be a bit aloof. So I haven't done that. I never, for instance, played with my son when he was very young; I found it a bit boring. **If he had been a girl, would it have been different?** Probably it would have been a bit different. But I think one should get involved a bit more, but nobody got involved with me and nobody ever played with me. I had the most phenomenal mother in the world but she never bothered with all this. I hope I grew up quite normal! One shouldn't also overestimate all this interfering non-stop, but really it would be better to get a bit more love than to be in one's pockets all the time; this can be very irritating and I think it's bad for children because they are so infantilized. Western society now is being like children and in Russia it's even more so. You are completely and utterly a child until you die. It's part of the awful circumstances and hardship. In many ways people are complete infants; in many ways they don't think for themselves. They might be physically very exhausted, but mentally very childish.

Do you think there were any problems that were specifically related to women?

Women in Russia were treated like dirt. Even today a woman at forty is of no consequence anymore, although they are probably changing now a bit. But women are not treated very well at all and they do awful jobs. In the

65

factory where I worked it was horrific. [The factory she worked in made tape recorders, etc...] Also women were cleaning the roads in minus 20 degrees because the black ice was fatal. You know you could kill yourself slipping on it. So women were doing all menial awful jobs and they had to look after the family as well. It was a very, very bad deal. The quality of life was abysmal and there were not the facilities we have in the West. Giving birth was always a big thing; here people give birth and they don't even talk about it. It was different times!

Did religion play a role when you were in Russia?

Not really. Anti-Semitism was always there and one felt that one was Jewish. I remember the panic in the 1950s when Stalin had a plan to send the Jews to Siberia and one of the Russian writers advised him not to do it because foreign communist parties would be very angry about it. So one knew one was different, but concrete religion didn't come into it. Although my uncle, my father's elder brother, was always in the synagogue on Fridays and Saturday mornings and they prayed for Stalin and for the Politburo. They didn't want to go to Birobidzhan (Stalin's plan).

When Stalin died in March 1953, do you really remember crying?

Yes, yes I was personally crying. Everybody around me was crying. I remember it very well. Yes, and we heard about the doctors' plot [the alleged doctors' plot to kill Stalin] at that stage. My Russian friends were telling me not to worry. Their parents told them not to trust Jews, they said, but 'I'm a friend of yours so don't worry', because there were people like that. Not everybody was anti-Semitic. It was very rare, but there were normal people, but you always have a few normal ones, good ones. I didn't go through any particular hardship or horrible things that you might find interesting. I am not a very interesting example!

How did you spend your free time when you weren't at school?

We read, because we couldn't do anything else. You couldn't listen to jazz, you couldn't dance the boogie woogie, and you couldn't dance any foreign dances. It was all very traditional, of course. We went to dances; we danced the waltz, the foxtrot, the tango, nothing more than that. And we read a lot of rubbish, but we read classical things as well so it was not all bad. But we were all reading and reading, unless somebody did sports, which I wasn't a sports person, or chess. I remember I went to a dramatics society and they would put on Soviet plays and things like that. So that was what people did as well.

How do you picture the ideal woman in the Soviet Union?

The ideal woman would be a member of the Party and serve the state. I think physically people didn't take much notice of the ideal women in the Moscow metro, but ideologically a woman should serve the state, be a mother and be also a Party member if she is worth it. The main thing is you have to be worthy of it.

What did femininity mean?

Femininity did mean clothing and girls did look after themselves. It was second nature so they did try to make the best of what they had. People took a lot of trouble over their clothes because in Russia it's still very important the way you are dressed. For the theatre you would wear special shoes. If it were winter, you'd change; it was very important. One always tried to get Western clothes - that was very important.

Strong woman in Russian culture

Women are very strong because they have to put up with a lot. Very often they support their husbands who think that they are poets and intellectuals. They sit there the whole day thinking about the Russian soul while women really work. Women can be very energetic and very good managers. My mother was just working in an office, but she was the one that kept the family together. I don't think she was alone in this.

Did you think about pensions?

Not really because nobody thought about money because nobody had anything. People didn't bother about money so much because nobody had anything. We had a bit of a guarantee from the state for some basic things but people really didn't understand or didn't bother or didn't think about it. There is one very important poet, Mandelshtam, who said that our fright of what might happen to us physically completely killed our fright of death. People never talked about it because nobody was afraid of death because there were so many more things to worry about, about how to get through the day. Here in the West, I found that a child of four knew that we are here only for a short while and our life - for all intents and purposes - is not that important. But there you never thought about it. You thought you were going to be forever; Stalin was going to be forever, everything was going to be forever. There was a completely sterile [approach], particularly when we were young, nothing was instilled into us, any wisdom about life in general, I don't remember, we read a lot but....

Validating Western views about the past: Emphasis on children and closeness to parents

I must say that the children are loved and are treated well. Another thing is that they are made into infants and their parents look after them until they are pensioners. On balance, children are loved, unless of course parents are (like today) alcoholics; then they just throw them out onto the streets. On the whole there is a degree of closeness to parents. People did look after each other because they were all against the state. People were united against a common enemy, probably not consciously but people looked after parents and one had to have respect for one's elders; there was a bit of that.

Life in London

You said that you wanted to go to Warsaw because you were bored in the Soviet Union. Was that really the main reason or did you want to leave the Soviet Union?

They were related to each other but I never regretted leaving; I never missed it for a moment. But I might be made this way. But honestly at that point I didn't know anything about politics. Later on in Poland and in England I did and I am quite ferociously anti-communist and probably on balance very right wing but then I didn't think so.

Why did you come to London?

I came to London on the 19th of December 1966. I had been in Poland for eight years. Before that I was in Israel almost a year and then I decided I probably didn't want to live in Poland. Again it wasn't so terribly clear although I was very grown up by then, but I think I didn't like Poland. I came alone to London. I came to improve my English and I promised that I would return but I didn't. I was actually teaching English then.

How difficult did you find it to adjust to:

Climate

Not a problem. I think that the British climate is first class. You don't have very different temperatures. It's quite moderate and even, and I can't stand hot weather. So for me it's fine. Israel was too hot.

Transport

Now I complain nonstop but when I came I have to admit that the contrast between the East and the West was great, so that one was not very much into this 'trifle', that is, transport. When you are younger I suppose you don't pay too much attention to it but I was absolutely amazed that the English were so meek about everything. Even if you didn't have the fare on the bus there was never a fuss. They would let you go; not today, I think, but I found that they were very meek, there were still mean [experiences] but everything was fine. Now they have to be a bit different, but then they were very relaxed. It probably comes from the fact that they think they are the best; when you think you are the best, you can become very sort of lackadaisical.

Language

I had to probably adjust for about a year or so. After all I graduated in this language, but of course I didn't understand many idioms or pronunciation. I still don't always catch everything, I must admit, but I do my best.

Property

My friend met me because I came by ship from Gdansk. She met me and she took me to the place where she rented a room. Then I rented for a bit and then I met my husband and I moved in with him. So I didn't (to be honest) have the time to be very much bothered with it. But another thing was that for about eight months I stayed with friends of my mother's relations in north London which was very nice. When I came and told them who I am, they said, 'Look, you move in and we will help you a bit.' I was very lucky. It was a phenomenal flat. I didn't realize what a good address it was. I was absolutely amazed by this house but I didn't have any heating and I couldn't sleep of course. I didn't complain but I was absolutely struck by this because behind the Iron Curtain it's always extremely warm, because heating comes from the central system.

With whom did you socialize?

We did socialize in the beginning. I was friendly with the neighbors but then I found that I really didn't feel quite 100% but that's not a criticism at all. I was disappointed.

School system

My son went to a preparatory school and then he went to an independent school. We decided this because we thought that a child of an immigrant will have a better chance if they have been properly educated.

Did you get to know the mothers of other little boys and were they English?

They were all English, funnily enough. They would leave their children with me and I would leave my son with them. It was a very useful exchange but I never got very friendly with anybody. I am still friendly with my own kind so to speak. I am rather an Anglophile, but it's difficult, because we are on a different plane. We are not worse, nor better-- just different. I find the English very eccentric because I cannot get through their logic. Maybe it's because they are islanders -- this must have a lot to do with it!

Was it a problem being a mother without your own mother or mother-in-law?

My mother-in-law was in Russia. It was sometimes lonely, I must say. I was very happy when my mum came but one managed, one managed. I had a few friends from university so that was helpful and some very distant relations on my mother's side from Wales. It wasn't easy because one saw that it was a completely different society and we have to adjust. But I cannot say that it was very traumatic but I am probably a bit of a flippant person, que sera sera. I did miss my mother when I had my son because I wasn't very efficient and he didn't sleep well. I almost didn't sleep for a year and a half, so when my parents came to stay, mum said that I should give my son to her and I went to bed and didn't get up for about ten hours because I hadn't slept properly until then.

Shopping

I remember I worked in Whiteleys [a department store in Bayswater] for a few months. It was a proper shop and I remember that I was leaving, I didn't have anything and I was of course pretty poor. I was going through all the departments to the exit and everything was there on display and I thought, gosh it would be so easy to become a thief. I wasn't tempted, I am happy now that I didn't touch anything but I thought it was very tempting, because the things are all there. I didn't shop a lot before I was married, only occasionally. Since I married I have no interest in shopping whatsoever because I know I can have everything I want. You think that you might go back [to Poland, to Russia] so you try to stock up on things,

71

but the moment I found out I was staying here I didn't care. I am a hunter and I love shopping in the charity shops and things like that, just to try and hunt interesting things.

Do you miss Russian food?

Yes, this unfortunately has remained. I miss proper bread, proper hamburgers that we used to do for a thousand years. I miss berries, fresh berries from the forest, proper mushrooms and proper sausage, because food here is still abysmal. Now I shop in a Russian shop. It's called the North [*Sever*] off the North Circular; it's a dreadful place, it's just a bunker really, but we go there for all sorts of things. It's actually horrific but we buy our *pelmeni* [kind of ravioli], and our *blinchik* [pancake; fritter], that's stayed with me in spite of all sorts of three star Michelin restaurants, and also sour cream and proper, proper yoghurt, and cottage cheese, curd cheese, and radishes.

Housing

We lived in a house, then we sold it; then we lived somewhere else, and somewhere else, and then we moved to Germany for two years, and then we came back and got a house in north Kensington where we have been for the last twenty seven years. Unfortunately we are moving to south west London because my husband has retired and we find, as I don't have a pension, it's wiser financially to move. I don't have a pension out of my own stupidity and being careless and because I was brought up to think that these things didn't matter. It's just stupidity; there is really no other word. So selling the house we will release the capital. It's strange after over twenty seven years to move to other premises but we have to. It's okay -- we will take it as it comes; we took so many things like that. I will have to tell myself that I am okay.

Role of husband

You know he was married before me, so I am the third wife. It's normal in the Soviet Union: you marry at twenty and he married at twenty, and then another [marriage]. He was quite okay in the Soviet Union, quite a prestigious worker, and everything on balance probably could have been a bit better but I never thought in those terms.

Is he more involved or helpful with shopping, cooking, cleaning, childcare?

Around the house? Russians? Never, good lord, never. I must say as far as shopping is concerned, he will do shopping for me now. If I am not there, he will do it if I ask him, but he needs a list or something. The fact that he would help with the shopping would be the biggest role change. Russian men were not brought up to help! Of course, the double burden remained in my marriage; there is no doubt about it.

Does his job take precedence over yours?

It would always take precedence, here, there or on Mars, anywhere. Work, then his car and then I probably come number three. **Would your son do the same thing?** I understand from my daughter-in-law that he is not very good at home. He doesn't bother with many things. But they have no children so she has a bit of time to do more. He sometimes helps but not a lot and only under pressure.

Does religion play any role for you once you came here?

Not really, I must confess. I was brought up terribly anti [religion] and atheist, but I am not an atheist of course but that's how I was brought up. So not really no, no. It really doesn't play a role and besides I found the Jewish God also extremely, extremely severe -- not like other Gods, so kind and forgiving. My husband is very much inclined to religion, I must say. **So you didn't bring your son up in a religious way?** It's a terrible thing to say but no, he knows he's Jewish and he doesn't make any bones about it. I don't think that he has ever been to a synagogue; it's a terrible thing to admit we are so lapsed. On the other hand we are not at all lapsed -- we are much more associated with Jewish culture and everything the way we understand it, but not religion per se. It's a mixture really and he

73

knows he is Jewish and his wife was good enough to take his name. A girl who has a beautiful name, to take our name -- people are eccentric.

Would you go back to Russia?

If God is kind enough, no. I even don't want to go back now for a holiday. I don't know what has happened to me. I used to go quite regularly, but I don't feel like going at all.

What do you miss the most?

Probably nothing now. Don't forget I left a long time ago. I am very much connected and I do go, and the language is always discussed for hours a day. I took part in the English /Russian dictionary (the Oxford one). I go there but I don't want to go as much as I used to. You know what is probably nice: Russians are easy communicators so for a while it's nice, but not for a long time. But you can really feel that people are open, quite open and very gregarious, let's say sociable.

How would you characterize British society?

Well I don't find that they can communicate at all, so that's why I find that teaching Russian to English people is an additional chore because they don't want to say anything in English, let alone in a foreign language, whereas other people from the Continent are much more used to interacting. For instance, Germans are phenomenal linguists and it's easy, but the English I find very difficult to understand after so many years. I mean I have nothing but praise for the English on a human level, but I have never got through to them somehow.

What do you value most about living in London?

Of course freedom, the fact that nobody meddles into your affairs. People are very polite and very helpful if there is a crisis. But then they leave you alone, and people don't impose themselves or their opinions. That's very nice because I am exactly the opposite. I think London and New York are my kind of town. I like big cities. I like places where nobody knows me. I love to go to places where nobody knows me and I can walk or do whatever I like. London is a wonderful place. England actually is also fine.

Nadia (66)

Life in Russia

There were specific problems for women, like the double burden. Everyone was complaining about that. It was accepted as an automatic role of a woman to be a grandmother, an active grandmother. If she didn't want this role and if she didn't have an excuse, like having a job or a disease, then of course it would be sort of a social condemnation.

Nadia emigrated to the UK in 1965 with her first husband who was a South African. She originally went with him to Glasgow (Scotland) and subsequently to London with her second husband. She studied linguistics and philology at Moscow State University which prepared her for a career as a university lecturer. With her first husband she had two children. Her mother (from Vologda) was an historian and her father (from Tambov) an economist at the Institute of Foreign Trade in Moscow. Both are deceased. She is the middle child in a family which consisted of a sister and a half-sister. Her older sister is now living in LA and her younger sister in Kiev. She grew up in Kiev but her grandparents played no role in her childhood as they had died when she was growing up.

Childhood

As a teenager I was interested in pop music. We listened to Radio Free Europe but not very frequently. I also listened to Voice of America and the BBC. I started to listen to the BBC when I was thirteen or fourteen. **Could you trust the BBC?** It was just interesting, it wasn't a matter of trust. It was just more news and I was more interested in the cultural programs. There was no problem listening to the radio in the late 1950's apart from the reception. Sometimes there occasionally would be very bad interference, but not always. The cultural programs were relatively clear. I even remember some of the programs I listened to, like when Marilyn Monroe visited Britain. I also listened to the English language programs. I think I was actually more inclined to listen to the BBC because they had a fantastic jazz program. Jazz started before World War II and I think that although there was jazz in the Soviet Union, the American jazz was just better. Soviet jazz existed but it was actually 'toothless' jazz. Voice of America was really good for American jazz.

Did you study English at school?

It was a normal school, not a special school, but I chose to study English. I studied three languages -- Russian, Ukrainian, and English.

University

At that time I didn't have any specific idea as to a career. It was basically going to university for the enjoyment of studying. The underlying idea was if you wanted social mobility in your life, then you have to go for higher education. In other words, education was good in itself. I choose what I studied because it basically was my affinity with English culture. I started my studies at Kiev University. I studied there for one year and then I got married. My husband was studying in Moscow University. So I got a transfer from one university to another. In fact it was quite complicated. The programs were slightly different. Also, in Moscow there was a problem of a *propiska* [residence permit; identity card]. It took some time to obtain.

Marriage

My first husband was from South Africa. He was studying for his PhD in London, South Africa and Moscow. His studies were arranged by the African National Congress. He was in Moscow writing his PhD in the field of economics. I met him in Kiev at the university when he was taking a Russian language course. We were married in 1960 or 1961 when I was nineteen and he was twenty four.

Discussion of sex, sex education and birth control

Sex education itself was, I would say, quite sporadic. You basically discussed it among friends. I think it mainly was a hygienic education with my mother. It was mainly about the sexual side of life, that is, what you don't do. This sort of discussion wasn't forbidden but it was basically an emphasis on hygiene. If you get involved with sexual activity you have the consequences of it -- pregnancy and what not.

I knew about contraceptives, basically that was the sheath [condom]. They were very badly designed and of poor quality in those days. The Russian word was 'galoshes' because the rubber was so thick and they didn't fit very well. Children used to find them and play with them! Since only sheathes were available, therefore pregnancy happened!

Abortions

Strangely enough, abortions were accepted as a form of contraception but there was no discussion about it. People just said I have to go and have an abortion and that was that. In my group at university there were several girls of my age who had children. In fact having children at Moscow University was quite a normal thing. The floors were covered with children. We used to babysit for each other.

Giving birth

In those days, children were a part of the marriage. As soon as you married you were supposed to have a child, at least one, but better one and a half! My son was born in Moscow in 1963 and my daughter was born in Glasgow in 1969. For my first child, the maternity care was good because it was at Moscow University. It was quite impressive because you had to see your doctor once a fortnight for measurements, weight, etc.. The maternity hospital was this wonderful building in Moscow. I was in this hospital because it was in the area in which I was living. The experience was uneventful really. There was a ward for women and when it was your time, you are invited to the delivery ward without your husband. It was actually quite strict in terms of hygiene. They were quite determined not to allow husbands in for several days, sometimes ten days. You hold the baby from the window so the husband could see the child.

My delivery was quick but someone else arrived and I was put to the side. In other words, after I delivered my son I watched another woman give birth. I thought that was really very interesting. At Moscow University in those days we all had to go through medical training as part of our military training. The men went for the real stuff and the women, because I was in the English section, did either translations or military or medical things. I was doing the nursing training for five years as part of my military training. I really was lucky. The child was small, he was only 2 kg 800 g which for Russia was small and I was young.

Role of husband

He was a white South African who was in the anti-apartheid movement. This didn't produce a shock in the family because if a foreigner was interested in 'left' politics rather than just an ordinary businessman, for example, it was sort of a respected position. He was already '*nash*' [one of us], or almost '*nash*'. My husband did help with childcare, such as babysitting and things like that, but not really with shopping because Moscow University had a well-stocked shop. There are also two or three good cafés or restaurants so in those days (we left in 1965) you could still get salmon and caviar! And friends who had access to the American or British embassies would bring us coffee; the Americans would bring us cigarettes. But a working woman with a child would have had a much harder experience than we had as students.

Living arrangements

We never lived with my parents. We lived together in the dorm, in the hall of residence. So we never lived in a communal flat. To some extent it was a rather privileged situation in that we had a whole block to ourselves which consisted of two rooms, small rooms but they were two rooms. The kitchen was a communal one in Moscow University as nobody had a kitchen. There was a toilet, a shower, and two rooms. Usually in those days it was shared by two students. Because we were students and my husband was actually a research student, we got this block together. Before our child was born we actually had one large room, a research room. But when the child was born we had two rooms.

Were there different gender roles in the Soviet Union?

It's difficult to say about the Soviet context. I think I was more conscious of different roles here in the UK than in the Soviet Union. At the university in Moscow, we had so many female students who were reading physics and maths. There was no kind of gender roles there. The higher your education in the Soviet Union, the less was the impact of your gender. Of course rising to the top was somewhat different. The medical profession was primarily female but the medical profession wasn't high in the social scale anyway. They're like the teaching profession. So in this respect women were predominantly in these spheres. It's difficult to make comparisons because these professions are more valued here in the UK. In the non-productive sphere you were not so high up in the social scale. The state obviously determined what was valuable and what wasn't valuable.

Were there any problems specific to women?

Yes, there were specific problems for women, like *the double burden*. Everyone was complaining about that. It was accepted as an automatic role of a woman to be a grandmother, an active grandmother. If she didn't want this role and if she didn't have an excuse, like having a job or a disease, then of course it would be sort of a social condemnation. In the average family, the two families (husband's and wife's) would take part in looking after the grandchildren – they would probably share it, except for distance. Culturally, the young couple would probably move back to be near the wife's relations.

Childcare

In my case my mother provided a lot of help when my son was born. Although she lived in Kiev, she came and stayed in Moscow because my grandfather lived there. So she stayed there and came to look after the child periodically. Then I had a babysitter, a woman who worked in the university as a cleaner. She babysat for children at the university. When I was writing my final diploma, my mother took the child to Kiev. Mothers really played a significant role! In fact, everybody that I knew in Moscow – students as well as non-students – had the help of their mother or a grandmother. Grandparents looked after the children all the time. Very often the retirement age for a woman was fifty five so that left healthy years for the upbringing of the grandchildren. I think it was like an institution, actually integrated into society, that the grandparents would be there to help. Of course a lot of parents, elderly parents, lived in the same flat. I guess I would have been an anomaly as I lived separately. When my mother came to Moscow, she had to stay with my grandfather. She would come to look after the child several times a week and sometimes would stay overnight with us. My husband's parents also helped us from South Africa and they sent us clothes and food, so their contribution was also significant.

Infidelity

I discussed this topic with women but not with men. It was rather an ambiguous attitude. There was one case among friends of mine whose husband was caught by her sleeping with someone else. It was really very surprising. Otherwise among my friends or even in my family there was no infidelity. The attitude towards infidelity was basically ambiguous; I wasn't sure how to think about it.

Was religion any relevance then?

No, because my parents' marriage was a mixed kind of nationalities. My mother was half-Jewish and my father was also mixed (he was from Tambov in the Ukraine). So there was no baptism, etc.. My husband came from an orthodox Jewish family but they were more like reformed Jews.

He, of course, was not religious at all. His group were the boys` in South Africa that were doing revolution rather than synagogue.

How do you picture the ideal woman in the Soviet Union?

I don't know anybody of my circle of friends who would picture the ideal woman as a strong, peasant type. The ideal woman would be more like a fairy tale image in this context, a woman who looks well, who knows how to be smart, who has the right type of clothes, that sort of thing. And the one who has no problems with study, the one who knows which subjects to choose in order to pass the exams. **Femininity** is included in this way – you can't go out of the house without dressing yourself up – the shoes and everything have to be properly matched. The environment at Moscow State University was so interesting because the girls looked like pictures.

I remember one Italian student who was a friend of mine and I asked him whether he was missing his home. He replied, 'Just look at the girls – how can I miss home! They're wonderful!' The girls at Moscow State University had access to a lot of rare commodities because of their background. Their parents were either going abroad or were well able to buy clothes at special shops. A high percentage of the girls were from the elite. It's not a difficult subject [linguistics and philology] to study and you don't have to be exceptionally bright (although you had to pass the exams). The bright girls were studying in the science faculties and they came from varied backgrounds; they were selected according to their real abilities. My faculty was basically – if you know somebody you [could] squeeze in! This was definitely part of *blat*. It's the *blat* of a different kind in that it actually works because of your social position in society. If you were the daughter of a Party secretary somewhere else, you would be given preferential treatment during the entrance exam.

Strong woman in Russian culture

Women were strong but in my day it was the period of destalinization, the opening up of all kinds of things from the West, such as the images of Bridget Bardot and Marilyn Monroe. After all the films were already there.

So the strong woman image was already shaken because that was the time when a lot of things were changing [the end of 1950s]. Lots of films were shown from abroad. When I was growing up after the war, there were lots of Western movies, such as the whole series of Tarzan. Errol Flynn movies were shown. We were really full of these Western images and images of the women, such as Lana Turner. Some of the films were German, including some of the films made in fascist Germany. In *The Indian Tomb*, a very famous German film in two parts, Liana played an Indian princess in this love story. We also saw all of the movies of Goring's mistress.

During the war we stayed in the Urals, not in Kiev, but after that from 1946 onwards we were living in Kiev. My whole generation was brought up with the images of very sophisticated ladies from Hollywood. This was a contradiction of that life: on the one hand you had the images of the peasantry (the sculptures of the women in the Moscow underground) and on the other hand after the war you had all of these movies. So, a woman was strong in character but she also had to be feminine at the same time. So if you look at girls of my generation they were pretty confused.

Life in London

Why did you leave the Soviet Union and come to London?

I married a 'foreigner'. It wasn't a forced decision as it was normal to go with one's husband. I wanted to go, I liked it! We left in 1965. At first we had to stay in London to wait for my husband's and my jobs to begin in Glasgow. He already had a job and I was having an interview there. It was just a matter of waiting a couple of months and there was someone in London who had an empty flat.

How difficult was it to adjust to:

I'm very pleased I came to this country. Let's put it this way, I wouldn't change things in my life.

83

Climate

In the beginning it was summer. It was all right. After that there was the absence of a proper winter and that was a bit confusing. Otherwise it wasn't a problem.

People

People were welcoming, both in London and in Glasgow. Of course I was at an institution which introduced me to people and I'm sure that it would have been different if I hadn't worked.

Language

I spoke English already, that is, about 90%.

Property

My husband's family found us some property. My father-in-law had gone to Glasgow and bought us an apartment. Money helps! Of course then property prices were affordable. The flat was only four times my salary and since we both worked, it wasn't so much of a problem.

In Glasgow we had a five room apartment, but it was rather cold. There was no heating whereas in the Soviet Union you had a very well-adjusted heating system; when the radiators were working you had to open the windows because it was too hot. In Glasgow it was just an electric off peak heating appliance(s). That was a bit of a shock!

School system

It was reasonably easy to get my children into the school system. The university had a crèche for young children and my son went for half a day. The other half a day was spent with a Russian babysitter of aristocratic origin. Then he went to an ordinary state school. In those days there was a selection system and as a five year old he had to go for an interview. It was exactly the same with my daughter, but she went to a private but affordable kindergarten and then to the same school as her brother.

Transport

Transport was good. We lived next to the university in Glasgow and so didn't use the transport system that much, but when I taught evening classes I still remember that it was good.

With whom did you socialize?

In Glasgow, we socialized with fellow students and with friends of my husband. There was a Russian contingent, an American contingent and a British contingent there. They were very accommodating and supportive.

Shopping

I found shopping rather enjoyable. Lots of choice, much better choice. I did buy makeup and tried to adapt to the styles here. Now I don't spend much time shopping as it's boring and there's not much of a drive anymore. I would call myself a reluctant shopper. I used to like to shop but now there's so much technology around that it depresses me so that when I go to the shops and I see all this new stuff, I think, Oh god -- I can't do that. The whole of China is working for GUM [State Department Store] in Moscow!

Russian food

In the beginning I missed Russian food, especially lovely caviar. You could buy it in the center in Moscow anywhere, even though the price was high but you could still afford it. I also missed the bread, the cheese, the smoked fish.

Role of first husband

I think he did less here than in Russia because he had become more involved with more 'manly' things, like active politics and academic work. My first marriage lasted about twenty years. My son was already at university and my daughter was already a teenager when that marriage ended.

Whose career took precedence?

His career took precedence, but it was also my choice. I considered it my duty first and foremost to look after my children. Then, when the children were slightly older, I could concentrate more on my career. While they were small, it was set in my head that the children were the priority.

Did you bring up children by gender roles?

Actually I didn't differentiate the roles at all; I just knew what they had to have, sort of in terms of education and guidance. I didn't think that my daughter would be any different from my son. My daughter was probably more sporty than my son because she went quite early onto skateboarding.

Concepts of femininity

When I was in the Soviet Union, femininity was more appearance than substance. Here, with the sexual revolution it was something else. So that was a bit shocking. In the 1960s, I thought - and perhaps it was my mother's influence – that personal hygiene was very important in sexual relations. I thought that this liberated sex was a bit too much and who was gaining from it? Whether it's good for ladies or not, I wasn't sure, but I was always kind of asking this question.

What does equality mean here?

In the Soviet Union, it was like everything else. You had the official ideology about equality, claiming that women were equal to men, so you couldn't object to it. What you were actually objecting to in life is that it didn't work out like this. But then nothing did: it was part and parcel of many other things. In the Soviet Union it was basically that women were dissatisfied with their husbands because they didn't help them with domestic work and were rather selfish.

Here it was a different story. I would say that here husbands were more understanding by and large (that is, people in my circle), whereas the official ideology was a problem. In my days, in my environment, the husbands here were involved, not as much as they are now, but it was not an unusual thing to meet friends who were shopping together. My daughter was born in the UK and unlike my son's birth in Moscow, my husband was allowed to be at the birth. This was a big difference.

Has religion played any role in your life?

I encouraged my children to go to the morning [religious] sessions at the school, but they found friends who didn't go to religious assemblies, so they opted out. So religion has not played a big part in my life.

Going back to Russia?

No, not for good. I don't know whether I'm settled here but I am settled out of Russia. When I came in 1965, Russia is not the same as it is now.

What do you miss most?

I never really missed anything, except my family. People yes, that is different, but as a country in those days I wasn't at all shocked that I left or anything. I didn't have nostalgia for the land itself. With friends I tried to correspond and keep in touch as much as I could. I never lost touch with many people. I visited when my parents died and then I didn't go back for almost twenty years. That twenty years was basically a period of integration into life here and maybe that was good because I was young enough to say, 'I'm here and I'm going to live here. End of story.'

How would you characterize British society?

In the early days, what struck me was that Britain was a society in which British people were very fair and very rational. A lot of people were very comforting. They would actually discuss things with you and they were sane. Now it is different. I would say that a lot of people of my generation are quite disturbed, quite dissatisfied. And not really happy. In the 1960s they were quite a contented, quite a happy lot. Now they are not. Whether it has something to do with age or not, I don't think so because a lot of things have disappeared which were actually social cushions for people, like social provisions. Of course, the NHS went from bad to worse. As for pensions, I have been lucky enough to receive what was mine. I know a lot of people not in the university sector who lost their pensions. The social provisions as they used to be don't exist anymore. As far as I can judge, the schools have also gotten much worse. This is what I learn from my own grandchildren. In this respect maybe people had less money, myself included in those days, but there were things that were available for which you didn't have to have much money. Now you do need to have money for most things. In the Glasgow context, the unrest in the deprived areas has now penetrated towards the middle class areas. In the 1960s and 1970s it was quite segregated. ....

What do you value most about living in the UK?

I think I understood that as soon as I came here. It is the degree of personal safety because you can exercise any political affiliation or anything and your life is not threatened because of it. Actually in the Soviet Union even in those days, that was the main problem. I left during the remains of the Khrushchev time, before the dissident movement really started in the full sense, and that was a liberal time in the USSR. Even then, you could express so much and no more. That personal safety, despite your political activity or affiliation, is very important.

ADDITIONS: Cinema in the Soviet Union

What I find surprising when people discuss **what life was like** in the Soviet Union is that they think it was a kind of uniform picture, but the **escapist movies** existed to the same extent as they existed for the

American public. I remember those queues to the cinema because the next foreign movie was coming. We saw a lot of French movies and Italian neo-realist movies. We were brought up on this. The French movies were famous classics, such as *The Red and Black* (*Le Rouge et le Noir*). The release of the films was all over the Soviet Union. Like *Rome, Open City* and other neo-realist Italian films. As for British movies, we saw, for example, *Room at the Top*. So in this respect I think Soviet cinematography couldn't have supplied enough films to show to this huge public. Therefore the films were always imported and always shown. Eisenstein films were shown, like *October*, or as I call them, historical untruths. *Alexander Nevsky* was a popular movie and Part One was also shown. The movies of the 1920s and 1930s were shown in clubs as special shows but not on the widescreen. Even if they were shown on the collective farms, the projection was so poor that you wouldn't be able to see the film properly. There were groups, there were jazz groups, but there was a lot of objection to these groups but you could still go and listen to the groups. But the cinema was the revelation.

Life after Stalin's death in the late 1950s was actually quite interesting. The destalinization process, the appearance of writers, the journal *Novy Mir*, were fantastic -- all these discussions and the tensions -- it was a good time!!

Kira (62)

Life in Russia

I had abortions and they were awful. I think the stories are true about how awful the abortions were. There were queues to get the abortions. You had to go to the polyclinic and get some paper and then go to the hospital....For many years for many women, it was just a pain killer in the womb. It was a very very painful procedure. But if you had money and/or if you had some connections, you could ask for painkillers before the actual operation.

Kira left Russia in 2000 but only came to London in 2004. She grew up in Sverdlovsk in the Urals and earned a PhD in chemistry at Moscow Institute for Chemical Technology. As a student, she was introduced to her future husband with whom she has one daughter and one grandson who are presently living in Moscow. In London, Kira is training to be a licensed guide for Russian tourists. Both of her parents were engineers: her mother taught at a polytechnic institute and her father was the manager of several successive factories. Her youngest brother is a computer expert living in Melbourne, Australia, whereas her oldest brother [a 'cripple'] lives in a residential care home in a small village near Tver. She only remembers her maternal grandfather because her maternal grandmother died when she was five. Her paternal grandparents were Jewish and were killed at the beginning of World War II.

My family

My family moved to a small town outside of Moscow called Rzhev, a town which is famous for very important battles in World War II. My father was a director of a factory and he had some troubles in his job in Sverdlovsk so he moved to Rzhev. The rest of the family didn't want to move; we had a nice apartment in Sverdlovsk, many friends, a house - we had everything. My mother had a very good position in Sverdlovsk at the polytechnic institute. My father was a member of the Party; my mother was not. In 1955 there was some motion among engineers. Somebody at the factory (the Party, that is) wanted my father to go to the kolkhoz [collective farm] where he would be the chief [director] at the Machine Tractor Station [MTS]. My father agreed because we had a private house in the suburbs of Sverdlovsk. My oldest brother went to a special school. There was only one such school in Sverdlovsk and it took maybe one hour to get there. The Party promised my father that they would get him an apartment in the center of Sverdlovsk, but he should go to the MTS. My father agreed, but he didn't go to the MTS. He sold our private house and he took the money (which was our money, of course). My maternal grandfather had bought the house. He was a very famous man in Sverdlovsk because during the war he was the chief engineer in Uralmash [Ural machine building plant] where Yeltsin was. My father wasn't very popular after this. Some area (*raion*) organization of the Party blamed him, of course. So after that my father moved because he couldn't find a job at that same level in Sverdlovsk. He moved to the north of Sverdlovsk *oblast* and he got a very nice job there. He had a good salary and my youngest brother was born there. But the Party decided that it was not good to have him in the same area, so he had to move to another part of the country. And it was suggested to him to go as chief to a factory somewhere near Moscow. So he went to Rzhev. Then my mother got a job at another institute in Rzhev and I went to school there.

I was interested in reading books because I went to the music school. I played the piano and did a bit of sports, but not too much. I myself was an excellent pupil and ended secondary school with a gold medal. In Rzhev in the 10th grade I was taught chemistry by a very nice teacher. I liked this teacher and I liked chemistry! At that time it was very popular to study chemistry. Why was it so popular? Because of a slogan. Earlier in Lenin's time the slogan was, 'Soviet power is electrification'; in Khrushchev's time, the slogan was, 'Soviet power is the chemicalization of the whole nation'. So I followed the propaganda! I am sorry, but I like my job very much, I like chemistry very much, but ….

In Rzhev our apartment was a three-bedroom apartment. At that time our apartment was one of the best in Rzhev. It was where the elite lived, but I absolutely did not like it. I missed my friends from Sverdlovsk. After two years when I was seventeen I left and went to the Institute in Moscow. For five and a half years I studied at the Moscow Institute for Chemical Technology.

Marriage

During my first degree I got acquainted with my future husband who was in the maths department at Moscow State University [MGU]. We were both students when we met and when we married I was twenty one and he was twenty two. My uncle had a friend before World War II and his son lived with my future husband in the dormitory at MGU, and that's how we were introduced. Like me, he earned his PhD. He was first in his course; he had a fellowship named after Lenin – the highest in the USSR at that time.

Discussion of sex, sex education and birth control

There was no sex education in school. Nor did I learn about sex from my mother. But now I try and teach my daughter. In those days unfortunately I didn't use contraceptives (and maybe that's how I had my daughter, but let's not speculate). Of course I was afraid of getting pregnant, but I did it regularly!

Abortions

Yes, I had abortions and they were awful. I think the stories are true about how awful the abortions were. There were queues to get the abortions. You had to go to the polyclinic and get some paper and then go to the hospital. I learned about this from my girlfriends. For many years for many women, it was just a pain killer in the womb. It was a very painful procedure. But if you had money and/or if you had some connections, you could ask for painkillers before the actual operation. I know of some cases where a young woman died because they used some domestic approaches to get rid of the baby and my mother also spoke about women she knew, one who bled to death after an illegal abortion.

Giving birth

After thirteen months of marriage, our daughter was born. I was young when I had my daughter. I gave birth to her in a hospital near Moscow University. I was in hospital for about seven days. I can't confirm that it was an unpleasant experience.

Living accommodation

As my husband was studying for a PhD, we lived in the dormitory. Our room was about 6 meters square and it had a shower and a toilet. We got a better place once we had the child. When my daughter was a year and a half she went to the crèche and I went to the chemistry department at MGU. We lived there and we had friends there. The first year that I worked I was the senior laboratory assistant/demonstrator, then I became a scientific researcher and ended up as a senior scientific researcher.

How did your husband obtain his position?

When my husband was a PhD student, there was an interesting and very serious problem. He was the first in his class of 400 students, but he was Jewish. He finished his undergraduate degree in 1978 and there was no political discrimination at that time. But after one or two years (I don't remember exactly), there was a war between Israel and Egypt and a policy of discrimination began in this field, especially at Moscow State University. My husband was the student of a very famous mathematician, named Markov, and of Kolagor. They tried to get a position for him at Moscow State University. They promised him this, but the Party didn't allow it. There were some negotiations. The director of MGU was I.G. Petrovsky. Professor Markov went to Petrovsky with the recommendation for my husband. They tried to get him the job. (It was suggested to my husband that he join the Party but he refused.) The head of the Secretariat of the Party tried to get the position for a member of the Party. They asked Petrovsky to give them three positions, one for my husband and two for members of the Party. They put pressure on Petrovsky to get more members of the Party into the faculty; Petrovsky said no. One of these people was third rate. They didn't like it. Then Petrovsky tried to help my husband get a job, because it was very difficult to get a job being Jewish. And then my husband got a position (a *dotsent*, docent, lecturer) at Tver University (at that time, it was Kalinin).

The problem, however, was that I had a job in the chemistry department and I began to do some research for my PhD. Tver was 160 km from Moscow. We didn't know what to do. But suddenly (a very unusual case) my husband was recommended to get an apartment in Tver and we didn't have a choice because we didn't have an apartment in Moscow. So I ought to have gone to Tver too. But the chief in my department suggested I work for a PhD and become a graduate student. So my husband was in Tver, my daughter was with my in-laws in Grodno (it's 8 km from Poland), and I was in Moscow at MGU. When I was a PhD student, my in-laws took care of my daughter for three years. My father died when I was eighteen and my mother was living in Rzhev. So, I lived in Moscow and my husband lived in Tver. But every weekend I went to Tver, cleaned the apartment, cooked meals and left things for my husband for five or six days. But when I was more advanced with my PhD, I didn't have time for that. Then I went to Tver once every two or three weeks. After all, I had to work in the laboratory and conduct experiments, all of which took a great deal of time (often a continuous eight to ten hours at a time).

Definition of a good mother

Of course I worried about my role as a mother. In the summertime we went to Grodno and took my daughter for the holidays. My daughter was worried about me. I phoned her every week; five or seven days we spoke to each other. My husband also visited Grodno. We have a very nice relationship now; we like each other very much. She's now living in Moscow with my grandson.

Women's problems

Maybe it was difficult to get a job after university because of being a woman. After I graduated from the Institute, I had to go to the factory (dealing with semiconductors) to work, but they preferred men to work there. It was very serious shift work, from morning to evening. They knew that a young woman would get married and have children, so they didn't want to teach her the ropes because she would then leave. This was true of several professions.

Was religion any relevance?

Religion didn't play any role in my life at that time. I did describe the problems my husband faced by being Jewish, but it wasn't a religious problem. I think it was just discrimination. I also had discrimination in my search for a job. I was invited to an interview for a research institute outside of Moscow. They asked about my mother and about my father, my grandfather, etc.., and then goodbye! The person they took was absolutely and totally Russian. They inquired about my parents and learned what my mother's and my father's names were: my mother's name was totally Russian and my father's name indicated that he was Jewish.

How do you picture the ideal woman in the Soviet Union?

All my life I have not been interested in politics. For me,[an ideal woman means] it's an interesting job, interesting friends and to look good.

What did femininity mean?

I don't have this idea of femininity. I wanted to look good, I wanted to have some career and I had it. For Russia, yes, I succeeded. **What about clothing?** My uncle, who was Jewish, was a communist officer in World War II, and during the war both his legs were cut off. But before the war he was an engineer at the Leningrad Polytechnic Institute and when he returned after the war to Moscow, I lived with my aunt and uncle when I went to the Institute. My aunt at that time was a very important person because she was the Secretary of the Party organization. And then she was the head planner at an atelier (with 20-25 people) which made winter and spring clothing for men and women. This was in the center of Moscow. Sometimes I was able to get clothing there; once a year I got a present from this place. Especially when my father died, she really took care of me and really loved me. She was very helpful to me. She taught me to cook and clean (my mother did as well). She was a real Russian woman from Siberia. After some years, there were second hand clothing shops where some of my friends worked, some in some famous shops.

Life in London

Why did you leave Russia?

When I was fifty five I was working in Moscow. I had a good position, but because I went to America for two or three months, they wanted to retire me. I didn't want to retire. My husband went to America only for a university semester. So I was retired without my permission. My boss, who is younger than I was, had really promised my job to his wife. So I decided to go to America with my husband!

Why did you come to London?

We came to London in 2004. We came because my husband was invited here as an academic. He originally had a contract for five years, but three weeks ago his head of department said they would keep him in this position. So I think he will now stay.

How difficult was it to adjust to:

Climate

My first year here I was ill, so I didn't like the climate. My friends explained my illness by the change in climate. Now I think it's just normal.

People

In August I applied for a course at City University so that if I pass, I will get a license to be a guide, a guide for Russian visitors, for excursions in London. I have learned a great deal about the history of London, etc...

Language

For me speaking English is a real problem. All my life I've loved English. I understand English and I read it without any problem, but speaking is difficult.

Property

Finding a place to live was very difficult. For one month we lived in a hotel on the understanding that we would find a place to live originally. We lived in one apartment but I was looking for another one. I actually looked at forty four apartments and then our estate agent suggested an apartment. And now it's good.

Transport

I think the transport system here, that is, the tube and the buses, is better, because the metro and the buses in Moscow are very crowded. In my last years in Moscow I had a car and I didn't use public transport. Here I use public transport. And now I have a Freedom Pass [for women Londoners over the age of 60]!

Lack of family

This is probably the most important difficulty in adjusting to life here. I really am missing my mother and I'm worried about my mother. She is all alone in Tver.

Socializing with whom?

I don't really socialize with many English people and I don't know my neighbors. I find the English very friendly and I have some acquaintances at the course with whom I talk about 'world' problems, for example. My husband is very special and is quite introverted. At his job he met another professor from MGU whom he didn't know before and we spend some time with him and his wife.

Shopping

London is a very expensive town. For the last twelve years, my husband has worked in Paris every summer and that's where I try and buy many clothes. I also buy clothes in America where it is much cheaper. I do shop here but not too much.

Russian food

Sometimes I go to Russian stores here. I miss *tvorok* [cottage cheese, curds] and mushrooms.

Role of husband

Since I have had a fall [she is on crutches for the interview], my husband has had to do several things. He goes to the shops, buys food, and I have a girl who cleans the apartment.

My husband's [academic] area is in theoretical computer sciences. When he was working in America, he was very nervous because he didn't know how long he would be employed. So he couldn't start his research because he was working all the time. Now he can do more.

Are women's careers as important as men's?

In my mind, I was first: my job took precedence. I was responsible for our life, for our daughter, for holidays, for tickets, for theater, for food, for cooking, for cleaning. My husband has two doctorates and I have only one. Sometimes he helped take care of our daughter.

Religion

No, religion doesn't mean anything to me.

Are you going back to Russia?

I kept my flat in Moscow which I'm renting out now. So I don't know and I'm not sure.

What do you miss the most?

I miss my daughter and my grandson, my apartment and my nineteen year old cat who recently died. And of course I miss my friends.

How would you characterize British society?

In America at the university there was much more socializing than here. Every month there would be some sort of get together. Here there's nothing like that. My husband is not a very sociable person; I'm the one who usually arranges our social engagements. Sometimes he's invited by his colleagues to the pub.

What do you value most about living in London?

I like the architecture in London. I like just walking in London. It was a surprise to me that there are many concerts here. I like the Albert Hall; I like the Barbican; I like the Queen Elizabeth Hall. There is a nice cultural life here. It reminds me of life in Moscow. In Moscow I went to the theater rather than concerts; here I go to the theater as well.

I would have preferred to live in Moscow and go somewhere else for two or three months rather than vice versa. My daughter graduated from Moscow State University in computer sciences and now she's doing computer research. She's very involved with her son who is fourteen. Very soon he will have a bar mitzvah; she is more Jewish than I am. Her Polish husband has asked her why she wants her son to be Jewish.

Women in their fifties

All of these women have lived their adult lives in the UK. With the exception of **Maya** who left the Soviet Union in 1975 when she married a British engineer, they all married their Russian husbands in the Soviet Union and left the country with them. Three of the five women came to London during the perestroika period because their husbands were either working for a Soviet or an international company which sent them to London or they were posted to London by the Ministry of Foreign Trade. **Masha**, the last to leave, accompanied her academic husband first to France, then Canada, back to France and finally to the UK.

Their stories all paint a vibrant picture of life for women in Soviet times. They all remember their university days (including their various methods of entry into university) and the reasons they got married, one aged 20, three aged 22 and the last at 24, although she had met her future British husband when she was 21. **Maya** implicitly points up the different pace of social change in the Soviet Union and the UK when she states that 'Getting married was basically a way of having sex and so people got married very young. And they got divorced quite easily.' **Masha** explains early marriage in Russia as an attempt 'to gain independence from your parents. Once we got married we lived with my parents for the first two years but still the status was different.'

The women's accounts of the generality of maternity experiences are stark and uncompromising, privilege typically providing the only exception. **Liza** describes giving birth to her son in a Moscow hospital as an abominable experience. **Galina**, however, going to a very specific maternity clinic -- she compares it to the prestigious Portland Hospital in London -- gave birth in a privileged place. **Victoria** compares giving birth in both Moscow and Denmark, saying that 'it was completely different worlds!' Several of the women discuss the abortions they had, sometimes comparing them to the more severe problems their mothers faced in earlier times. Some of the discussions describe how the general attitude of the medical staff was very negative and dominating. 'They had to subjugate you. You had to be obedient and go by their word.'

Even though Soviet ideology said men and women were equal, several of the women view Russian society as very male dominated. According to **Liza**, 'In the sense that you had to go out and earn your living; that was your privilege as an emancipated woman, whether or not you wanted it.' **Maya** relates that 'it was equality from the point of view that women could work and do the same sort of job as a man.' She also tells how, unusually, her grandmother never really worked, a fact which was very atypical at the time; in her passport, instead of a notation for profession or occupation, she was listed as a dependent (an *izhdivenka*). **Victoria** notes the problems of promotion or lack of promotion for women, but now sees that as a given in capitalist as well as Soviet society. **Galina** tells of entrance requirements to university as being gender dependent.

Regarding the balancing of work and family, **Victoria** says that 'we never thought that balancing work and family was difficult. It was just a fact of life that you have to cope with.' However, **Masha** and **Galina**, the two women who were academics in Russian universities, indicated that their profession always gave them flexibility at work, although they too felt the stress of balancing work and family. **Liza** went back to work part-time when her son went to kindergarten but as she describes it, it didn't work out as planned. All of the women lived with or tried to live with their parents or their in-laws once they got married. As **Victoria** explains, 'there were no options; you either lived with one set or the other.' And they all agreed that their parents would help out the young couple by looking after the grandchildren, taking them to different activities, helping financially, even helping to eventually purchase a flat. In **Galina**'s case, she and her husband brought their daughter on Sunday evenings to her parents' flat; they returned and collected her on the Friday. So grandparents played a major role in bringing up the children. As **Masha** puts it, her daughter 'had three grandmothers around her and had their full attention and full support; my son, brought up in the UK, only had me!'

Another area of shared experience concerned what one might describe as culture shock. Arriving first in the UK in 1975 as an educated and cultured young woman, **Maya** was transported from city life in Moscow to small town English society: she was an urban girl thrown into a little English

101

village. She lived there for almost four years before coming to London and that 'probably was the hardest time of my life!' What she couldn't adjust to was the fact that she 'wasn't accepted ... for who I am, I was a foreigner. ... It never occurred to me that I would be a foreigner for the rest of my life.' Her language was pretty good when she came, but she was 'absolutely terrified to discover that everybody assumed [from her accent] that I couldn't speak [English].' **Victoria** discusses her inhibitions about speaking English because 'I knew that whatever I said people would know I was a foreigner' and **Liza** found her English to be 'entirely inadequate.' **Liza** was 'very intimated about my language' and the first five years 'wrote down every expression I seemed to like.' English was not a problem for either **Galina** or **Masha**.

Did religion play any role for them? For three of them, religion presently means nothing ('we are steadfast non-believers!'), although **Maya**, being an atheist all her life, occasionally goes to the local Church of England because of her children. **Galina** goes from time-to-time to services at a Russian Orthodox Church, but says that, while she is a religious person, she is not a churchgoer. Olga is Russian Orthodox and she and her children are baptised.

The Russian men of this generation all seem to help their wives. Put in a different way, they appear to have conceived of (and tackled) housework, childcare, cooking, etc.., in terms of a partnership. As **Masha** puts it, 'he was always very helpful, maybe because we were married so young and we built our family together.' A slightly different view is cited by **Galina** who indicates that for the first time when she came to the UK her husband was 'absolutely indispensable because I couldn't even go to the shops without him; we had to do our shopping together ... apart from family, you come here and you don't have much outside of your family. That's why you feel more dependent.'

Three women came during perestroika with husbands who were international civil servants. Subsequently they were more or less initially involved with the Russian community in London, rather than with the embassy personnel or the trade delegation. By coming in Soviet times, they were not free to choose where to live and they met each other in the housing provided. As for jobs, **Victoria** relates how those who had a command of English were the fortunate ones: others 'just couldn't [get a job] unless they were cleaners of something; there was nowhere else to work.' **Liza**'s detailed story of how she eventually was allowed to leave the required regimented life --'every step was kind of regulated for you' -- is most illuminating. What sets them apart from the others, both within the age group and in the other age groups, is the fact that they thought their postings would not be permanent and they would have to return to Moscow. The events in the Soviet Union changed all that. Perhaps that is reflected in **Liza**'s noting that 'I guess I belong to neither society at the end of the day, so there is a price to pay.'

When asked what they miss most (besides the food), **Victoria** says 'the closeness'; Russian culture is really very cosy. **Liza** misses 'the feeling of a clan, being from a big close-knit Jewish clan'. **Masha** misses her friends but is thankful for email today. **Maya** also misses not having friends and family here, but at the same time maintains a nostalgia for her house in Moscow. This is reiterated by **Galina** who misses 'the atmosphere, hearing Russian spoken,' especially from her cherished Moscow. These thoughts are certainly endorsed by most of the other participants in the other age groups.

Maya (58)

Life in Russia

It's very common in Russia! Marriage - divorce, it's all so different there because people don't take it quite so seriously as they do here. I think in a way it's because it was practically impossible to live with a boyfriend because everybody lived with their families. Getting married was basically a way of having sex and so people got married very young, the only reason being to have sex together. And they got divorced quite easily. Infidelity would be one of the reasons. There's plenty of infidelity of the women's part as well as the men's part.

Maya left the Soviet Union in 1975 when she married a British engineer. She herself had a degree from Moscow Institute of Engineering and Economics. Her father was a civil engineer in the army and her mother a medical doctor. When her mother contracted cancer and died at a very young age, Maya was first brought up by her grandmother, then by her father and stepmother, and then by her grandmother again. Her older brother now lives outside of Moscow and has a degree in physics.

Grandparents and stepfamilies

When my mother died, my maternal grandmother brought me up because when my mother returned to Moscow for treatment, we stayed with my grandmother. Once my mother died my grandmother tried to hold on to me, but my father wanted me back. By then he had moved close to Moscow and he remarried the very same year that my mother died. So I lived with him and his second wife for a few years and then I went back to my grandmother with whom I stayed until the time I went to university. So yes, my maternal side played a big role in my development. They did not, however, really accept my stepmother and they were very hurt that my father had remarried so quickly, especially because he married his secretary who didn't have a higher education. Nobody in my family did not have a higher education! Nobody accepted her and they felt she was a gold digger. She already had two children whom she brought with her to

104

the marriage. I was in that not very healthy atmosphere (for a child) between these two groups. But I did have my brother (who is four years older than I am) with me, although he really didn't want to know me until I became older at about aged eighteen. When his friends noticed me as being pretty, then he started to notice me as well. Before that I felt I really didn't exist as far as he was concerned. As far as my two stepsisters are concerned, I still remember wondering as a child why my stepmother loved her daughters more than me. I thought I was so good and I obviously accepted her, but that feeling always stayed with me.

Youth

We didn't spend our childhood in Moscow because my father was an officer and he was sent around the country. I was actually born around Lake Baikal. Then I went to Moscow with my mother who developed breast cancer when she was very young. As a teenager, I was very much interested in theater and cinema. My best friend from university was interested in the same things so we went to the theater at least once a week. We used to get spare/extra tickets

[*lishniye biletek*], that is, we were reasonably young and pretty and we never had trouble getting these spare tickets.

Accommodation

As a colonel in the army and a chief engineer, my father was sent to various scientific establishments in classified towns. That's why he had privileged living quarters and never lived in a communal flat. We had a housekeeper who had her own room. But my grandmother in Moscow lived in a communal flat which was much more common. I loved the flat she lived in; she shared it with quite a variety of people. There were four neighbors in the flat. This flat was in the center of Moscow and all of these flats were communal. In my last year, we were all transferred from these flats to the outskirts of Moscow due to development. So then I lived in the 'sleeping' area of Moscow, basically where one goes to sleep because it's on the outskirts of Moscow. I hated it! So I much preferred the communal flat with its tall ceilings and outlook and being right in the center of Moscow.

University

I chose my university very pragmatically. In fact I'm very proud of how I chose my university. I left school with a silver medal and could have chosen Moscow State University. But in the first place the Institute I chose was very close to where I lived in the center of Moscow. And secondly, if you had this medal, you only needed to take one exam. I chose economics because it's in between; I was very good at maths and I was good at literature which I like. I wasn't passionate about anything in particular. I just wanted to live in Moscow and get a degree. I couldn't wait to leave home. I loved my grandma, I loved the place where we lived. I just wanted to enjoy life; I obviously wasn't ambitious to go and try for other things.

I started university in 1968 and was there for another five years. I also had an extra thing after university; it was called *asood* [automated management systems] which was new at the time, so I stayed on at university.

Marriage

I met my husband at an international scientific development (which had a nuclear particle accelerator) where my father and my brother worked outside of Moscow. It was a cooperative adventure between Russia, Switzerland, France, etc.. My husband, who is British, worked for ICL at the time. As his first job after university, he was working as an engineer to support the machines. My English was pretty good and I basically acted as a translator for any young people who wanted to chat with each other.

We met when I was 21. My husband to be was only a couple of years older than I was. So when we married I was 24 and he was 26. We got married in Moscow in April, 1975, and we came to Britain in September 1975.

We were married in Moscow in a beautiful palace of marriage in which Russians married foreigners (which was much more beautiful than a normal registry office).[I assume that there must have been enough inter-nationality marriages to have a special marriage office set aside for foreigners]. My father was heartbroken that I was going to marry a foreigner. As far as he was concerned, he was against it and he was devastated. Because he didn't know I had an English boyfriend until we decided to get married, his first reaction was -- no way. He was very worried not just about the effect it was going to have on him, because he was still working but retired from the Army, but he was afraid for my brother who was still a physicist and for my half-sister (my father was married before he married my mother) who was married to a professor who was in charge of a scientific laboratory. So he was terribly worried that it would affect everybody. And of course he was terribly upset that I was going to leave. He really loved me so I knew he would come around. He was a very correct sort of person and he had all of these communist ideals. Of course he visited us here in England and absolutely loved everything. When he saw the children it was wonderful. But I did feel sorry for him, especially after I had my own children.

Discussion of sex, sex education and birth control

I learned mainly about sex from girlfriends. I also learned from books, but Russian literature was never that explicit nor was the foreign literature that we read. As for contraceptives, we used condoms and I didn't use the pill until I came to the UK. Yes, there was a fear of pregnancy.

Abortion

I've had a couple of friends who had abortions. I can't remember, but I think they had a general anesthetic. I knew all the details of who the 'culprit' was but not so much about the medical information. Abortions were however much more accepted in the Soviet Union than here. A common perception was that abortion was certainly a form of contraception. One of my friends was not able to have another child after the abortion.

Infidelity

It's very common in Russia! Marriage - divorce, it's all so different there because people don't take it quite so seriously as they do here. I think in a way it's because it was practically impossible to live with a boyfriend because everybody lived with their families. Getting married was basically a way of having sex and so people got married very young, the only reason being to have sex together. And they got divorced quite easily. Infidelity would be one of the reasons. There is plenty of infidelity on the women's part as well as the men's part. It was a pretty emancipated society as far as I could tell. Women worked, not only because they had to - not at all - but because it was considered to be the thing to do. It never occurred to me that I wouldn't go to university and that I wouldn't work afterwards. Women would have the same salary as men so that there weren't those material differences that would make the woman stay with the man.

Were there any problems specific to women?

Women worked. It was still considered to be right that the woman brought up the children, cooked the food and did all those sorts of things. But at the same time she worked full time. It was equality from the point of view that a woman could work and do the same sort of job as a man. In my experience (and I'm probably not a good interviewee for you), when we left university we were all paid the same sort of money. As an engineer, we were all given the same 100 rubles. Then it was basically up to you how you progressed. I can well imagine that men went ahead. Women didn't have the same time or energy to devote to their work. I didn't actually have the experience of living a married life and living as a Russian family. I met my husband when I was still a student and we didn't marry for two and one half years. But we were together. When we did get married, it was really a different existence because I didn't have the same problems, like after work buying something and having to stand in a queue. Also I didn't have a role model because my grandmother never really worked which was very unusual for Russian families. In her passport, where professions/occupations were listed, she had *izhdivenka*, a dependent. I've never met anybody else in Russia who had that in their passport. My

108

grandfather was obviously well paid, being the breadwinner; they had three children. They married very young and she stayed at home with the three girls. She stayed at home with the girls and he provided. This was very unusual.

Religion

Religion had no relevance at all.

Party member?

My father was a member of the Party. I was a member of the Komsomol, but when I got married I was really thrown out of the Komsomol. Before I met my husband, I was able to travel within the country but not outside of the country. My father couldn't travel because of his job, so that obviously affected us.

How do you picture the ideal woman in the Soviet Union?

What would I consider as a role model for myself? I definitely would say that education was always very important to me, so the 'ideal woman' must be educated. Culture is very important so she must go to the theater, cinema, read modern literature, preferably also know the culture of another country.

When I met my husband, my English was quite good. I also had a lot of misconceptions about what people were like. For example, if someone had gone to university, I assumed that they were cultured and that they read a lot. My husband as a recent graduate who studied engineering at an English university gave up literature quite early in his education. Whenever we had conversations about some literature (and I was a very snobbish and cultured young woman and I knew quite a lot about foreign literature: there were some progressive magazines even in my time in the Soviet Union and my aunt was in publishing so I always read *Novy Mir, Novy Vremya, Yunost*), I'd mention a writer and my husband never heard of him. I always gave him the benefit of the doubt. It took me at least a year in

109

England to realize how different we actually were simply because of the assumptions and ideas that you have about how a certain person should be.

What did femininity mean?

I remember a woman should make herself as pretty as she could make herself. Femininity was incredibly important. It doesn't matter how educated she was (no, it does matter) but also she must take care of herself, she must be beautiful, she must be attractive. This included makeup and clothing. I used to go to a tailor and would bring him pictures from magazines. Even when I was still at school, my clothes were made for me. When I was a student, there was a 'toilet' not far from where I lived where 'speculators' sold Western goods. Everybody in Moscow knew about this place. It was chock-a-block with people selling Western goods. The idealized image of femininity was like the Moscow metro (peasant and working women). That really was the Party line and that's really what they wanted. It's like the posters that you see from the 1930s and the statues come from the same sort of period, the 1930s.**Strong woman in Russian culture**

Women are strong, but Russian men really are quite macho. There are certain things they wouldn't allow their wives to do; that's in their culture. So we have macho men and strong women! Another difference is that so many men are drunkards. This is a huge problem and so it's down to the women to hold the family together. Alcohol is a big problem.

Life in London

Why did you leave the Soviet Union and come to London?

I left when I married in 1975. Originally we didn't come to London but we went where my husband was working in Berkshire. We lived in a village between Bracknell and Reading.

How difficult did you find it to adjust to:

We lived there for almost four years and that probably was the hardest time of my life. Hopefully I will never experience anything like that again! It certainly wasn't Moscow!

Climate

I didn't particularly like the climate, but my first summer in England was in 1976 which is the summer we're still talking about as the hottest summer for whatever amount of years. But in the first winter (before the summer in 1976) for the first time in my life I got chilblains. From time to time, I miss snow but not so much now. I don't particularly like the climate – there isn't much to like.

People

It's not the British that I found difficult to adjust to. What I couldn't adjust to was the fact that I wasn't accepted. The fact that I wasn't accepted for who I am, I was a foreigner…. It never occurred to me that I would be a foreigner for the rest of my life. I always thought it would just take a few months and I would be assimilated pretty quickly. And it would be fine! It's the labelling, and also the year that I didn't work (that was my first year in the UK) was quite definitely the worst time of my life.

Maybe if I had been in London it would have been different. Where we lived (outside of Reading) there was actually nothing for me to do. I had no children. I used to be very gregarious, I used to go to the theater, I had lots of friends, I had a very full cultural life in Moscow. I was very lonely there. And here I couldn't relate to the people. Basically all the women were young mothers who, when they invited me for coffee, would just talk about their children and shopping. I was not interested in these things. And I didn't have anything to say that they would be interested in. So it was a city girl finding herself really in a little village. It was a very different environment for me.

The British are really much more reserved and they didn't really look for friends. It took a while and I did acquire British friends. Once I started

111

working, I could sort of be on the same level as they were. People would get used to my accent and then they don't notice it. It's at the parties, meeting people on the street--that's where you get a reaction to you as a foreigner. Being a foreigner in any country is difficult!

Language

My language was pretty good when I first came. But I was absolutely terrified to discover that nobody could understand me -- no, it's not that. Whenever I opened my mouth, people started speaking very slowly to me. My language was very literary so when I used to go to the little local corner shop and I'd ask for something, I used to use words that I would use in Russian, like exaggerate or exacerbate. Basically the words were too long or too complicated; my English wasn't a very colloquial English but it was pretty good. I felt terribly insulted when people started using their hands to explain things to me. This basically was the shopkeepers and people who didn't know me. They could hear the accent and they immediately assumed that you couldn't speak. I was so taken aback because up to that point I was never embarrassed about my language. I acted as an unofficial translator and I spoke pretty well and was pretty relaxed about it. So coming to this country and discovering that people on the street immediately would start talking to you as if you were a child, it really knocked my confidence. I really stopped talking for a bit. But when I started to work, my confidence came back. I just said to myself, 'Forget about your accent and just speak.'

I always thought I would work. I was looking for a job as an economist. But in this country economists work for the government. And as a fresh graduate from Moscow University they weren't going to employ me. So I replied to an advert in the local paper. It was for some general administrator; it was the only advert that required a good level of general education. It was at the English headquarters of Avis Car Hire. I was incredibly lucky because I was interviewed by a technical director of the company. By the end of the interview, he said, 'Our programming department is looking for trainees. How about you take a test, an IBM test for aptitude?' I went home and said to my husband that's what they said: it

112

was my only interview! I was called back and took the two hour test. Within ten minutes of finishing the test, the programming manager came in and said I had the job. And I never looked back! First I was a programmer there and then I became a business analyst and was there for twenty five years. I stopped work for health reasons. For the last fourteen years I was a freelance business consultant; I worked all over in the City. It was very interesting but very demanding. I did a lot of interviews with people who needed programming assistance.

Property

We had plenty of problems. The problems stemmed from where and when we wanted to move to London. (My husband would have been quite happy to stay where we were, but I wanted to move into London.) At first we didn't know where we wanted to move, but then we decided on moving to Hampstead as it is quite a desirable part of London. We doubled our mortgage, sold our detached three-bedroom house and bought a two bedroom flat there. This didn't make any sense to my husband at all. But it did make sense to me. And I think the best investment we made was this house. The term 'gazump' was invented when we were moving to London. To make a long story short, on the day of exchange the buyer sold to somebody else. I had already given in my notice at work and already arranged the start date for my new job. So I had to say sorry to my old job and sorry to my new job. It really is an awful system!

Childcare and school system

In the beginning I needed childcare and that was a big problem. In Russia you sort of take it for granted that the grandmother will help you out. But it's very different in England. We always had good relations with my in-laws, seeing each other maybe once a month for lunch or at the weekend. But they didn't live near us. So I couldn't rely on my in-laws and therefore I had nannies. I earned good money so money wasn't really a problem. When my children were full-time at school, I had au pairs.

I had a conversation with my eldest child's primary school teacher and then she said, 'He's no problem. He just sits at the back of the class and reads his books.' He was aged six at this time and I felt something was not quite right. I'd like him to actually participate in the class! So that's why we basically decided to go to an independent school and from the age of seven my children went to an independent school. Before this my husband would never have considered an independent school as he went to a grammar school.

Transport

Funnily enough I didn't mind it at all and I was still quite young. I was so pleased to come to London. It really got on my nerves when I became older, including the last three or four years of my working life – I actually commuted every day.

Now the transport has actually deteriorated. Nowadays I really hate the transport system.

Lack of family

It obviously doesn't help the situation not having a family, especially when you have children. I miss my friends more than my family. It's not my particular friends; it's just the lack of friends. So moving to London was great because I had a job and I had friends there. That changed my life a lot.

Shopping

I wasn't overwhelmed with shopping when we first came because we lived in a small English town. My first month in the UK I stayed with my in-laws which was once again a small provincial town which had no exciting shops. I guess you could say I was under-whelmed. By the time we moved to London I had already lived in England for four years so I was more used to it; there was no 'wild' factor in shopping. My husband never liked shopping so to go to London shopping wasn't on the cards.

Russian food

In the beginning I did miss Russian food and I did try to find some Russian food in Bracknell! Nowadays there are all sorts of Russian delicatessens and Sainsbury's sell things either Russian or East European. After all there were no supermarkets when I first came to this country, only corner shops.

Child rearing and values

I had been living here for eight years before I had my children. My children didn't speak Russian because it wasn't natural for them to do so. I didn't have a children's language in Russian; I brought my children up using books. I didn't have anyone to help me. Everything I read was in English. I didn't really know much about children at all. So as far as child rearing was concerned, I didn't have a mother, I was never close to my stepmother so I can't say. The only value I'd say I applied is the value of education. (But even then that's not the case.)

By the time I had children, my values were Western values rather than Russian values because I didn't have the experience of being a working mother in Russia. And I didn't have a role model because I always had a grandmother who looked after me and didn't work.

Role of husband and our different responsibilities

Compared to my Russian friends, my husband always helped a lot. He couldn't sit and watch me doing anything without lending a hand. But one difference between us (and I think this is true for most working women) was the fact that if one of my children was ill, I couldn't switch off this fact when I was at work whereas he could. Let's say I had a problem with a nanny, for example. I would stay at home because I couldn't bear to leave the children with strangers. So that's an additional burden. Also when I was freelancing, I had a rule that I would always leave on time so that I would be home by six o'clock. It didn't matter how important a meeting was, I had to be home. I would come in early or I would do the work the next day but I had to be home. So these certain things I just couldn't be without (like giving my children a bath). This is the extra burden that I had. My husband just didn't think like that!

Concepts of femininity

I suppose I did carry with me this image of trying to be pretty at all costs. In Russia in terms of makeup and clothing, I always thought I had to make an effort. Russian men expect Russian women to present themselves. They do care about it.

Religion in the UK?

Religion now does play a role primarily because of my son. My eldest son went to a Christian camp and got converted. So my son has had an influence on us. My husband was brought up a Catholic and went to Catholic school but he never actually did anything. But my son at the age of eleven made us go to church and our youngest son also went to the youth club and got involved. Being an atheist all of my life, I don't think I'll ever get converted, but I do go to church from time to time. My generation knows nothing about religion; we are incredibly ignorant about religion --we're a blank slate. So I'm still finding it an educational experience. I find it quite interesting and I find a lot of ideas incredibly useful. There are many things I don't agree with and I don't have faith. But I enjoy going to church because sometimes I find the sermons very interesting.

I wouldn't go to a Russian Orthodox Church because basically it's ritualistic. It's almost like a mystical church. I think some of the Russians who go there go there for nostalgia reasons. Here the Church of England church we go to is very down to earth and very relevant to our lives. It makes you think!

Would you go back to Russia?

I can't imagine at all going back to live in Russia, unless something drastic happens. I still have friends and family there, but I've changed a lot and I've lived here a very long time.

What do you miss the most?

Nothing material, but I do have some nostalgia when I remember the house I used to live in in Moscow. From time to time you remember the faces of your childhood. I do regularly go to Russia and what I do miss is getting together with my old friends and relatives which is something special. I've passed the food stage!

What do you value most about living in London?

So many times over the years my husband was very tempted to sell up and move out of London. But I've always held on to London. I still like the theater, I still like the cinema. I love being in the center and walking around the streets. I like the way London has changed in many ways. I love the South Bank and how it has changed over the years.

How would you characterize British society?

As far as the British people are concerned, I think all the clichés are correct. An Englishman's home is his castle; there's no question about that. The British are reserved and polite. As far as society is concerned, I like the liberal attitudes which definitely suit me personally. I like to see both sides of an argument. Russians tend to be black and white; there is never a grey area in Russia. With my Russian friends who have been here ten or fifteen years, it's still this or that; it's never seen as grey. The British are very good at grey areas. There is always another view, always another perspective. By meeting my Russian friends I can see how I've changed and how little they have changed over the years. I recognize my much younger self when I hear their views. This liberalism, this acceptance, this tolerance suits me. Most Russians are not really very tolerant; if you start digging deeper you'll bring up questions about race, for instance. Of course when I'm talking about British people I'm talking about a particular strata of society, a particular class of society. (We're not talking about the BNP.) But I'm also talking about the same class in Russia which would be much less tolerant and much more extreme in their views.

Victoria (58)

Life in Russia

Surprisingly when you lived in the Soviet Union, you thought that everything abroad was wonderful but then the realization came that no, that's not exactly so. The underground system in Moscow is fantastic and it still is; it's beautiful and very efficient. The trains come -- they just come all the time.

Born in Moscow in 1950, Victoria graduated from the prestigious State University of International Relations [GIMO] having studied international relations and economics. She has worked as a foreign trade economist and organizer of cultural charity events. She left the Soviet Union in 1987 with her two children when her husband was posted to London on commercial business. Her 92 year old mother taught at **GIMO** and her now deceased father, after having been taken into the military for eight years (including World War II), studied at Leningrad's Academy of Fine Arts and became an artist. Her paternal grandparents whom she remembers were, respectively, a lawyer and a housewife. Her maternal grandfather died in the Civil War and her grandmother was a librarian. She has no siblings.

Living accommodation

Although I was born in a communal flat, it was a flat overlooking the Kremlin. It had big ceilings, crystal chandeliers, parquet floors, but the room was divided by cupboards because on one side lived my grandparents and on the other side of the room lived my parents and me. But there was a big corridor and three or four other families were living there; in that corridor I could ride a bicycle and nobody objected. So I had quite an interesting childhood because I was the only child in the flat. When there was somebody who made *piroshky* [pasties; pastries], I would get double. At the age of seventeen my parents bought that flat in the cooperative. That was the only way of getting private accommodation, to become a partner in a cooperative; you would pay 30% and the rest you would be paying all of your life. But that belonged to you and nobody could take it from you. This is how my father and mother ended up in their own flat.

School and university

I was very much interested in literature, politics and economics because at that time it was the beginning of economic rethinking. Under Kosygin [Soviet Premier] they were contemplating reforms which were very much discussed in the classroom. I didn't go to a special school but we had a very good teacher who specialized not only in history but in society, a subject which was not yet introduced at that time. At that time it was sort of a novelty. I graduated in 1967 from secondary school and I was very interested in politics and economics although I was not involved in these subjects.

When I went to university [GIMO], connections were important -- *blat*! My mother taught English there all her life, so that was probably the major influence on me; otherwise I could have gone somewhere else. You know even now normally, unless you are somewhere in a very provincial place, you stay where you live. If you were in Moscow, you wouldn't go to study in St Petersburg because all the major universities are in Moscow. If you are in St Petersburg, obviously you would stay there. I lived at home; there was no option. People would come from other cities and stay in a hostel. I can't say they were considered second class, but it was not sort of very fashionable. I can't say there was an attitude towards those people but, somehow in the back of our minds, they weren't Muscovites. So it was not a good thing to stay in a hostel.

I wanted to have a good education and I was very young (about seventeen) so I just knew that it was a very interesting place to be, a very sort of posh place to be. Probably at that time I didn't know that word, but I just knew that it was very difficult to get there, both to Moscow State University and to university so to get there meant that you had opportunities.

What did you do once you had graduated?

120

Nothing special. I worked for a state run commercial company which dealt in foreign trade and I went to work there for a little while. Then I didn't work and I stayed with my husband. After that I came back to Moscow and I worked for a market research institute; they publish a bulletin of commercial information.

Marriage

I met my husband at university as we were studying the same thing. We graduated and got married in 1972 when we were both twenty two. He is from Moscow.

Describe living accommodation

We lived with my parents once we got married because at that time there were no options -- you either lived with one set of parents or the other. My parents lived in a one bed roomed flat so one room for them, the other for us; actually it was only one room where I lived with my husband. With the help of my parents, a year after the birth of our first child we were able to buy another flat in the same co-operative block which was very very difficult because there was a queue and people wanted to jump the queue. We could have bought somewhere else in a new area, not as central, but we didn't want to go to another area, to relocate. We had a small cottage [a dacha] in the country and when the children were born I would spend the whole summer there. We also spent some time in Estonia, near the Baltic Sea.

Discussion of sex, sex education and birth control

My mother never taught me anything about sex, never. I learned about sex naturally! I was able to get contraceptives. Probably they were only Soviet made condoms but they were there. It very much depended on where you lived and what background you came from, because even without contraceptives, if you had an intelligent husband, you wouldn't get into trouble.

Abortion

Yes, I actually did have an abortion. No, I had two miscarriages, so it was sort of more or less the same procedure. The first one I did not have any anesthetic so it was a very nasty experience, but the doctor who operated on me was very kind, trying to soothe me and distract my attention by trying to talk to me. Apparently an anesthetic was not available then. After my daughter was born, I had a coil and with that coil I got pregnant; the coil was very uncomfortable. Then I had to have a kind of abortion because it started like a miscarriage; then I had a local anesthetic. That was done in Russia about 1983, so you can measure the change because my first miscarriage was before my son was born in 1972. So within, say, ten years things changed at least in the hospitals. Although obviously it was a very unpleasant experience, I can't say that any of my Russian friends or acquaintances described it as horrendous. It was barbaric because it was done without anesthetic but otherwise I wouldn't say it was deliberately torturous. It was a necessity and it was done professionally. Because doctors would do it very often on an everyday basis, they were true specialists.

Giving birth

My son was born in a specialized maternity hospital in Moscow. It was surreal as I was not expecting it. My Moscow experience was okay. Obviously there was not that much attention and care as you have in a Western country because here when a baby is born there are several people looking after you. In Moscow it was just a big open space and a lot of ladies giving birth. The personnel were struggling to look after everybody but somehow they did it quite efficiently. Actually after birth care was amazingly nice. There was an old lady coming with some iodine buckets or something, just changing the tampons and washing, but she was so nice, she was so sweet to us, and she was sort of saying, 'Don't worry, the worst is now behind you!' She was very kind, but this very much depended on who is there. But they were paid peanuts, just nothing. My husband obviously saw the baby from the window -- no other contact with the outside world before you went out. I was in hospital about six or seven days. They wouldn't throw you out the next day as they do here. After care was hygienic, it was efficient, but it was sort of no nonsense, let's put it that way. My daughter, on the other hand, was born in Denmark. Comparing the birth of these two children, it was completely different worlds!

Within the Soviet context, did you bring up your son and daughter differently?

Yes, definitely. I still have my regrets and probably I will have them till I die. With the first child, because we were very young (we were only twenty five and we probably we did not understand how important it was sort of not to dominate the child) we probably were too strict with him. It was very much in the Soviet mentality: children should behave, they should say 'fine', 'please', 'thank you'. Now it's just another extreme but I think our son was not the kind of person who needed that, because he is a very intelligent boy; there should have been some other things that we paid more attention to other than that. I think it was because he was our first and he was a boy. Obviously we were not experienced, we were not relaxed, we did not know how to bathe the child, what was right and what was not right, and we were meticulously following the timetables and routines for feeding and things like that. But with my daughter it was a completely different attitude. I already knew [things] so I could very easily give her a bath holding her head in my hand. And the same with feeding: whenever she was awake then I would give her my milk. So I really enjoyed the baby.

Did your parents help at all?

My mother did help when I went to work. She would come and stay. We would have a rota so I would go to work late in the day; she would come and stay for a little while. Then my husband would come back and so on, and my father would go and take my daughter from the kindergarten and go for a walk with her. As we had a rota it was very convenient that we were living next door. As for my in-laws, my husband's father died when he was a child and my mother-in-law was absolutely hopeless.

Definition of a good mother

I would say caring and understanding and that's it.

Was infidelity different for men and women?

I don't think it was, but it was not as common as it is nowadays because families were closely knit, because life was harder.

Were there problems specific to women in the 1970's /1980's?

Probably it was promotion and getting further in your career, but it's still a problem. It's still the same. Now I understand that it doesn't matter if you are in the Soviet system or in the capitalist system, the problem is the same. Probably even in the Soviet times there was more equality then than there is now. There were some levers for women through the Party and the trade unions to get through but now it's just a wild market.

Was there a 'double burden' in the USSR?

Even the generation of my parents, Russian women -- compared to the women in the West -- did not have a choice. It was not their choice that they *wanted* to work and to look after their family at the same time. You just had to: you wouldn't survive on the one salary. That's the reason for the double burden because you had to do that.

Did religion play any role in your life?

No and still it doesn't but obviously religion was suppressed and there was a good thing about that and a bad thing. The bad thing was that it was suppressed and the good thing was that it was not promoted as it is now. Now I just can see that it is being imposed on people and I don't like that at all. It's just again another extreme, but some good came out of it because religion divides people a lot and in a multinational country as the Soviet Union was, we were not divided. At least in the territory of Russia we lived very peacefully with each other, with people of different nationalities. I don't know how people in, say, Uzbekistan felt. Maybe they felt oppressed, but at least they were educated. In Soviet times people had equal opportunities no matter what nationality they were. Even more, there were special ratios for people coming from the Asian republics, especially in universities in Moscow. They would be given special treatment in particular for obvious reasons [language being one of them] because their education was not that brilliant; they could not have competed with the Muscovites so they were given special treatment to get into universities. From that point I think it was a good thing.

Were you a member of the Party?

No, although I was offered once but I did not feel that I wanted to do that. I was in the Komsomol going to university. I didn't want to join the Party and I knew that if I needed that later at work that I could join, because I am sure that most of the people who joined the Party just had to do that. It's just like, I don't know, getting higher education or getting promotion. It was the same thing. Most of the people whom I knew didn't care about that because that was just a procedure; if you were not part of the Party then you would not get promoted, no matter where you were, a scientist or dealing in commerce. You wouldn't be promoted. It's like a trade union card. That's how I think of it. My husband was a member of the Party. We travelled outside of the USSR because of my husband's work for a commercial organization, which dealt in grains.

How do you picture the ideal woman in the Soviet Union?

In the Soviet Union, the ideal woman would probably be a woman who could successfully combine her roles as a mother and a worker, a working mother. **And how does that relate to femininity?** No matter whether we had restricted opportunities or not, Russian women would always look after themselves, have a manicure, tint their eyelashes and eyebrows, go to the hairdresser and wouldn't go out into the street as women very often do here, sort of half asleep. It's still the same now in Russia. Women normally wouldn't go out without makeup and being made up. As for clothes, I didn't go and stand in a queue for ages to get something. I would go to a local woman, a tailor who would make my skirts; I would knit my sweaters. Sometimes I would get some dresses through my friend whose mother worked as a hairdresser in a salon and that was where black marketeers would bring stuff. They would distribute through hairdressers and so that's how I would get some things. I even didn't go because my friend would tell me, 'My mother has brought back something; would you like some?' I didn't go specifically. Somehow it was not a priority for me but I always looked okay. Probably I wanted to have more fancy things, but somehow I didn't fancy too much. I didn't suffer from it.

Strong woman in Russian culture

Probably in Soviet times the peasant woman holding grain or working on tractors (like in the metro) was the female figurehead of the woman who was capable of anything and everything. But in actual fact, my vision of the society then was quite quite even. There were not that many [women] sticking out and obviously it was men dominating society (such as the male dominated Politburo). There were women who were in charge of factories and different institutions; there were a lot of doctors, a lot of scientists. So I think it was just the woman who was a professional woman with a family -- that would be my description of a strong woman.

Validating Western views about the past: balancing work and family

We never thought that balancing work and family as being difficult. It was just a fact of life that you have to cope with. We didn't feel that we were suffering but obviously families would help, so your mother, your husband's mother (depending on the situation) and your father and your grandmother, if you had one, would always help. It is still the same in Russia. Families are very closely knit and parents help a lot. Parents would not only help to look after your children, but they would help you financially; they would always help the young couple, always, at least in the middle class families. Grandparents would help to take them to different activities -- ballet, singing, drama, and painting -- because the development of the child was always important and grandparents did not just come and see them.

Life in London

Why did you leave the Soviet Union and why go to London?

I went because my husband was posted to London. We came in 1987 when Gorbachev was in power. All the changes had just started and my husband worked for a company which was the only company in the whole of the Soviet Union that was dealing in grain. It was really a very big company, dealing in huge volumes. At the time there was lots of talk about spies. In any foreign delegation of course there are some spies, but in Soviet times most of the people who worked in the trade delegation were genuine business people who dealt in actual trade; otherwise there was no other way of trading in the Soviet Union. They were the only people who did that. My husband worked for the grain organization and they had a post in the International Grains Council, so this is how he came to work here.

Normally you would come for three or four years and then go back and somebody else would be looking forward to taking our place. But when the whole Soviet Union collapsed, my husband's company was privatized. It was a very, very hard time in Russia. So my husband didn't have much choice: he decided to carry on working in London and because of that, his work would pay 75% of the school fees for the children. It would have been mad to just take the whole family back at that time and to refuse all these things. On the other hand I think professionally he lost a lot because some people who worked with him are now very rich.

How difficult did you find it adjusting to:

Climate

At the beginning I had a lot of headaches. I didn't know if it was my age or just probably getting used to the climate. I still miss winters because here the whole year is very similar. Of course, there are fluctuations in temperatures; spring is very beautiful here, but otherwise it is just the same weather. Obviously in Russia you feel those actual changes in nature. For example, when spring comes you can see the drops of the melting ice coming from the roofs; you hear the spring noise of melting snow through our streets where the children make small boats out of matchboxes. They put a match on top and a small flag for a sail. So that affects the Russian character, all these fluctuations in weather. The changes in winter --and the snow-- are very extreme, including the brightness that you get from the snow that substitutes for the lack of sunshine in the winter. Obviously there are winter sports as well so you don't need to go to the Alps to go on sledges or go (a)cross country. That is what you do normally every weekend, or go out with your children every evening and take them on sledges or take them to an ice rink. This is what I miss a lot.

Language

At the beginning I had a lot of inhibitions because I knew that whatever I said, people would know that I was a foreigner and that I would make mistakes. Somehow for me personally it mattered, even to such a degree that I felt I behaved differently, in terms of mannerisms and (sort of) in the way that I was trying to present myself in English and in Russian. Now I am over that, thank God, and I am what I am. But for me it was a very, very long period of time.

What about finding property?

We were not part of the Trade Delegation, but we ended up in the same block of flats [as two other interviewees] because we came in Soviet times and at that time we were not free to choose where to live. The building did not belong to the [Russian] Trade Delegation but somehow they were getting the income from the people who lived there. We were put in that house and then after perestroika we were free to go; then we all just started to move. We were renting at first and then we eventually bought a place.

Schools

At that time children were not allowed to go outside to non-Russian schools. But gradually the rules were eased and funnily enough it was the smaller children who were allowed first to go into the British education system. First my daughter went to a Church of England school and then she went to an independent school, whereas my son was actually the first Russian boy to go to the local independent school.

Transport

Surprisingly when you lived in the Soviet Union, you thought that everything abroad was wonderful but then the realization came that no, that's not exactly so. The underground system in Moscow is fantastic and it still is; it's beautiful and very efficient. The trains come -- they just come all the time.

Did you find it difficult adjusting without your family, without your mother?

No, it was easy. I didn't mind. To be honest and not with disrespect, my mother is not the typical Russian mother. She keeps very much to herself, but she had to help me with the children because there was no other way. She still lives in Russia but visits here for half a year and spends the other half in Russia.

Childcare

My daughter was six and no, we didn't have nannies. I wouldn't have been able to afford that. The salary that my husband was paid was taken from him; he would have to bring it back and pay it into the account, I don't know where, maybe at the Embassy, and that would leave him with a small portion of the money. But we got that accommodation almost free because we just paid the bills.

I started working almost immediately. I worked part-time as a secretary at the Embassy and the Trade Delegation because again, at that time, we were not allowed to work anywhere outside of the Soviet organization. So those who had a command of the English language were the fortunate ones. Others just couldn't [get a job] unless they were cleaners of something; there was nowhere else to work.

With whom do you socialize?

I would say that half of my friends are English. We are very fortunate to have fantastic neighbors and we are very good friends with them. We are closely knit and we see each other and organize parties and socialize. So being Russian isn't a problem at all.

Shopping

I wasn't overwhelmed by it at the beginning. But sometimes it's a bit too much, too much choice. **Do you miss Russian food?** Yes and no, because Russian food is very tasty but very heavy. We cook some of the Russian dishes quite regularly, for example, soups. There are variations, we can make vegetarian without any meat. Russian food is very tasty and English food as it is not that great. But now, just in front of our eyes, they have developed a system of so many cuisines and restaurants in London – a big change -- so you are spoilt for choice.

Role of husband

My husband or the husbands of my friends in Russia have always helped, always helped with children, with cooking, with cleaning, with everything. We always did that together but again I think it's probably a class thing. Middle class men would help, but it's interesting that when my father was looking after me, he would stay at home more than my mother and he said that he was the only man with a pram in the street. People would give him strange looks; he was the only one. But my generation was not a problem anyway, at least not in Moscow.

Did you bring up your children with different gender roles?

Not in gender terms but in terms of a general attitude. Here I had sort of a less aggressive behavior because life is much more comfortable and you are not that stressed. Obviously it affects your relationship in the family and you don't get angry with your children as often as you would, because you are not that stressed. It's just the general atmosphere; it affects you the way other people behave around you. It's a pattern of behavior that affects you because I like people here being polite and probably better bred.

Concepts of femininity

I haven't altered my views but I think here women start losing their femininity which is understandable but it's not helping. Women are losing their femininity because they have to compete with men. To be able to do that, they have to become almost masculine, more masculine.

Does religion play any part in your life?

No, nor were my parents religious.

How do you spend your free time?

I go to the theatre, to concerts, to all sorts of things. I take advantage of London, but now in Russia you can get the same advantages -- no problem. In the past we couldn't get tickets but not any longer. Now again it's another way because now all of the tickets are sold out. In the past you had to have connections. You had to know someone, that's where *blat* (connections) comes in. In the Soviet times *blat* was a very important thing to have in every aspect, whether you wanted to get tickets to the theatre or you wanted to get some nice meat or clothes.

Do you think you will ever go back to Russia?

I don't think so. The more we stay here the less feasible it is. You know it's a completely different country. Not that I dislike the changes. It's just that several things have changed completely and it's not easy to adjust yourself to the way of life there. There are still a lot of difficulties people have to overcome, whereas life is much more comfortable here. My mother still lives there and we bought another flat in the same block as my parents which we still own.

What do you miss the most?

I miss the closeness. I should say the Russian nature. I know that even foreign people who used to live in Russia miss it because Russian nature is really very cosy.

How would you characterize British society?

More polite and more patient. **Not so aggressive?** That would be another thing. **Do you think there is such a thing as British society?** I think there still is, but you may see a lot of changes happening in this respect. I think some disintegration is in the process and you asked me about what I treasure. I think what I like is the law abiding part.

What do you value most and least about living in London?

Security is in the 'most' category and as for least, probably that closeness of people in Russia. When you are in a relationship with somebody, it is much more casual and a much warmer relationship.

ADDITIONS:

How do you translate the values you had in the Soviet Union into living in the UK?

I would say that it was not such a drastic change. I don't think that people in the West realize how rich the cultural life was in the Soviet Union and how much we read. Probably we were better educated in English literature than the same generation here! What we found quite striking was [the fact that] we thought that it was the paranoia of the Soviet system to see every foreigner as a spy, but when we came to live here, people jokingly were saying that Russian spies have come here. It happened many times and it was not funny for me personally because I never liked spies and I realized that peoples' minds were poisoned with the ideology here, probably equally on this side too. They had no idea how we really lived. They just had some patterns in their mind and that was it. But life in the Soviet Union obviously was oppressive, but because of that it was rich in some other things. We were a very well developed people, not like a grey mass. There are quite a lot of people who suffered from the collapse of the Soviet Union because there was an international community there; now people find themselves isolated in different republics, not necessarily in the Russian [republic], but like the Uzbeks and the Kazaks. I hear a lot from the native people [in those republics] that they remember the old times with great warmth. So it's a very complicated thing.

When the Soviet Union collapsed, my personal view is that the West should have immediately integrated Russia into the Western community and made a good friend of Russia, helping her to become powerful. But Russia felt first she was to be destroyed and then pushed aside. Now I think that Russia is looking more to the East than to the West which is very sad. But it is very bad for the Western world too.

Whether we like it or not, China, India, etc.., in no time will dominate the economy of the world. It is sad that probably gradually the Western world and Western culture will lose its position. What you realize when you come from Russia to the UK is that Russia is not treated as a European state, but we all feel absolutely European. People who live in the European parts of Russia, even in Siberia, feel themselves European. That's absolutely justified because they have the same culture, the same religion and the same values. But for some reason there has always been some rivalry because Russia is so huge – the [Russian] bear! …Russia could have made the whole of Europe much more powerful; it's a shame. But it's not meant to be.

Liza (55)

Life in Russia

British society is just fine as long as you don't start to pretend to be part of it. That's when you really get slapped on your wrists. I don't remember how I got this idea; I think it has been proven over time if I or anybody crosses the line. It is a fair enough society if you obey by the rules. It has been fine for us.

Liza left the Soviet Union in 1988 when her husband was posted to London. She is a graduate of a pedagogical institute in Moscow, the city where she spent her childhood. Although she was trained and practiced as a language teacher, she is currently working as a translator. She has one son. Her mother, who dropped out of university sometime after she became pregnant with Liza, spent her life as a proof reader in the leading editorial house in Moscow. Her father became a civil engineer. Both parents now reside in the States as does her younger brother, a computer specialist.

Grandparents and the availability of food

My maternal grandmother actually brought me up. My maternal grandfather died in World War II to which he volunteered rather than be conscripted. As my mother was working, my grandmother brought me up which was really quite typical of that time. A lot of my friends were brought up in a similar fashion: their parents were both at work and they were looked after by their grandmothers. My grandmother did the cooking but she preferred reading. She of course did the shopping as well which I don't remember as being that onerous in my early childhood. She would pop out and be back in 20 minutes with food for the day because, of course, we didn't have freezers. We had a window sill, so it didn't make sense to buy for a longer period. The availability of food was alright at that time [the middle to late 1950s]. After that things started to disappear. But if you compared the West with the Soviet Union in the late 1950s and early 1960s (that is, judging by the movies and books), the comparison or rather the gap in living standards was not that dramatic in those times. It was reasonable and stuff was available. But the West did leap ahead and left the Soviet Union behind as it sank into the past. I first came across a very small supermarket in the late1960s; they were few and far between.

Choosing university

From the very beginning I knew I wasn't going to be a mathematician or an engineer, although I did well in all subjects. For me my interests were always in history, the humanities or languages. My grandmother, who was a major influence on me, was an Anglo maniac, believe it or not! She introduced me to English culture the best she could. I think at the age of seven or eight -- after I stopped doing ballet (for all the wrong reasons) and as a compensation for that -- I had a private tutor in English. My teacher was a very likable girl; I didn't like English very much but I did like the girl. Then in Moscow there appeared specialized schools, schools specializing in maths or foreign languages. My grandmother got it into her head that I had to go to one of these schools. Little by little it became obvious that I would carry on in the same way.

But then of course, being Jewish, I had my limitations. I never suffered. Don't get me wrong, people often ask me what it was like to be Jewish in the Soviet Union. It felt fine. I never had any problems, probably because I was fair-haired and I didn't come across immediately as being Jewish. My last name was quite telling, but I never had any bad experiences. But my parents made it clear that I shouldn't try the state university (or the international relations university where my husband graduated from) because it was a no-no situation unless you had friends in very high places which my parents, of course, didn't. No *blat*, not even *znakomstvo* [circle of acquaintances]. They weren't the type of people – they honestly couldn't be bothered. So the choice was downsized to where I actually went, that is, to the State Pedagogical Institute where my two fields were English and German. It wasn't very challenging because it was so language oriented and humanities oriented. So for the last two years (after grade 8) I was in a very competitive but very humanitarian environment.

135

Then I went to the pedagogical institute and was there for five years. I never thought that I was going to ever teach; I didn't fancy it one bit. I never realized that I would come to absolutely love it. I absolutely adored teaching probably because I never did it for a living. I did it as little or as much as I wanted.

University and accommodation

Like every Muscovite, I did live at home; it would have been unheard of not to have lived at home if you had family in Moscow. My routine varied from year to year because we had alternatively to do shifts: sometimes we'd have classes in the morning, sometimes we'd have classes in the afternoon or evening. I don't think there was any such thing as routine. Until 1973 my grandmother had a flat in central Moscow which consisted of two rooms in a communal flat (quite typical of the time). But when I was in my last year my parents (after twelve years of queuing) got an individual flat. It wasn't private; it was given by the state. It was an individual three room flat in a godforsaken suburb of Moscow where you had to wear Wellingtons [boots] twelve months a year. There was a room for me. At that point my mother insisted that I come under my parents' auspices (my brother was already living with my parents). Before this flat, my parents had a very small room (12 or 13 meter square) in a communal flat and that's why I was much better off staying with my grandmother.

Marriage

My husband was from Moscow. I met him it in my last year at the university during my winter holidays. He was a year and a half younger than I was and so hadn't finished his education at the Institute for International Relations [GIMO] in Moscow. He was very ill advised to marry a Jewish girl at the time. His mother is half Ukrainian and his father is Russian. I got married in 1975 after I graduated; I was 22. Lots of the other girls started getting married in year three when they were 19 or 20, so I was quite old! Now my husband is a senior economist with an international organization. I think they are loosely attached to the United Nations. He was posted by the Soviet Union but he is an international

136

staff member. He just stayed with that organization when the Soviet Union went down the drain.

Discussion of sex, sex education and birth control

I knew about contraceptives. I knew about the pill (I don't know which one) but it gave so many women allergies and I was very allergy prone so I didn't take it. I've always had this aversion towards condoms so we tried to be careful. My mum and I never never discussed sex together. My son and I can discuss sex but of course that's a different generation and it's a mother and her son, although I'm sure my mother and my brother couldn't discuss sex either. As for sex education in school, I don't think we had any. I don't really remember how I learned about sex. I did a bit of reading, mostly classical literature like Maupassant, so I got the emotional side. I guess if you don't know much you are getting a lot from literature. Of course I was also essentially at a girls' college and they were getting married one by one, so we learned about contraception. I suppose that's how we did it. And then there was natural curiosity!

In my husband's final year at university he was telling me that several of the students were sharing the same girl. I think we had a similar girl in our class. I mean that there would be a more progressive or daring girl who had already learned things and was willing to share, physically or verbally. They/he/we were eternally grateful to her. I don't think he [her husband] had a clue of what to do at all, but she was probably his first experience.

Abortion

Women certainly discussed abortion. I myself had one before I went on the coil. In fact everybody knew about abortions because contraception was either non-existent (or like the condoms, the 'galoshes' or rubber boots you spoke about) or they had to do this [have an abortion]. Abortions were quite easy to get, that is, up to so many weeks. It was indeed a very unpleasant experience. If we talk about the personnel performing the abortions, I don't think it's just these people. I was very scared of any medical personnel in the Soviet Union, people in white gowns; that is, be it a dentist let alone a gynecologist, the general attitude was very dominating and negative. They had to subjugate you. You had to be obedient and go by their word. That's how they were taught to behave towards patients. So the people who performed abortions were part of this medical environment.

Giving birth

My son was born in a maternity hospital in Moscow. The whole experience was not that good because I was not yet twenty three. The ambulance came and they looked at me and said as this is my first baby I wasn't due to deliver for another 12 to 14 hours, but I went into labor in the ambulance. They, of course, were going by the book. I didn't actually deliver in the car. They were oh so scared when I went into labor that they were completely lost. They weren't just drivers, they were actually medics. My mom was there as well but she couldn't do the delivery. So they had to divert from the hospital they were originally taking me to and went to the hospital that was nearest to us. But when we arrived at that hospital there was no stretcher or anything to help me to the delivery room. So I had to run myself, so as you can imagine it wasn't a very happy experience!

When my son was born ten minutes later, he was the color of blue sky and he came out bottom first. I'm sure it was better this way than if he had come out head first. When they saw him the first words they said was, 'Oh look, he's alive'. This was my very first experience and you don't forget it. It was my first experience with the thorough cynicism of the system: I had never come across anything like that before. My mum of course now feels that we should've organized a private hospital; she's never really forgiven herself for that. We were very lucky that my son was born but then they gave me a dressing down because it was their lunch hour. They said they couldn't be expected to assist babies around the clock. So it was really an abominable experience! I was in hospital for about five days. My husband didn't even know that I had given birth because he was only a student and we needed money so he was running around like a rabbit as an interpreter. When he did finally come, he was not allowed into the hospital but I remember him holding flowers which I saw from the window. I don't remember holding the baby up for him at the window because we only got the babies at feeding time and he usually wasn't there at that point.

Accommodation, grandparents and bringing up the baby

For the first few months of our marriage we tried to live with my parents-in-law because my husband was not yet twenty one. They had no other children and it was difficult for them to part with him, especially since my mother-in-law didn't work. She did go to work now and then out of boredom. My father-in-law was a professor of Chinese studies in Moscow. They were quite well off by the standards of those times. At that time we had a communal flat, but we had only one neighbor, so that was an advanced communal flat. People were moved out from the central areas in Moscow but the ones who stayed in the communal flats in the central areas were the old babushkas [grandmother, old woman]. The babushkas didn't want to leave their homes so they put two babushkas together in the hope that one of them or both of them would die quite soon. And once that happened a family could have a flat to themselves. My grandmother was moved out to this new area of Moscow with someone from her same house. And then we occupied her room or two rooms with another old lady who was fantastic. Although she's been dead for nearly twenty years now, hardly a day goes by when I don't remember her. She was quite a character and she really taught me a lot; I'm very grateful to her to this very day. We were very lucky to have her, although it would've been better if we each had had our own flat! We lived for seven years with Baba Katya. And then we exchanged our accommodation for two separate smaller flats and that's how we got our little flat in Moscow.

My parents and parents-in-law did help with the upbringing of my son, every now and then (but not as much as you would expect in the Soviet context). They were all working. It was mainly ourselves who brought up our son. I didn't work until our son was big enough to go to the kindergarten. It wasn't feasible to send him to a crèche because there were no places. Even when he reached the age for kindergarten, we had to breathe down the neck of our parents who would know somebody who would know somebody to find him a place. We were in a new area with lots and lots of young families. The women were proletariat and we were Muscovites.

Definition of a good mother

I would have had no clue about how to define a good mother. I can't think of anyone who would've been less prepared than I was. I was very lucky to have a son because I had always wanted a son. Since I was so much in love with my husband, I really wanted an imprint of him. That was all I wanted. When he was born he had black eyes, that was all that interested me. I just wanted a tiny boy with black eyes and black hair, like my husband. Although my husband was younger than I was, I think he was much more prepared and more consistent as a father; I think you are just born that way. It took me awhile to get used to my new role. But with the benefit of hindsight, I should've waited to have children, maybe eight to ten years!

Did you think of having any more children?

No, not really because it was so tough. Well, I didn't, let us put it this way; my husband would have had any number that he would have been able to support. But I said, 'Let's stop here; that's it.' When we came to London, my son was eleven. If we had known at that time that we were going to stay, we would have done something, but of course we expected to go back. We thought we would stay three, four or five years in London and we wanted to grab the opportunity of being here. We saw it as an opportunity for our son to learn the language, to see the country, to get the experience that he might never be able to get otherwise. We thought if I had another baby, I'd have to stay at home and take care of the baby, and that would be it.

Were there any problems specific to women?

It was a very male dominated society. I think there was a very distinct set of problems which were considered male or female. There was nothing specific for me. The main problem for my husband (as he saw it) was providing for his family, of course, combined with going to university because when our son arrived, my husband was in year three. He had two years to go and he had a family to feed. And he had to join the Party because being at this university he had to be a Party member. There was no two ways about it. I wasn't a member of the Party, in fact, I dropped out of the Komsomol because I forgot to pay my dues! Of course to enter any institute you had to originally be a member of the Komsomol.

The ideology said men and women were equal. Do you think this is valid?

Yes, in the sense that you had to go out and earn your living. That was your privilege as an emancipated woman, whether or not you wanted it. But again it was easier said than done. As young mothers, an employer might look down on you because of sick leave, because of husbands and the rest of it and then of course you might get pregnant again, God forbid. No, it wasn't equal in any sense of the word except that the expectation of the society was that you would go out and earn your living, do all the public chores, go to the meetings, sit long hours there as if you didn't have a worry in the world and you don't have to pick up your child and take him home.

I haven't come across the term 'double burden' but I can understand what it means. Maybe I'm a special case but I've always had a very happy marriage and my husband has always been very helpful - with the child, with the cooking. I can't really complain, to be fair.

How do you picture the ideal woman in the Soviet Union?

I can't speak of an ideal Soviet woman. There were lots of women whom I admired in this or that respect, but nobody who would have fit the bill for an ideal Soviet woman. Seeing the 'ideal' women portrayed in the Moscow metro, I would've laughed my head off suggesting they would be ideal.

What did femininity mean?

141

I think it was really a combination. My school was not a privileged one but more privileged than most. I was surrounded by people whose parents would be travelling abroad. Indeed my father did travel quite a lot for a Jewish person although he was not a Party member. So we had some probably very twisted and very introverted thoughts about what was life like in the West. We were very much into Western music; we were certainly listening to the Beatles. So I think my ideas were much more influenced by the hippie culture and what little I could learn about Western culture (not from the peasants in the metro).

Until grade 8 we had to wear school uniforms; after that we had to obey certain rules. We had to wear dark clothes, be modest and still had to wear aprons for some reason. Any makeup was completely forbidden as was jewelry. At university, femininity was clothing, makeup, jewelry, hairstyle -- everything. The first thing I did at university was to cut my hair because I used to have plaits which probably went down to the floor.

Strong woman in Russian culture

The woman was supposed to be the pillar of the family. She was supposed to be wise (not strong, strong). Doesn't it work like that in this country? From my limited experience here, I think the wise bit is still at the nub of it. As a girl in Russia I think you are not expected to show your brains, but as a woman, yes, you are.

Validating some Western views about the past: balancing work and family

I didn't work when my son went to kindergarten, but for a few years I worked part-time. Then I was given an opportunity to make a career in teaching (including administrative work, etc..) After some discussion, my husband was working very long hours; sometimes he would come home after one in the morning because they were working with the New York time zone (there was an eight hour time difference). We decided to give it a try because by this time our son was in school. Indeed we tried for a year. I came home around nine-ish probably and it was so tough. What really did it was that something started to happen to his diction. He wasn't pronouncing words properly and he had always had the gift of the gab. I couldn't get my head around it because none of us had had any problems like this. I tried many [corrective] things and then quite by accident I went to see his new teacher. She was a lovely young girl in her very early 20s and when she opened her mouth, I knew where it came from. She couldn't pronounce .... She shouldn't have been allowed to be around children at all, to be in this profession. I guess this was the last straw because we had been struggling. It was really difficult and we never realized what our son was doing (because my son had to stay in the after school facilities, etc.). So on top of everything else when he started to mispronounce words, well that was it. And so I went back to teaching only and I've stayed at teacher ever since. It was a lot easier and although it wasn't easy, we could survive; we didn't depend that much on my salary.

Prime emphasis on children

I don't think this is a fair statement in that parents love their children equally. Russians probably have different ways, such as we put more clothes on the children to keep them hot!

Life in London

Why did you leave the Soviet Union and come to London?

My husband was posted to the UK in 1988 as he was working for the Ministry of Foreign Trade. It was on the cards for him as a career step to have a posting abroad. And London was chosen for us, very luckily. We couldn't have dreamt of a better choice!

How difficult was it to adjust to?

Climate

It was hell to adjust to living here. The climate was probably part of it because I felt cold for about a year. I think it was the damp.

Language and its consequences

I found my English to be entirely inadequate. But I think I still was quite an inhibited person, so I was not really willing to come forward with what I had. I was waiting for my English to mature to get to a certain standard before I started to socialize. I felt really thrown out of my environment.

Living in the Soviet community and the consequences

Of course the Soviet community didn't help either because we were not part of the community in a major way, like we didn't belong either to the Soviet Embassy or to the Trade Delegation which would have been the two major centers. But still we were Soviet citizens and we belonged. My husband had to attend the Party meetings and pay his dues. I found it very intrusive because I really felt that I was being watched all the time. I don't think I was. We didn't even live with the community. There was a special house which was not within the compass of the trade delegation or the embassy; it was not one of those. Every family who lived there was in the same position as ours as they were all international civil servants. We were given a specific flat. But somehow it was extremely regimented. Every step was kind of regulated for you. You had to go here, you had to go there. You had to accompany your child everywhere.

The school was the embassy school which I think was inferior to an average school in Moscow. At that time we couldn't go to an English school; we had no freedom to choose. The lack of choice – you had to toe the line -- was absolutely killing me. It began to grow better after I called upon my inherent cynicism. I went to work in March and in June we sent our son to Moscow for the summer because he hated London. In London he was 'attached' to his mother, e.g., he had to hold my hand, he couldn't go here or there, he wasn't a free person here, etc.., etc.., whereas in Moscow there were grandparents, comprehensible cinema, etc.. I went to work for the consulate for a year. They paid well by our standards but I really hated it. Then they called on me to teach at the embassy school where for some reason I felt quite challenged. The chairman of the local Party committee was in charge (this is the height of perestroika and pretty

144

relaxed by this time). I was summoned by him and questioned about why I didn't want to work at the school. I said, 'To be quite honest, I don't think my English is good enough and not good enough to teach English in England; it's ridiculous. My English is not up to the standard as yet.' Obviously it sounded so stupid that they didn't know what to do with me. So I was left alone, in peace, although they made my life in the consulate absolute hell. Then I was summoned again and told to be prepared not to come to work the next week. But then, nothing happened. And that is when I learned my first lesson of living abroad: if you are bold enough, you come to no harm. Mind you, again it was perestroika and I am sure it would have been different, say, five years earlier. So I stayed at the consulate; it just blew over and in fact, a year later when I wanted to leave the consulate because of the travelling, etc.. (and I thought I would rather stay at home for a while), I had a huge problem leaving it. By that time my English had improved and honestly I think in the bad days my English was probably better than most of the other women. I was a professional anyhow, so they were clinging to me.

The way I left the consulate is very, very typical of the Soviet system. I think there was a spy case at the same time. Something was found in Moscow and a few people were sent back to the UK. As a reciprocal measure a few people were sent back from the Soviet Embassy. Next thing we were all summoned and told that now that the summer holidays were coming up, we should watch the children day and night. No way should they be allowed to be on their own. That was my chance because who would be there to look after my son since we weren't living with the rest of the [Soviet] community. So I went straight up to the man in charge and said I absolutely have to resign because I can't leave my son on his own. And that's how I was able to leave (what could he say as he read my thoughts!)

Property

We lived for three years in the flat which was provided for us. I was very sorry to leave it because we had been there for three years, but I didn't like it because I didn't like the feeling of being exposed. There were five

145

families around the same age, in the same boat; all the families were working for this or that international organization. The women were working part-time or not at all. We came home around the same time of one or 2 o'clock and from that time onwards, it was 'Knock, knock, who's there?', somebody else with a cup of coffee. We are still friends with those who are still here. They were all very nice people. But I somehow felt very exposed and vulnerable. I wasn't used to socializing so much, probably because I stayed at home so long after my son's birth. I guess I am an introvert, a more private person. I sort of felt like I was in a market place. I felt extremely insecure because the embassy or whatever could command me to go to school or to go here or there or whatever.

By then our husbands didn't have to take money back to the embassy which they had to do in the first years; they were given permission to keep their salaries. The first thing we did – the change came on 1 January 1991 – was to move out to another place on the 19th of January. So we wasted no time at all!

Finding a place was difficult because we were out of our depths. We had no idea what the prices were or what the renting market was like. We were the very first to move, but I was 100% certain that I wanted to move out. And we did move to our own, little rented place and I felt a lot better.

Transport

I found the underground quite charismatic, but not very efficient. Much less efficient than in Moscow! It always brought the *Forsythe Saga* to my mind. (I felt like the heroine out of there.) I used the buses because I could go straight to the consulate on the bus but I didn't like them so much. But I guess at that time the trade delegation and the organizations around ran minibuses or private cars.

Lack of family

It's not specifically missing this person or another, rather it's the feeling of not having a family because we used to be a very big, closely knit Jewish clan. I miss the feeling of a clan. When we moved into our tiny house here in London, the first thing I wanted to do was to buy a big dining table because probably in my subconscious is the memory of my most secure times in Moscow when we were all gathered around the big dining table at my aunt's place. I was absolutely adamant that we needed a big dining table.

Schooling

My son went to an independent school because my husband's organization paid up to 75% of the fees. In fact our son went to both types of school because we were thinking that more likely than not we were going back to the Soviet Union. For quite a few years I was still feeling that I was a tourist on an extended trip.

With whom did you socialize?

In the beginning, most of the people I met were not British. The people I met were connected to my husband's organization which was an international body, so they included Germans, Americans, Australians, New Zealanders, etc.. The only thing was I was very intimidated about my language. The first three to five years I had a notepad and I wrote down every expression I seemed to like, for communication purposes. I did this mostly for teaching when I thought I would be going back to the Soviet Union. Of course I was also quite inhibited and tense with the language.

Shopping

Shopping was mind boggling and I wondered why I had to expose myself to that! I had it from very many people that this choice was exhausting and suffocating; you can't breathe, literally. You don't want to see it and you don't want to know anything about it. Give me my one available TV set and let me go! Now I consider shopping business rather than enjoyment. I don't find it very entertaining, unless I have company and we go and have lunch.

Russian food

We cook Russian food sometimes. We have always been very open minded. Even back in Russia with limited availability we tried as best we could to branch out into different cuisines. Of course when I came to London they didn't have Russian shops like they do now. When visitors came from the Soviet Union, they brought loaves of Russian bread.

Has your husband's role changed here?

His role may have changed not so much because of the city but because of the situation. He absolutely adored what he was doing in the Soviet Union; it was him 100%. When he accepted this posting, he didn't expect it to be permanent. This is not what he would have chosen to do. So more and more he was probably finding interests and sense in the family rather than in the job. He's never done cleaning because he is not good at it. I'm sure he wouldn't mind but we have our own roles to do. But cooking is his domain. He is doing more and more cooking; he has more time, he has books galore. (It's his Ukrainian blood! Like singing for the Georgians!) He doesn't mind doing most things either. He's always been inclined to do things around the house. If his work had been more rewarding, it probably would have been different. Maybe I'm a special case but I've always had a very happy marriage and my husband has always been very helpful - with the child, with the cooking. I can't really complain to be fair.

Have your parenting roles changed at all?

Being here has probably affected our role as parents. Parenting in the Soviet Union was seen in a very different light. It's no, 'Honey and darling' there. It's, 'You do this and you do that' mostly. So in this respect we have re-thought our roles, probably too late (definitely too late), but this has certainly affected both of us and we often talk about it. This has certainly changed a lot (I hope it has) and we have spoken about it with our son. I now find it very abrasive when my mother commands me to do something; it isn't advice, it is a command. I was brought up this way and so was my husband. So this is a very different concept of parenthood altogether – more joint, more respectful.

Would your husband's job take precedence over yours?

I wouldn't think he would insist on it. There are periods when I am working around the clock because translations are always due 'yesterday', you never have enough time or hardly ever. He's always very understanding, probably because he knows it's only a temporary arrangement and it's not going to stay this way. Otherwise he would probably take a different stand. But it has never been a problem.

How did and do you spend your free time?

Now mostly music and exhibitions, at the Barbican, Covent Garden, Institute Français, local literary society. In the Soviet context, I certainly went to exhibitions especially when some of the works which were originally in storage were finally on display. As for concerts, it was very difficult to buy any tickets for something worthwhile (because of the deficit), so I don't think we went unless we came across nice tickets to something we really wanted to see. Of course the tickets would have been quite cheap compared to one's income and the exhibitions were accessible to all (everyone could have afforded them). We went so seldom to the theatre and to concerts. 'Culture' was certainly more affordable if you had access to the tickets -- if you had *blat* or *znakomstovo*, basically the latter being more essential, especially now! If you had these contacts, then 'culture' was quite accessible and there was a lot of it.

Religion

We are steadfast non-believers. It would be very difficult for us to choose a religion because my husband by all rights should be a Christian and I, although I come from a non-religious background, would never convert to Christianity. If I really was forced to choose which religious institution I had to go to, it would definitely be a synagogue. In the family I am probably most interested in religion, although our son is better educated in

149

this area because at school in London he had to go to religious education. When he went to the independent school, the head suggested that he attend a different religion every term, so he spent one semester with the Muslims, one with the Jewish lot, one with the Anglicans, etc.. I think this was very good of the school to suggest it. He is interested in each of them and now he has some knowledge, unlike me who has very little knowledge. I think my husband takes no interest in religion at all. But we have some religious friends, some of whom have intermarried and who find time for both sets of religion: each one of the couple has stuck to his or her own religion but with all of the respect of the other party.

Will you be going back to Russia?

I constantly think about going back to Russia. Before Mr. Putin, I think it was more or less decided that when my husband retired we would go back, regardless of what my son decides to do. As far as my son is concerned, I don't think he would go back. But we will probably make a home from home here and be settled permanently in Moscow because we have all of our friends there. Somehow we have managed to keep all of them. And most of the cousins (some have left) are still in Moscow.

What do you miss the most?

Family and friends. Definitely not the birch trees! The sense of 'motherland' is the people, that is, being surrounded by very reliable people I have known all my life.

How would you characterize British society?

British society is just fine as long as you don't start to pretend to be part of it. That's when you really get slapped on your wrists. I don't remember how I got this idea; I think it has been proven over time if I or anybody crosses the line. It is a fair enough society if you obey by the rules. It has been fine for us. At first we were surrounded by Russians, but we were welcomed by our neighbors. Now we live in a tiny little close where everybody more or less knows everybody else. The following day after we moved, we got an invitation for a drinks party. I think the reason behind it was that the neighbors wanted to know what to make of us. Russians do get a lot of bad publicity and we moved in February of 1994 and it was way after the peak of the popularity of the Gorbachev era. Those were the years when Russians were associated with the Russian mafia. So our neighbors wanted to get to know us a little bit and to get some idea of what to make of us. I think they were pretty apprehensive, but never ever declared it in any shape or form. From the word go we have never had any problems. That is not to say that we have made friends with each of them, but you wouldn't expect that. We are private enough people who don't throw huge parties, so we wouldn't be a major disturbance to them. We did have a really mad party in the summer, and there was singing in the garden. The following Christmas on the Christmas cards I got compliments on the quality of the singing! I don't know if they were being cheeky! To be fair, there are not so many English English among our friends. Mostly our friends are international. And so are our neighbors.

What do you value most about living in London?

What I value most are two things. It is relatively relaxed and convenient (I mean the creature comforts) which can't be compared, even now in Russia. You have to go through painstakingly organizing your life in Moscow to get the same standards. Here it comes naturally; you don't have to be anybody to live like that. In Moscow, it is possible but it needs a lot of work to create the infrastructure. Secondly, which is probably very cynical of me, in Russia whatever happens, even now, it is my personal pain and my personal shame, mostly both combined. Here I am still a foreigner. I may regret certain things and I may be cross about certain things but it is really not in my back yard. I don't feel like it is my personal problem. So in many ways my feelings and my emotions are spared here rather than in Moscow. Without underestimating the rest of it, I absolutely love London. I think it is a fantastic place to live.

ADDITIONS:

At the end of the day, I guess I belong to neither society -- Russia and the UK -- so there is a price to pay. So that is fair enough. **If you thought you would stay here, would you feel differently?** Definitely not, I think we will probably stay here. It will depend on the pension because life here is very expensive. If we can afford it, we will probably stay here because we don't like Mr. Putin's regime and we don't like the general changes and the tendencies that Russia is following at the moment. I don't think going back at the moment would be an option for me. My husband still has parents there, so we will have to balance out our wishes.

Galina (55)

Life in Russia

I was very interested and I did have a Bible, brought illegally from abroad. I read it and I knew it…. my maternal grandmother was sort of religious but her husband, who was the Lenin of his community, was so against religion that he was like a fighting atheist. She had to hide all the small icons not because of officials but because of her husband, and he was always mocking all the stories about the resurrection of Lazarus.

In Moscow, Galina attained a doctorate degree in international relations from a very prestigious university. She left the Soviet Union in 1988 when her husband was posted to London. Her daughter was born in Moscow but her son was born in London. She currently is a personal assistant to a Russian family. Her mother worked in a financial ministry as a civil servant and her father was a very high official in one of the ministries. He was a member of the *nomenklatura* [list of appointments reserved for the Party]. Both of her parents were Party members and are currently living in Moscow. Her older brother attained a higher education degree and is in business in Moscow. See her most interesting discussion about her grandparents.

Childhood

My childhood was spent in Ukraine. Although both parents received their education in Moscow, my father and his friend wrote a letter to *Pravda*, the newspaper, asking to send them where they would be most needed after university. So he was sent to a small village in Ukraine. At the age of twenty four (or twenty five or six), he had a very responsible job. He was a boss already at this age and that's probably why he made his career quite fast; he didn't sort of settle in Moscow. He just wanted to be useful, to be where he was needed, so that's why we spent our childhood in the village. Then we moved to a Ukrainian town. I even went to school where all the subjects were taught in Ukrainian.

Role of grandparents

My paternal grandfather went to war, was captured at the beginning of World War II by the Germans, and was released within a week by regular Soviet troops. The fact that he was captured by the Germans ruined his whole life! He couldn't find any work after the war, although of course he didn't have a higher education. He was a normal man; he could have worked at a factory or anywhere, but he wasn't admitted because he had this 'dirty biography' by being captured (although he stayed only a week, he was not even in a German prisoner of war camp). He was sort of surrounded in a field and in a week liberated by the Soviet army, but still this episode, as I understand it, ruined all his life. So he worked as a driver and he drank and my grandma left him, although they had five children. My father started working when he was thirteen because he was the eldest in the family: he was the man in the family and that's why he has always been so responsible. Although my grandparents were divorced, they lived close to each other and I knew my grandfather very well. My grandma usually took care of him [the grandfather]; neither ever married again. It was sort of a very sad page in their lives. She couldn't stand him being in the same family! She worked all her life; she worked everywhere she could find work. They were living in a suburb of Moscow because she came to Moscow to earn her living when granddad went to the war.

My mother's parents were more or less happy with their lives. It was an incredible family. They were always together; they couldn't spend a day without each other. My granddad was studying, writing poems. They lived in the village where my mum was born. Then all the inhabitants of the village left and it disappeared. So they came to live in a small village-like town, which is neither a town nor a village. My granddad worked at the factory, a shoe making factory, and I think my grandma was working for the same factory but she worked at home. They had four children. My grandfather was very keen on education although he was only educated up to four classes. He read much and he was respected by everyone in this small town. Everyone knew him and they came to him for advice. They even called him 'Our Lenin!' When he died at the age of only 68, the whole town came to his funeral. Although from a village, all of his children got a higher education. In my father's family, only he and his sister got a higher education; the other three did not.

Did your grandmothers help your mother to take care of her children?

No, my mum left home when she finished school. At the university she lived in the dormitories as did my father. I think it was the other way round: my parents always helped their parents. Sometimes I was sent there for the summer. I used to go to a Pioneer camp for one month, but my brother hated Pioneer camp. So usually we ended up at my grandparents who have a small house, a garden and an orchard. It's by a river but it was not the big city, it was still very small and pleasant so we went there; it was a help of course for our parents.

University

I went in Moscow to the Institute of International Relations [GIMO] in 1973. As it was the most prestigious university, all the *nomenklatura* [see glossary] kids went there, although my father was of no help because it should be *nomenklatura* of the *nomenklatura* to get there. **Did you chose it because of your father?** Actually no, my parents were totally against it because they told me that I would never get in. I was an excellent student but it was quite obvious that my marks didn't count, because they would just put me not A but B at the entrance exams, only because no one was behind [backing me up] me; it was like this. That's why my parents said, 'Just go find something else, where you can be among equals' because you should have someone in either the Ministry of Foreign Affairs, the Ministry of International Trade or at the KGB [secret police] or the Politburo [Political Bureau of the Central Committee of the Communist Party] or anywhere: then you were sort of 'backed up'.

But you were in the Komsomol yourself by then?

I was the leader in the Komsomol organization in my class, but even my parents didn't believe that I could get in. But I did. I got in and I chose it

155

because I was always good at languages. I was at a specialized school which taught English language from the beginning. So that's why I decided to have a higher education with something connected to the international. I didn't want to teach language; that's why I didn't go to any philology or pedagogical institute. I didn't want to teach but I wanted to use it. Actually I chose the institute from which my mum graduated, namely the Moscow Financial Institute, now it's the Financial University. It's an excellent education but just in finance; it's the best in Russia and still is, but they do have an international department so I wanted to apply there for the international faculty. But I had a friend whose father was in the Ministry of International Trade who was applying, and he knew from the very beginning that he would go into this Institute of International Relations [GIMO]. And they had entrance exams a month earlier. [Usually all universities in Russia have entrance exams in August; but some faculties, the most prestigious, have them in July.] This means that if you fail, you can still apply. And he told me, 'Try, what do you have to lose, let's go together.' To apply to GIMO you had to gather all sorts of recommendations from the Party organization at your school, from the Komsomol, from the Party organization of your district in Moscow, and you had to have several interviews because they had to decide whether you are fit or not for this. So it took plenty of time and it was so boring! My friend said, 'Listen I'm so bored, let's go together; at least we can chat while we are waiting, so you don't lose anything.' And it worked: that's right, he took me in, so I went with him, had my career, had my husband - - so this friend made my life! I was absolutely happy at the Institute.

Marriage, work and living accommodation

My husband and I both started university at maybe 19. We got married when we were 22. We have the same education, absolutely totally the same-- same languages, French and English, same absolutely everything, same year. But I had chosen to do post graduate work and he went to work because he said he was fed up with learning things and he wanted to work. In the Soviet Union you had to go to work obligatorily after graduation. I of course went before I sat for the entrance exams for my post graduate degree (*aspirantura*); I had to work and I went. I hated it from the very beginning; it was so dull, so boring but he loved it.

Where did you go to work in Moscow?

In Moscow, I went to work in the same company, a foreign trading company, as my husband. He loved it, I hated it and when I started my *aspirantura* and I had to sit for the very, really very, difficult entrance exams, I knew what I was doing. I was so happy because I knew how to do it, how to prepare. And he said, ' You are crazy; we have just finished these exams, you want more!' That's men and women! I didn't stay at this university for post graduate work; I went into the research university which was within the frame of the Academy of Science in the USSR. It was and still is the Institute of World Economy and International Relations, IMMO. I enjoyed every minute there. (Yevgenii Primakov, who was Prime Minister, was the director of this Institute.) That was three years of *aspirantura* [post graduate degree], then they took me on as staff. I left when I came to London.

When we got married my husband moved in to live with my family. Then we were lucky enough to find and rent a flat; it was very difficult to find something suitable. Then we moved on our own which was really nice and we lived there until my husband went as an interpreter abroad for two years. I decided whilst sitting alone in the flat and paying for it to return back home. When he returned we moved in with his grandfather who lived alone. His grandmother had died, and it was very difficult because we had to prove that we didn't have proper living conditions. At that time, my brother was already married and he had a child, and we had a child; so we wrote that we lived under impossible conditions. So that's why we left and we were allowed to move in with my husband's grandfather. Thus started our world separately.

Discussion of sex, sex education and birth control

I never talked with my mother, with anyone. I didn't learn anything in the schools. Just from my girlfriends! There was a fear of pregnancy all the

157

time. I was aware of contraceptives, but we didn't have any contraceptive pills. Of course we had, but I was absolutely uneducated in terms of pills so I was sort of afraid of them. I never asked my doctor to prescribe any pills for me, so the only contraceptive which we used was a calendar. I was just counting days and that was it. I knew about condoms but it didn't appeal much, neither to me nor to my husband. By the way when we arrived here, the best present we bought here was condoms and we brought them back; this was already 1988 and it was the best present! Tampons were not used either.

Abortions

We never discussed abortions. Absolutely not. Abortions were certainly a form of contraception. I did have one abortion, but I never even thought about trying something illegal, because you could pay and go into a good hospital, or you could have tried to do something without any registration at all. So I went into a good hospital which used an anesthetic and everything. But when my Mum needed an abortion, they were still prohibited. That's basically why I am alive -- it was exactly 1955. She said 'It's my biggest nightmare, I always dread it. If it [abortion] would have been allowed, you would never exist.' They were difficult times -- with my father and all the rest; they already had my brother and she probably was thinking about leaving him or whatever....

Giving birth

My daughter was born in Moscow and my son in London. I didn't have any [problems] while I was pregnant. I was feeling fine, I was totally healthy and there were no aggravations. I was quite old by our standards as I was twenty six: by Russian standards it's quite, quite old for the first child . But my brother's wife was pregnant at the same time and she had all kinds of problems. It was her second child, and her first child was born prematurely and he died. Her second child, a wonderful girl, is the same age as my daughter. My sister-in-law had plenty of problems and a very bad experience so that's why my father insisted that she go to a very specific clinic, which is like the Portland Hospital here. It was not private -

- nothing was private. It was still free of charge but you couldn't get it from the state, so you had to be somehow recommended. My sister-in-law saw consultants there and she stayed for some time at that hospital; then she was an in-patient and then released home. Seeing all this trouble, I sort of got worried and I said to my father, ' Listen, can I get in there too when I will give birth?' I never had any consultations there as I was monitored at my local. I was absolutely happy with it because I didn't have any problems, but still that's why I gave birth at a privileged place. Actually we gave birth within four days of each other and in Russia you stayed about a week at least at the hospital. I was first as my daughter is four days older, and I didn't know that my sister-in-law was there while I was staying there. There were no mobile phones and no communication at all and one day, out of my window I saw my husband and my brother. I thought how sweet that my brother had come to visit me. Then I found out that he came to visit his wife! Men are not allowed in at all -- not even flowers!

Parents and childcare

My mum definitely played a major role. The regulations were such that I could stay at home with my child until the child was one year old and I would receive some monthly payments, like child benefit. I could stay another six months without being paid if I wanted to. But work was very important and my place at work was saved for me, so I could return anytime. But when the child reaches eighteen months old, you either returned to work or your place was not guaranteed. So I decided to return. Nursery was not the best idea for a little child; I was not that fussy about my kids but still nursery was absolutely not on. In the Soviet Union then it was out of the question. (My nieces never went into kindergarten because for their mum, even kindergarten was out of the question.) By that time my mum was already 55, at pension age, and she said, 'OK, it's more important for you; you need it, so you return to your work and I will sit with my granddaughter.' Although she was very important at her work and she loved her work, she suggested this. We lived separately by that time, so on Sunday evening we brought my daughter to my parents' flat and returned home and collected her on Friday. She lived with my parents and they enjoyed it immensely. My dad of course worked and my mum took

159

care of her granddaughter. When my daughter turned three, she went into kindergarten near where we lived. We took her in the morning to the kindergarten and we collected her in the evening at 6 o'clock on our way back from work. But when my mum tried to go back where she had worked, (she said, 'No, you can't cross twice the same river'), my dad already was used to coming home for lunch because they lived across the road from where he worked. He very much enjoyed coming home for lunch, seeing his wife and his granddaughter. And so he said, 'No, no, no, no, no you come back home, I want you to be here.' So she never worked again and was quite happy. If it had not been for my daughter, probably she would have worked till 60 or maybe more.

How would you define a good mother?

I think it's not whether you work or you don't work. Work is not that important for being a mother, it's more important for being a wife. That's why when I worked, I was sort of more interesting because I had my separate life; we had more to discuss at home because you can't discuss shopping or washing or whatever. But for children, I think it's not that important [working], because one's education is absolutely important for raising children; the more you are educated the better it is because education doesn't disappear. I told my daughter, 'Listen, you take it for granted, you come to me and say, "Mum, help me with French, Mum, help me with this, help me with that."' I know everything, I seem to know everything though I am only doing the washing, the cooking, the shopping -- all this rubbish stuff. So education doesn't disappear, it is important when you are raising children.

Do you think there are specific problems that are just related to women?

You know it was so difficult in the Soviet Union that when we came here I thought that I would never work again! But it took me less than two months in London to understand that I just can't sit at home; I have to do something. But while working in the Soviet Union, I was lucky enough because I was an academic so I needn't be present at my desk every day (well I should be every day!) but I could tell my boss that I need to go to the library. Everyone knew this 'library' ; 'the library' is sacred! They knew that if I needed to produce some written work I could do this on Saturday or Sunday at home. I had a typewriter so I could easily do it at home. That's why if my daughter was ill, I could stay with her. I had a medical certificate which allowed me to stay with her. But still it wasn't like my husband who had to be at his desk at 9 am and he couldn't leave earlier than 6pm. I didn't work like this. Of course I had to be at my desk at nine and couldn't leave before six, but still I could come at 9.30, leave by 5.30.

Do you think this is because of your job or because of your gender?

I think it's because my job was much easier. My mother-in-law was a professor at the university and I think that's the best job for a woman in the Soviet Union because she had long holidays and she had very short working hours. It was sort of much more effective because if she was teaching, she was teaching for two hours. I could be drinking coffee, but I still had to sit there. That's why she was always at home and my husband's brother had two kids to raise and she was absolutely happy in doing this only because she was a professor all the time at the university. She had four hours in the morning and then about two hours with post graduates late at night.

Ability to travel

My father was in the Party but his work didn't allow him to travel and didn't require him to travel because he was in the Soviet economy. But he went once or twice maybe; I remember Bulgaria, Vietnam, Finland. I didn't go. My husband went to Madagascar, and I went to see him in Madagascar; he was a French translator and I went to see him. I could have accompanied him, of course, but I didn't want to because I was doing my thesis; I was at my post graduate course for three years and I had to sort of cancel it for some time. My husband's father was of course a member of the Party as well, but he worked in foreign trade. He travelled a lot, absolutely. It just was not a matter of Party membership; it was a matter of what you did as a job. But if you weren't a Party member, you had much less chance of going abroad, no matter what your job was.

Equal but not equal - education

Not totally equal or equal but not equal. Here is an easy example. The 1973 entrance exams to this Institute of International Relations (I don't know about state university honestly, but I guess that there would have been the same scheme needed for entrance at any prestigious university) had an entrance number of points. It is five points, five is the highest, that's an A, four is a B, and I so on. There were four entrance exams for the Institute. If you have all fives you get twenty points and a fifth set of points is the median point of your school certificate. (When you count all the subjects and then divide by the number of grades, you have the school number). Actually the biggest combination you can get is 25. But the numbers for admission were absolutely different. The lowest number was for undergraduates who had work experience after school and who were members of the Communist Party; it was about 17. Then came men and women undergraduates with work experience. Within my type --which was straight from school, not a member of the Party, but a member of the Komsomol and a girl -- my entrance points were twenty four and a half; that was next to impossible. They gave me only an allowance of 0.5 which could only be achieved **if you were a boy?** Yes. Boys had twenty four points, at least they could have if they were great at school and they had this median of five on their school certificate. They could have one four at the entrance exam and I couldn't; one four and I am out absolutely, because I needed to have twenty four and a half. So that's equal but not too equal! **Do you think there were quota systems for boys and girls?** I guess yes, but I never knew it for sure and when I entered as a post graduate, I was told if there were two equal candidates, a man and a woman, they are going to take the man because women will have children and all this! But in terms of opportunities, of course, it was total equality, absolutely.

Did religion play any role in your life?

No, I was very interested and I did have a Bible, brought illegally from abroad. I read it and I knew it. We had Jesus Christ Superstar, the rock opera, which we knew by heart. I think twice we went for Easter celebration services but it was very, very, very quiet and we never told anyone. It was more like a tradition. We had these Easter meals prepared by my grandmother. My maternal grandmother was sort of religious but her husband, who was the Lenin of his community, was so against religion that he was like a fighting atheist. She had to hide all the small icons not because of officials but because of her husband, and he was always mocking all the stories about the resurrection of Lazarus.

Did you join the Party?

No but I would have joined the Party if I had stayed. That was where there were quotas, quotas for academics were very small. But I definitely should have joined the Party before I was allowed to start my doctorate because I am a Doctor of Economics and economics was considered to be a political science. To be a professor in political science you must be a member of a Party; if you are a biologist, a chemist, a physician or whoever, you can stay like this but with the political sciences you would never have been allowed to start your research.

How do you picture the ideal woman in the Soviet Union?

I wouldn't say ideal, I would rather say lucky woman. To be an ideal you have to be quite lucky, because the ideal woman --a woman with a career, with an education, with a husband and with children, who is well dressed, more or less okay in financial terms, living in a separate flat, in a good flat-- for all this you must be quite lucky.

What did femininity mean? Does femininity come into this when you say well dressed?

Of course that's why you can still separate Russian ladies from any others. Especially at our age, we are used to making the most of our looks without any help. Only living here [in London] can you be dressed in an old T shirt, some baggy jeans and you go off to see your kids at school. Once a Russian lady is out, I mean a proper lady of course, she tries to look really well. It was a skill to get some really nice clothes. It was so funny, especially when I worked. My girlfriends, if they saw something really good in the shops, they bought for the three of us. And we came in proudly the next day --all three of us, all three in the same shoes; we were so proud, you know it was wonderful! We even had a saying between us: 'it was a present for money'. One weekend my girlfriend went to her dacha and at the country shop she bought a very nice French facial cream for ten rubles. She bought three, one for herself and two for her two friends. Of course I gave her ten rubles but it was what she called a present for money: I couldn't myself buy it as I never saw it. My friend's mum could make clothes. She was a dressmaker, but she was not a dressmaker by profession, although she was so good at this. I have several handmade clothes which were very beautiful, because we had these patterns from foreign magazines.

Validating some Western views about the past: degree of closeness to parents

The closeness to the parents was basically that you don't have any other place to live, and so you have to be close to your parents.

Life in London

Why did you leave the Soviet Union and come to London?

We didn't leave the Soviet Union. My husband, whose profession was foreign trade, was sent here to work as a professional for three years plus one, exchanging with another person who would come after him. He was sent to London to a particular job; he knew absolutely everything - about where he would live and what he would do. I accompanied him. My place at work was saved for me because I was sort of on a mission as well.

How difficult was it to adjust to?

Climate

The climate is wonderful! No problem. But I like Moscow climate more because it does have winter and it does have summer. But I am used to this climate now.

People: How did you adjust to the British?

Well easily, easily. I think that it's honestly the best people in the world, taken as a community. It was difficult of course because we are different, but when you get used to and get to understand the British, I honestly believe that it is one of the best communities in the world. They are very friendly and although they do not interfere at all in your life if you do not ask, but once you ask, you can get every possible help.

When we moved here the first thing we asked the vendors to do was to introduce us to the neighbors and they did. They invited this neighbor and that neighbor and we had a drinks party. And so we knew everyone. I can't understand how you can live within a community and not communicate. So then we made friends everywhere; we knew all the people living here, especially those who lived here when we moved in. We don't know the new ones yet, but still we know some children through supporting Arsenal--you know it's our local team! And I know the ladies. This Russian family knew no one until we came and she asked me, 'How come you know everyone?' and I said, ' Listen, I made an effort to know everyone!' whereas they only watch Russian television. So that's what I love about being a part of the community.

So you really have socialized with everyone in your area? More or less. I think I've socialized enough not to be frightening to other people, like some Russian lady, living here, drinking vodka. When we moved in we made friends with some neighbors and they said, 'You are nice.' We said, 'Why should we not be nice?' And they said everyone knows there is a Russian family here and we've never had a word from them. [A Russian family lives two doors down who moved in prior to Galina.]

165

Language

Well I was absolutely fluent in English, so it was no problem at all. The same is true for my husband because he wouldn't have been sent to London if he wouldn't have spoken English. The only problem was that when I was working, I was working more with French because I was a researcher on French economy. (I have never been to France; I never saw this economy before; I only read about it but still I was using it in my work. I was using French more, especially when the scientific delegations came from France, we were exchanging views, conferences, etc..). So when we came here, my first intention to speak a foreign language was to speak French.

Property

When we first came we were given a place to live and we nearly didn't pay anything for it. We were not living within the trade delegation, but lived outside, quite independently [in north London]. But still the house belonged to the trade delegation so when we had plumbing or electrical problems, we reported it to the trade delegation and they sent a person to fix it.

Looking for property in London as an experience was great fun because when we came from Moscow there was no property market at all and it was a nightmare there: you couldn't buy property. You would only be given this property and the only time when you were using the market was when you tried to exchange your property. So that was the only market and that was a nightmare. But here it was such fun; it was already perestroika and we had money. We were allowed to return to Moscow or stay here if we wanted to stay. We could have stayed in the same flat, but the older market relations were now changing, so we had to pay rent to the trade delegation; it was much lower of course than the normal rent but the conditions were so much worse at that flat, and the flat was smaller. We decided not to throw money away because the prices in 1992 or 1993 were so low for property here that it was quite sensible to buy something, pay a mortgage and not pay rent.

Transport system

The London underground-- awful, very unreliable, awfully expensive! It's not a system at all. Buses are better, especially after the introduction of these bus lanes. But we don't use them much, so that's why I am not a person to ask. You should ask my daughter; she travels to and from her work and to all these clubs and wherever she is going, she only goes by public transport.

Did you miss being without your own mother or mother-in-law? I didn't miss my mother-in-law because we never lived together. I was absolutely fine talking to her over the phone and they visited us. Perestroika was a very great thing! It allowed our parents and close family to come to visit; so they lived here for a month. My parents visited longer when my father retired so it was quite nice. but I wouldn't say it was hard to adjust without them. We communicated, we wrote letters or phoned from time to time. Then they were allowed to come. It was more like my mother missed me. Now especially, it's the other way round and I am very worried that I am here and can't help her much.

Children's schooling

My daughter was six and my son was born here. In 1988 no one was allowed to go to British schools. There was a school in the embassy, a very good school. It even had a Moscow number and produced proper certificates; the education was excellent there and it was free, but now it is private. (They charge if you are not a diplomat or a member of trade mission, but you can go. I know families who send their children because they don't want their children to go to university here as they are planning to return to Moscow. Therefore it's more reasonable for them to have a Russian style education.) But my daughter was not yet school age and it was already sort of perestroika-ish timing. We had a very good rule at that time: *everything was allowed which was not prohibited*, so if it was not prohibited then it was allowed. And going to British schools at that time was not prohibited: it was not said that you must not go to British schools. At the age of seven every child here, if he or she needed an education, must be

167

sent to this [Russian] school, but we had this year, so we sent our daughter to a British school. We didn't have money to pay for a private school so we sent her to a state school. Of course she was unhappy at the beginning because she didn't know a word of English. When the time came for her to go into this school, perestroika was getting more and more widespread and you could have combined two schools: you could have taken the Russian school as an external [student]. So you just come, you pass exams, they register you but you don't go there every day. So we did it like this for maybe three years. She stayed at a British primary school and went from time to time to pass exams in Russian, maths and something else at that Russian school. Eventually we dropped the Russian school because it became more and more difficult to catch up with the program because the program was very difficult. And so she stayed at primary school and then went into secondary school. By then we had chosen a private school -- it was different. My son goes to the local secondary school, the one which frightened me when I brought my daughter to see this school eleven years ago. I was so terrified, I can't explain it, I said, 'No, I will never leave my daughter here alone.' And now my son is at the same school and he is absolutely happy. When my daughter first went to school, it was still a conservative time, conservative values and all the rest. And now we do have sort of more liberal times.

Shopping

Shopping was exciting, but very hard, because we had to shop for the whole family that we left behind. The sales were like hard work. I never go now, I don't need anything, so when I need something I just go and buy it. But at that time we needed to supply [things] for everyone. We needed the sales because we didn't have enough money to buy proper things for normal prices. I used to miss **Russian food**, but not now. We have so many Russian shops you can buy everything.

Has your husband's role(s) changed since you have come here?

For the first time he was absolutely indispensable because I couldn't even go to the shops without him; I could only go to the corner shops which were not sufficient. So we had to do our shopping together. You know you sort of feel like you are more dependent being here. You don't have many friends. Of course we were very lucky when we first came here that we were given a flat in this trade delegation house. There were four other families living there and we really got along nicely. We were close and we still are because we were very similar; our husbands had the same work, the same problems, the same everything and we were more or less alike. We had the same education, we came from the same town and that's why we quite easily made friends. But apart from this, you come here and you don't have much outside of your family. That's why you feel more dependent. You wait till your husband comes home to discuss things, and my husband was working in an international company not among Russians but other people, British and non-British alike. So he was not very much at ease in the beginning himself, and that's why the family becomes closer.

At first I tried to do all my housework during the day so that in the evening I could spend more time – leisure time -- with him, with our daughter together. Then at some stage, maybe a year or a couple of years later, I understood that he probably had an impression that I am not doing anything at all. So I left a bit of my homework till the evening for him to see that I am busy myself. But the best way was just to go to work; this just leveled everything. But I know several families who, when they returned to Moscow, got divorced because here, you sort of think, 'Well if I decide to divorce my husband, where shall I go? I have to rent a flat, I can't just go and go to my mum's; my mum is in Moscow.'

If I had a full time job, **his job would still take precedence** over mine. I would never have been paid as well as he was paid in this country. In Moscow probably yes, but not in this country. Here I have to certify all my qualifications and he didn't have to because he was employed at an international company. He was employed when he was still in the Soviet Union and they knew all his qualifications; they understood that he graduated from a very good university and if I said, 'I've got such and such qualifications and they would say, where are your GCSEs (Oh, for goodness sake!) and where are your A-levels?'

Were you conscious of treating your son and your daughter differently according to the gender?

Yes, because I still believe that at some stage the most important thing for my daughter will be her family, however educated she will be by that time. She could be President of the Academy of Sciences but still I believe that her first priority should be her family. Otherwise she will be unhappy at the end of the day; that's my strongest belief. She has a training contract with a very good law firm which has paid for her law education. She is very, very hardworking and clever and very well educated, but still I believe that. I said, 'Look at me. I had all my education and I never regretted it. I had wonderful work while I had the possibility to work. I am now sitting at home and still I can discuss things and I'm not dumb; it will not disappear.'

Of course my son will be the boss in his life, maybe because he is much younger (by eleven years), but maybe because we are living here in a society which is very, very individualistic. We don't push him at all. If he wants to play the guitar, he plays guitar, although we always dreamt of him being the best at school, but we never insisted that he goes to some private school where he studies and studies and studies. He went with his friends to secondary school. Next year he does his GCSEs and we will get him tutors so that he can get As. So we believe that he will be the boss of his family; he will take all the responsibility. He will be the main provider.

Femininity and equality

The concepts of femininity have changed since I have come to the UK. I think women in the UK are quite different. I never tried to apply for a job or something like that, so I can only judge by what my daughter is telling me. I think yes, women are pretty equal. I've never heard of any occasion when my daughter was treated inferior to boys. I have the impression that girls are being treated better than boys. If you compare my daughter and her boyfriend, she is better than him. Although he had an excellent education, he graduated from a very good independent school and went to Bristol University but still he is not finding it easy to get work; he is still dreaming about having the same contract as she has. So he did the same but at his own expense because he never had a training contract, so maybe....

Has religion meant anything more than it did before?

Yes, of course. We follow all the holidays (but not Lent). We don't belong to a Russian Orthodox church but we go from time to time. It's more mentally, as I put it. I am a religious person myself but I am not a church goer. I have plenty of friends who are very very religious; they are giving money to the church.

Are you thinking of going back to Russia?

I don't know, while I am needed here... you know the twist is that coming here I am thinking first of my family, my kids, and then about everything else. My father asked me where am I going to be buried, and I said, 'Where it's easier for my children to visit the grave.' My father is thinking his parents are together and they (my parents) will be next to them, and I say, 'Okay, what about Mum's parents; they are in a different place! So I prefer my parents to be together and if you prefer to be together with your parents, you will be in different places.' I am not going back now because we have the young to educate, so it's not now. We do have a place to live, we have a flat in Moscow, so when we decide to return we have a way to return. And of course we will go if we are needed there; we do have parents and although we have siblings but still....

What do you miss the most?

I don't know. Maybe it's an atmosphere, like when you walk and everyone is speaking Russian and you remember. I love Moscow and you remember streets and shops and everything has changed. And of course friends, but you know that we are in such an age that friends have stayed with you; they are still with you wherever you are. When you're younger of course there are friends, everywhere friends, but still I miss the life which I'm used to. This is different. But you know we left Moscow a very long time

171

ago so I now take it sort of as a place to visit on holiday place which is not really true.

How would you characterize British society?

It's a very appealing combination of friendliness and independence from each other. My first intention was to say that I don't see much of a society as a society. I see individuals, but no, there is a society. If you want to be involved, you have plenty of opportunities to be involved. So I don't know what more to say.

[indicated later in the interview] The British are not hysterical at all. They are a no panic nation. They can understand everything because I remember when there was an IRA bomb alert, and they usually gave a bomb alert, I remember central London closing and everyone was patient, everyone understood; no one was shouting, 'What's happening, I want to go home.' It was a Friday evening, everyone was late and they were patient, understanding. The police were doing proper things, because they had to close roads and all that.

What do you value most about living in London?

First of all it's a very pleasant place to live. It's green and where we are living we are used to all these small houses, quiet streets. It is still a big capital city with all the entertainment and all these events and everything. It's really a very interesting place to live. I was never thinking about going somewhere like a very pure village. I would rather stay here. It's still quite a secure place to live; we have bought electronic gates and all the rest, and it's` great for children with all these facilities like swimming pools, the schools, etc.. The system of relationships is very appealing to me. My son started school when he was four and he is still friendly with the children from his school. We are friendly with their parents. If you need something material, you call central London; you see it, you have it all. In terms of supplies, you can get everything here, nothing is a problem at all, nothing --food, furniture, clothing, anything. You don't really experience any

172

problem in getting something. Even with money, it's easy here: you know what you can buy and what you cannot.

In Moscow there are either good and extremely expensive things or some market Chinese stuff. They don't have places like Marks and Spencer where for reasonable money you can get decent clothes, decent food and decent whatever you wish. It's better, of course, than the market things. When my parents came here, although they can buy anything there, they found things here that are more quality and for more affordable prices which we do not still have in Moscow; we don't have affordable quality shops as far as I know. Here you just know you can buy a helicopter or you can buy such a car or any car. But 'value for money' is an expression which is understandable here but absolutely foreign in Moscow; there isn't value for money!

ADDITIONS:

Strong woman in Russian culture, under socialism and today

You know that if you take it statistically, women took all the hardships of perestroika stronger than men did. Plenty of men just got lost totally, because they used to go to work, get smallish salaries, basically doing not much, and they thought it would continue forever. And when they were forced to choose either to go and become, say, Abramowitz or whoever, very few honestly actually made this choice. Most of them just went with the flow. Some were lucky with this flow. Some were not able to grasp the opportunity. Whilst the population can hate our Abramowitz(s) of today, I do respect them because they were clever enough and brave enough to see this opportunity and to grasp it, to make use of it. Of course there was plenty of fraud and everything but it was an initial accumulation of capital as we economists know and if you take initial accumulation of capital here in Britain, you better read Dickens: it was basically the same, although it was 200 years ago. In the Soviet Union it happens now. So that's why I think the problem was created by the social system, the socialist system. Plenty of men just lost a sense of responsibility and women always had it because they always had to support the family, to raise the children. And

173

we have to restore it again, so that a man will be a provider, the main provider for the family and not a woman. So it was all twisted around during the years of socialism.

That's why I think any Russian woman (if you take our age and up) is a strong woman,. If you take young girls now, well I don't know. It is a strength in a sense, when a girl can decide what she wants: to either make a career, so she will work hard and get a proper education and all the rest; or if she is not good at education and careers and everything, she will make a perfect wife. Then she will find a rich husband, she will look nice, she will be a good mum, she will learn the art of making a beautiful house, designing it. What she wants, she is choosing!

The importance of education

It is less important even here. You are being educated, you work hard and then what do you get? -- you don't get anything, you are not guaranteed anything. We always believed that you must get educated and I know a Russian boy who is nearly thirty. He refused to go to university, though he did his A levels, and he went straight into either a bank or something; he started as a small clerk, getting proper training and he said, 'No, I don't need university; it's a waste of time, money and everything!' I believe that university is the most important stage not because of the future profession or anything, but just because it's a stage of life. Actually it's the best period in anybody's life. At university you are old enough to do anything and you don't have any responsibility at all apart from your studying, which you can manage. I love the idea here of a campus university which we don't have in Russia.

Masha (51)

Life in Russia

In 1991, we left for Paris. Then we spent two years in Toronto, Canada. Then we went back to France for one more year and in 1994 we came to England.

Adjusting to English society was an interesting experience. It was different.... In England it's more like implied rather than expressed so you need to adjust to social behavior here.... I think it's a difference, not a problem. We came here willingly and this country accommodated us, so it's our responsibility to adjust ourselves to the social norms of this country -- not the other way round.

Masha was born in St Petersburg where both of her parents come from. She is currently a university lecturer with two PhDs. Although separated from her academic husband, she has brought up her two children, one who is at Cambridge University and the other sitting his A-levels. At the age of 78, her mother is still an academic in St Petersburg because, although she retired at the age of 55, her pension was very small and insufficient for her to survive on. Her father was a colonel in the Soviet navy and was a good provider because his salary (and his pension) at that time was one of the highest. But when her father died, her mother had to provide for herself. On her mother's side, both grandparents were doctors. On her father's side, her grandfather was a professor of chemistry in the Caucuses; her grandmother never worked.

University

I entered the physical faculty at the university by pure chance. The examinations for the physical faculty were a month earlier than for all the other faculties, institutes and universities in Leningrad because they were considered to be so difficult, so students who didn't get into the faculty were given a second chance. My parents did not like this approach but when I got in, they realized that the alternatives were either that I stay

175

there or take another exam elsewhere. My parents were so horrified by my adventurous nature they said, 'Would you really like to sit another exam or would you like to go with us to the Black Sea coast and spend the month there?' So I went with them.

After university?

When I was at university I developed interests in medical physics and biophysics, maybe because my grandparents were medical doctors. They always wanted me to go into medicine. Still, maybe it was just my personality. I graduated in 1982 and I started to teach straightaway. I became a lecturer at the medical university. I liked it very much because I liked teaching. They gave me a special group of foreign students with the responsibility of teaching them Russian as well as teaching biophysics and mathematics as I would be the most appropriate person. I was the only person who spoke English. That was my first experience teaching Russian.

Marriage and accommodation

I met my husband at the physical faculty of the university We were both students in the same year. Then he got a job at the Military Academy and worked there for two years. Then he earned his Ph.D. at the Institute of Mathematics in the Academy of Sciences. He did research there when we married. I was nineteen, almost turning twenty.

In addition to the fact that I fell in love with my husband, there was another consideration [for marriage]. In Russian families in order to gain independence from your parents, the only way is to get married, to get independence. Once we got married we lived with my parents for the first two years, but still the status was different. We lived in a two bedroom apartment, but the living room was also used as a bedroom. In these three rooms we had my grandmother, my parents, and my husband, myself and my small daughter. My parents really helped take care of my daughter because we lived together. There was absolutely no problem when we wanted to go out or about us doing our degrees. My mother was always willing to stay with my daughter. My grandmother always cooked because she liked it.

Discussion of sex, sex education and birth control

There was no sex education in the school system. And I didn't learn it from my mum. In my family it wasn't appropriate to talk about sex. It wasn't considered intellectual enough, a low subject which wasn't worth discussing. It wasn't considered something you should be focused on. As for contraceptives, this wasn't discussed because this wasn't something appropriate to Soviet and Russian morals. I would rather discuss it with my friends and not with my mother. Contraceptives were readily available. You just had to make an appointment with the doctor and discuss it with the doctor. Both of my children were not accidents.

Abortion

I haven't had any abortions. Maybe because I come from a medical background, I didn't think it was difficult to keep things under control.

Definition of a good mother

My definition would include spending as much time with my child as I could and trying to interest her in the things I was interested in and trying to be interested in the things she was interested in, so that we would have a lot of things to discuss and a lot of things in common. That was how I was brought up and it was exactly the same attitude that I wanted to have with my daughter.

Were there any problems specific to women?

There were no real problems because I only thought that in principle if you had a very strong character – independent and self-sufficient and intellectual interests -- then you can survive with any problems you encounter. I never thought that my life in the Soviet Union was problematic because it was given. It was the life that I conducted. If you don't know any difference,....

What about the 'double burden' in the USSR?

In the Soviet context the double burden is a reality because the so-called equality wasn't equality at all. All the responsibilities for the house were left on the women's shoulders plus the same responsibilities that men had in terms of career and work. It's very much true.

How do you picture the ideal woman with the Soviet Union?

This is a very difficult question and really depends on your upbringing.

Strong woman in Russian culture

I think this concept is still valid in Russian culture and strong in character, not in terms of carrying heavy bags or household work. I mean not only a strong character but also a wise character. The main thing is not to show that you are strong. Not to show off. This doesn't mean playing dumb or being meek. Men should perceive you as you are, otherwise it would be a great deception afterwards.

Did religion play any role for you?

No. I am baptized and I'm Russian Orthodox as are my husband and my children. Religion didn't play any role in our family apart from these things. My father's mother was religious. In her will she asked that at her death she would have a ceremony in the church. Everybody went to the ceremony apart from my father who was a member of the Party. (Neither my mother, myself or my husband were members of the Party.) It was more or less compulsory for my father to join the Party as he was a member of the navy. I was told this story when I was quite young and it made a big impression on me. I thought it must've been awful for my father not to be able to attend his mother's funeral because of such a formal command. This was in 1958.

Ability to travel

My father couldn't leave the country because he was in the navy, but we [she and her mother] did travel abroad. My mother's best friend was working in Prague and we were able to travel together there. On the other hand after university my mother worked with the Supreme Committee of the Komsomol as an interpreter and she spent all her time travelling between Moscow and Copenhagen. She had a record of being reliable and that's why it wasn't a big problem for us to go travelling.

Validating Western views about the past: Balancing work and family and the prime emphasis on the child

I did feel the stress of balancing work and family, but probably not any more than anybody else. But that was specifically why I was always attached to the teaching profession: the teaching profession always gave flexibility. I didn't have to stay in my office from nine until five. I had to adjust my routine to the timetable and that gave me the possibility to do shopping on off-peak hours and to spend more time with my daughter. I had to teach about 20 hours a week which is about half of the 40 hour working week. I could do the preparation in my own time. I think it's always easier to manage your own time.

In many but not all families, the child certainly is the center of the family. In my family and in many families in my circle, this was always the case. Besides the myth that society takes full responsibility for education, that wasn't the case. I always thought that family played the major role.

Life in London

Why did you come to London?

In the four years after 1990, we changed countries three times: France, Canada and then France again. We were changing schools and languages. I couldn't get any permanent position because my husband acquired temporary jobs at the university and I always had to find some occupation for myself. We decided we had to find some permanent residence. The first permanent position that came up was in Sussex [UK].

Why did you leave the USSR?

We left the USSR in 1990 when the shops were absolutely empty and I spent all of my time queuing for food with my little son in a trolley. The second thing was the standard of living --- we were both university lecturers at that time and our two salaries were not enough to survive. It was necessary for one of us to get an additional job, say in the business sector (like most of my school friends did), but neither my husband nor myself were inclined to do this. But the main thing was that both of us were very tired of the socialist hypocritical and bureaucratic society and we did not want to comply anymore.

How difficult was it to adjust to:

Climate

The climate never was an issue for me. The climate in St. Petersburg is bad enough.

People

Adjusting to English society was an interesting experience. It was different. The French character is much closer to the Russian character in terms of openness and sincerity, in terms of conspicuously expressing your likes and dislikes. In England it's more like implied rather than expressed so you need to adjust to social behavior here. But I don't see that as a problem: I think it's a difference, not a problem. We came here willingly and this country accommodated us, so it's our responsibility to adjust ourselves to the social norms of this country -- not the other way around. I was always willing to do this and I was interested in doing this. I read books on this subject so that I could become more familiar.

Language

My husband was more or less fluent in English. He is a linguistically able person -- that means he picks up languages quite easily and quickly. For me English was never really a problem because my grandfather was fluent in English and he spoke English with me from an early age. My daughter was in a special English school in St. Petersburg and so she spoke English pretty well. She went to school in Canada so there was really no problem for her. For my son, however, there was a problem because he spoke Russian and French before he came here and for him Russian was the language that was spoken at home and French was the language that was spoken outside the home. But he picked up English within a month or two.

Property

Once again it wasn't really a problem for us because we already had experience in moving and finding flats and accommodation in other countries. In St. Petersburg we lived in one flat, a family flat, and we were pretty squashed. So here it's like shopping; it's a luxury compared to before. It was definitely a change for the best.

School system

Getting my children into schools wasn't a problem. We went to the local state school and there were places for them. They had changed schools three or four times already; they're both very sociable and it wasn't an issue for them.

Was it a problem being a mother without your own mother or mother-in-law?

That was very difficult at the beginning, very difficult because I was left on my own and because of my character. I don't trust many [people]. I didn't feel comfortable thinking my child was with somebody else while I was doing my own thing. That's why I always worked part-time. I wouldn't pick up the phone and call my mother because she doesn't live in this country, doesn't know this country and therefore couldn't give me advice.

I was never close with my mother-in-law, but I have great respect for my mother-in-law and very grateful to her for the kind of relation that we established which is probably ideal for her and for me. If I needed help, she was always there, but otherwise she didn't interfere. My in-laws never visited us in London but my mother did.

With whom did you socialize?

My children went to state schools where the other mothers were very friendly, but we never socialized. Maybe this was because when we came to London I started working on my second PhD and I just didn't have time. I always wanted to establish myself, to find a job, a career and to feel independent. For this I needed time.

Shopping

Shopping was paradise in comparison to Russia. It was a relief. Going once a week into a supermarket, buying everything, putting it in the car, then in the fridge. In Russia I spent hours and hours every day trying to find food for the family. It's paradise here!

Russian food

I don't really miss Russian food but there are some products that I do miss, like rye bread and *tvorok* [cottage cheese, curds]. Now they're more and more Russian stores and you can buy these products. So I don't miss them any longer.

Styles and makeup here

Every woman when she's on the street is very observant. Of course I never wanted to stand out, to be an exotic barbarian in a Western country. So I immediately tried to adjust my style, my makeup and everything to this country - not to be taken as a curiosity.

Did your husband's role change here?

Yes, very much so. When we were in the Soviet Union, he integrated into our family. He was never a leader. And when we went abroad, he became the provider and the welfare of the family very much depended on him.

He never tried to avoid this [cooking, cleaning, childcare] in the Soviet Union and he had less time here for doing these things. I can't say that he was the type of person who was trying to avoid these things or found them boring. He was always very helpful, maybe because we were married so young and we built our family together. We did our PhDs almost parallel so we always shared things. My husband never did more family and housework than I did because he didn't have the time. He worked full time and I worked part-time.

As far as our children are concerned, I would say that I spent more of my time with them, more energy and the major part of my thought was there, much more than my husband did. His role was not that decisive in terms of everyday management; for example, the subjects for GCSEs or giving permission for children to go to parties just because he wasn't that familiar with their environment, so that he could make a competent decision.

Are women's careers as important as men's?

I won't generalize but he knew that working was a very important part of my personality and my life. Even possibly if he didn't think that (I don't know if he liked it or not), he knew that to have a positive moral climate in the family, he should give me this opportunity. Otherwise there would be side effects on him. He had a full-time job and I had a part-time job, so his career took precedence.

Do you think you have brought up your children according to gender?

My daughter left Russia when she was ten years old and she was brought up as a typical Russian child. She had three grandmothers around her and had their full attention and full support. My son was born in 1990 and we left Russia when he was only one year old, so he was brought up only by

183

myself. My children are very different. The decision making was not in terms of more or less but in terms of allowing and not allowing different things. My daughter is very rational and pragmatic whereas my son is a romantic, emotional type. I'm not making gender decisions, I'm making personality decisions. My daughter was always very mature and rational so I was always 100% sure that she wouldn't make any mistakes. My son could make a mistake as he could be carried along by romantic impulses. For example, I would phone and check up on him more frequently than with my daughter, just to make sure that he wouldn't suddenly make a leap.

What does equality mean here?

Women should be treated the same, have the same education, have the same job opportunities. But at the same time women also shouldn't lose their role of decorating men's lives and I think men should have this attitude as well. I don't think women should just have a 'little job' because personally for me a career has played a very important part in my life. I'm interested in what I am doing and I don't want this to be belittled.

Thoughts about pensions

I think about pensions now because it's a big problem for me. I started my career very late in this country and because I worked part-time, for me it will be a big issue.

Religion

I'm Russian Orthodox. Now in Russia religion plays a major role and now it's more important. Here, I go to the Russian Church on special occasions and when I go back to Russia I also go to church. But it is not something that will guide my life. My children and I were baptized and they go to church with me.

How do and did you spend your free time?

I went to the theatre, to the ballet and to concerts. The tickets were very cheap and readily accessible. I went almost every weekend. In the UK, I really carried on what I did in the Soviet Union, but what I absolutely couldn't do in Russia was visit different places which I love doing (travelling). This is one of the biggest changes for me.

Do you want to go back to Russia?

No, it's impossible now. Academics are so badly paid in Russia that I won't be able to do it even if I wish. I also don't think I would like to be in a different country from my children; that would be very difficult.

What do you miss most?

Friends! I still keep up with my school friends and I see them once a year. Recently communication has become better. Previously phone calls were very expensive. So I used to write very long letters but that took an awful lot of time. E-mail in the last few years has certainly helped communications on a more frequent basis.

What do you value most about living here?

I value personal freedom in terms of the possibility to make moral choices: I value that people (as individuals) are respected in this society: this concerns even little children at school. I value that my independence and my privacy are respected by others and this is considered to be normal. I also value that here I can earn my living, being engaged in the work that I really like and that I'm interested in.

Hopes and disappointments

There have been no disappointments about living in a Western society. I have found it a very positive experience living in all different countries because I thought it was enriching not only intellectually but in terms of my personality. I'm quite happy here.

Women in their forties

The Russian women in their forties comprise the largest group of respondents. With the exception of two of them, all came to this country in the 1990s. Three actually left before the demise of the Soviet Union (with one woman actually emphasizing that she left the Soviet Union and not Russia), three came between 1992 and 1998, and one emigrated as late as 2000.

Their grandparents grew up all over the Soviet Union -- from Vladivostok in the Far East to Kiev in the west, from Leningrad/St Petersburg in the north to Baku in the south. Their fathers' occupations include, for example, a truck driver, an architect, an engineer, and a director of a restaurant, whereas the mothers' occupations range from a doctor, an economist, a dentist to a shift worker. As all of their mothers were employed, the grandparents, especially the grandmothers, helped bring up the grandchildren, especially during the summer months.

While the women themselves grew up in several regions of Russia, they all studied in either Moscow or Leningrad and obtained higher education degrees in such varied fields as languages (English, Spanish), applied mathematics, art, metallurgy, political economy, and civil engineering. Each of them would follow a different career path, stemming from but also deviating from these different subjects. Certainly when they settled in London, several of them left behind the fields of their educational training and considerably expanded their horizons.

Helena, the only one to have married a 'foreigner', namely an Englishman, thus enabling her to leave the Soviet Union in 1982, was the first in this group to come to England. Her struggles here are palpable, but she also describes many difficulties she encountered in Leningrad prior to her marriage. Most of the others married Russian men whom they met at university. **Marina** divorced her artist husband but later remarried him when he asked her to join him in London. All of the women have children, ranging in numbers from one to four children (including one set of twins). Some of the women gave birth in Russia, some in London and some had children in Russia as well as in the West, thus being able to make a comparison between the respective births. What they share in common is the fact that sex education was not available to them in the classroom nor did their mothers ever discuss the topic with them. Almost all of them had had one or more abortions, although for differing reasons.

Most of these women have strong but differing views about the meaning of equality as well as about the problems faced by Soviet women. Brought up in the USSR, many commented that as a woman you had to keep working as soon as you got home, that is, you had to sort out all of the domestic things after your paid labour elsewhere. As **Natalia** notes, 'The mentality of the society was – and still is – against women…. I think the mentality is pure Asian because the man is everything there and the woman will follow.' **Nadezhda** notes that contrary to Soviet ideology, she and her husband, equally qualified, were paid differently and he was immediately given a flat at their shared place of employment. Others wouldn't agree with her, saying that in the workplace there was no discrimination by gender. But **Sophia** argues that there weren't some problems specifically for women because everyone, men and women, were under communist ideology, 'a bad thing'. She blames communist ideology 'for every hour of unhappiness.'

What happened when these women moved to the UK? Of great importance here is that they came either after experiencing the effects of perestroika or after the actual demise of the former Soviet Union. This means that as a broad generalisation they were looking for a different, hopefully better, life, especially as some experienced very hard times in Russia in the 1990s. In some cases the decision was made because of their husband's job(s) or job potential in the West and some willingly followed their husband's change of career. **Sophia**, however, adamantly didn't want to go abroad. In other cases the decision was quite mutual as in **Larissa**'s case when she states that 'it was our mutual decision that we couldn't live in Russia anymore.'

Their reactions to speaking English ranged from 'speaking English is horrible and difficult' to 'the first five years were a nightmare because I was only with my young children' to 'I wasn't embarrassed by the way I was speaking because I spoke better than everyone else!' **Natasha** indicated that she had studied English at school and university and had some difficulty understanding English as spoken in Northern Ireland (before coming to London) but there some people from her husband's company were considerate, including 'a lot of Americans who didn't speak very quickly and were understandable.'

The school system certainly created problems for several of the women. Some always assumed that they would send their children to independent schools, and they did even though, as in **Nadezhda**'s case, the schools were very different from the kind of education these women had undergone: 'In the beginning I didn't really agree with these schools but now I think maybe it's right.' Others started their children in state schools. **Sophia** had the most trouble here (see the text). Still others enrolled their children in state schools and subsequently switched them to independent schools. **Helena**'s discussion of the reasons she switched her boys to the independent sector is enlightening as it highlights the current culture in some schools of 'football worship' at the expense of either focusing on more academic achievement or encouraging each and every student's potential, be it academic, sporty (not football) or other endowments. What this part of the interviews highlights is the 'inherited' Russian bias for obtaining a good/excellent education, including some recognition that education must also include knowledge of culture. Problems also arose for some in their interaction (or lack of it) with other parents at the schools. As **Natasha** explains, '[we] socialize with English people through the schools but …unfortunately we don't share many issues in common,' although her children have friends from school.

Several women missed their parents, especially their mothers, but this did depend on how good or bad their relationship was. **Sophia** confides that she and her mother have a difficult relationship but when they both lived in Moscow it was easier. Others seem not at all upset that neither their mothers nor their mothers-in-law are at hand. Many have had their parents (or an individual parent) and/or their in-laws visiting for either a short while or for two or three months. For some this certainly caused stress

188

and even distress. **Helena**, on the other hand, solved her lack of a mother in England by 'importing' her mother and father so that they now live two doors apart.

London is specifically praised by many for being a hub of culture and having something -- museums, concerts, art galleries, opera, theatre -- going on at all times. **Larissa** comments on London's diversity in terms of being an urban centre as well as having 'rural' outlets (including the marvellous parks system). **Sophia** is impressed by the quiet as compared to Moscow and correlates this with decreased stress. **Marina** indicates that daily Life in London is easier than in Moscow in terms of driving a car and shopping for food. **Natasha** is impressed with the security, education and environment she finds here. Only **Nadezhda** implies that she 'found freedom in London for myself, within myself.'

On the more negative side, London is criticised for the cuisine or food in the restaurants. [They should have seen it 30 years ago!!] **Nadezhda** isn't impressed with the way the police handle burglaries. Two women comment on traffic jams, the expensive transport system and the treatment of cyclists. **Marina** expresses her nervousness on being the only white woman on a bus as well as critically noting the noise in London. Only **Natalia** observes that there is too much political correctness now. She states that what she values least is what is going on politically, although this is a national question not specific to London.

While each of the women has something different to say regarding the question about how one would characterize British society, almost without exception their replies fall into the positive, if not super-positive, camp. Adjectives such as clever, intelligent, polite, tolerant, etc.., are used frequently. **Helena** speaks lengthily about Britain as a meritocratic society, whereas **Larissa** thinks that it is one of the best democratic models that exists. **Nadezhda's** main complaint is that British society is too patient. 'We came to live in one country and now it's completely different (for example, with respect to crime).' All of their responses are illuminating, not only about Britain today but about how they see present-day Russia. As a comparison, their adopted home comes out very well.

Helena (47)

Life in Russia

It's not an easy thing to marry a foreigner whom you don't know well and to come to a foreign country at the age of 21, leaving everyone behind. I left on the 17th of October 1982 because they didn't give me permission to do so for a long time. They chucked me out of college, out of university; they chucked my father out of his job and even my mother lost her right to work. The damage to my parents was pretty severe.

Helena left the Soviet Union aged twenty one to marry an English engineer whom she met in Leningrad. At that time she had already graduated from the Herzen Pedagogical Institute, having studied languages. She wanted to become an interpreter which she was finally able to do after a series of menial jobs in the UK. She also studied at the Polytechnic of Central London and obtained a post-graduate diploma in technical and specialized translation. Her parents joined her in London in 2001 after many years of trying to emigrate. Her mother, Anna, is the oldest interviewee on this project (see her own report). Her father and her grandmother were on the last boat leaving Leningrad before Lake Lagoda froze during the war; her grandfather stayed behind and died of starvation in the siege of Leningrad. Her father has degrees in radio electronics. Helena has no siblings but has two sons, aged seventeen and twelve. She is very forceful in her opinions, especially about the role that being Jewish has played in shaping her life.

Role of grandparents

My father's mother is still alive and living here, she is 100! My mother's parents brought me up -- we all lived together. Grandmother died at 68 from total mismanagement of her health care by the Soviets and grandfather died in 1983 at the age of 73.

Youth and my art education

My childhood was spent in Leningrad. From the ages of 12 to 16, three evenings a week and lots of weekends I studied at an evening arts school. This was the best thing that ever happened to me – the only education I regard as real education I received there. Art school was fantastic; I always call it a quiet forefront of dissidentism. Very quietly they were giving children proper education. We didn't draw a single portrait of Lenin and we didn't have to do all the Soviet crap. Instead it was the history of art. I still remember everything my teacher taught me in the evening art class. She used glass, Daguerre type slides from the 19th century, that she must have rescued from some archive. (We were taught much better than my children are taught in the best school in London.) Beautiful, proper history of art, a foundation course, and we did all disciplines of art. The teachers would say, 'Don't tell anyone but this artist is forbidden. but have a look at his illustrations …. real graphics … V. Favorsky (a formalist). Why was Blue Bird by Metterlink forbidden? Because he was called a formalist and was swept under the carpet with all other formalists. But have a look because this is what we called real graphics.' We tried our hand at all kinds of art; the next three years I chose theatre design. Every day of my life, whenever I go to another exhibition or a new city or even just read a book, I think -- if I didn't go to that art school I would be a total idiot, totally uneducated. Because Soviet school(s) in the 1970s …. The teachers didn't have connections so they couldn't get anywhere. Or the nihilist painter probably was refusing to paint Lenin! Teaching Russian children culture made my teenage years. Otherwise I was excessively bored. There was nowhere to go. It was freezing cold in Leningrad and so you had to go to each other's' houses. With my girlfriends we definitely discussed what we didn't have to wear and how we could share what we did have.

University

I wanted to do theatre design and my teacher said to take all of my work to the one place where you could study that. I sat in a queue with people who were twenty nine or thirty five and I didn't have any connections and I was Jewish. I came home and told my mother that I thought I would be there forever and I don't think I was that talented. So my mother said, 'Why don't you do what I did; why don't you study languages and become

191

a translator? Your English is very good.' You could only study languages at Leningrad State University or at the Pedagogical Institute. No one in their right mind would leave Leningrad to go to another city and in Moscow we wouldn't get a look in. At the University [in Leningrad] they said my documents were faulty, letting me understand [that she wouldn't be accepted]. The Herzen Institute did accept my documents; I sat the exams and I got in. We might have even known someone who taught there and she might have even helped us [blat?]. At Leningrad State University there was competition between Russians who might have had connections – the Jews in my year really didn't have a look in.

Then I thought I didn't want to study English; I knew people who taught English there and I speak better English than they do. …I listened to a lot of musicals …. Mother listened to Voice of America, BBC, all the time. I learned my English from musicals and from school. I met some girls whom I liked who were doing Spanish; they said why not do Spanish -- I wanted to do French but they didn't offer French. (They needed Spanish speakers for Cuba.) So I applied and got into a Spanish department and learned Spanish which was taught brilliantly for one year and then my time was wasted there. I didn't want to become a teacher. I wanted to become an interpreter -- I wanted to practice languages. I hung about shops helping foreigners to choose books or I offered my services to take them on tour. I tried to become a guide. I went to Intourist, to Sputnik. I passed the exam in English, but they wouldn't let me work. I passed the exam in Spanish, they wouldn't let me work. I passed the exam in Portuguese, they wouldn't let me work. Then finally they let me work and then I nearly got chucked out. I was in the Komsomol. I was dreaming of getting out of there [the Soviet Union] at least from the age of 16 (maybe even 14).

School was ideological crap apart from sciences; university was a total waste of time. The Herzen Institute had a quota of two Jews per year whereas the rest of Leningrad had none, so I had to go and read Spanish and English.

Marriage to a foreigner

My husband is English and I met him in Leningrad. He was a semi-blind date. I like music, the opera, and theater very much. He used to go to the Soviet Union very often because his hobby was paleontology as he's an amateur paleontologist. Otherwise he's an engineer. Initially he accompanied a scientist, a fellow of the Royal Society, because this man's wife died. Then my husband kept on coming back because he had fantastic friends, other geologists, and he said, 'Where else can I go where I'll be given champagne, get vodka, play classical records, go to the opera, and all that'. It didn't cost him a penny. They all adored him because, of course, he was a foreigner. He was a demigod! On one of those visits, my mother (who worked in the Arctic and Antarctic Institute which had very close relations with the geologists, etc..) was visiting someone and this woman said that she needed to send someone to the opera with him and my mother said, 'Well, Helena might go'. And so on the 30th of December 1980 I went to the Kirov Theatre where I desperately wanted to see the *Queen of Spades* and Russians couldn't get any tickets, only foreigners. I was wearing a woolly red hat like a carrot and that was how he was meant to identify me. I sat in the first row of the Kirov (for the first and last time of my life). And that's how we met.

He left on the first of January 1981 but he was still married but obviously the marriage wasn't doing very well (he didn't have any children). He rang the woman who introduced us, Rebecca, to ask if there was a safe number where he could ring me. So I went to the house of our friends who were refuseniks. We knew their phone was listened to but we also knew that they had nothing to lose. They could have contacts abroad, whereas my father (who was a scientist and therefore had clearance) had no right to have any contact with foreigners. So I couldn't receive any phone calls from abroad without damage to my father. I waited a long time and then he [the prospective husband] got his three minutes for which he paid a lot of money. He said, 'I'm starting the divorce process and am coming to Leningrad in April and can I see you then.'

So he saved all his money and bought a package tour in April. He came in the summer and we went together to Sochi with friends. Then he came back for Christmas in 1981 and we submitted our documents for [marriage]. The authorities give you a date for your marriage three months in advance and they gave us the 31st of March 1982 in Leningrad. So I married him, knowing him for four weeks and he married me knowing me altogether for four weeks.

It's not an easy thing to marry a foreigner whom you don't know well and to come to a foreign country at the age of twenty one, leaving everyone behind. I left on the 17th of October 1982 because they didn't give me permission to do so for a long time. They chucked me out of college, out of university; they chucked my father out of his job and even my mother lost her right to work. The damage to my parents was pretty severe.

Discussion of sex, sex education and birth control

There was no sex education in the classroom. And my mother wasn't all that hot on that subject. But my mother was very clever. She put some English novels in my room and said, 'Don't touch these until you get married.' So I read them straight away!

Contraceptives, fear of pregnancy, and abortion

Our biggest concern was not to fall pregnant. There were no contraceptives to be had. Fortunately I had a Portuguese boyfriend (before my husband) and when he went to Portugal he would bring back lots of condoms for me and my friends. Russian men are pigs: they wouldn't use anything even if you gave it to them! So the contraceptives were abortions. All of my girlfriends by the age of twenty five would've had five or six abortions each. I assisted at many abortions, that is, holding the hands of my friends, no anesthetics unless you knew a doctor. You could slip the doctor some payment, but nobody would give you a general or even a local anesthetic. It was pretty awful, in and out.

Living accommodation

My father and his mother lived in one room in a communal flat with only running water, no hot water. My mother and her parents lived in another room in a communal flat and that's where I was born. When I was born, my mother went back to her parents' flat and my father went back to his mother's flat. And that was awful. Then my mother's father managed to get us a small flat for all five of us, without my father's mum. Then because my father worked for the city government and the government needed clever Jews (they just can't do without them; he was doing something like financial accounting) he heard that this woman and her daughter, who lived in a ruin of a flat which was enormous, were desperate to swap it for one of these tiny, cozy done up flats and so we swapped with them.[Swapping accommodation was a common practice in Soviet times.] And we moved to something which became the curse for my parents. It was a four room flat with a kitchen, a bathroom, a separate loo, located in an old building with a long corridor where I cycled. My parents were doomed to live with my mom's parents and for my father this was no fun at all. Nor was it for my mum because grandpa and dad … it wasn't easy. My granny was an easy person and everybody adored her. My grandpa was a bit like my husband, very much like: this is how I am -- take it or leave it. And dad always had to be the boy who was told what to do! It was a curse but it was unthinkable to split up and unthinkable to move out. Therefore your life is determined by your accommodation in Russia and always has been.

Were there any problems specific to women? What does equality mean?

No Tampax or pads! No stockings! My profession, simultaneous interpretation at the highest level, was closed for women in Russia. So what I do here, Russian women couldn't do. In Russia it would have been closed to me anyway because I was Jewish, but had I been born Russian in Moscow with proletarian parents and gone to **the** foreign language institute to study languages, I would not be allowed to join UN courses, go to New York or Geneva for training, and join the Ministry for Foreign Affairs and become an official interpreter. Never, because I'm a woman! What I'm saying is there were certain professions that were closed to women.

195

However, I do not regard it as tragic. Because men were even less responsible for their offspring in Russia then they are here and because of drink, women had a hard lot. Emancipation is not all that wonderful. When women end up bringing up their families and doing really heavy work, you hanker for the times when somebody looked after you. There were a lot of cases when the women were abandoned; the men just ran away.

In our circle we used to say, 'the proletariat in the Soviet Union lives better!' What did I know! In our circle, men and women were equal; they were nice, Jewish, in families and all of the women worked. Men were engineers. They did slightly better than the women. Women had these engineering degrees which they hated and they hated their jobs so they didn't move on so much. But I knew quite a few women who did really well in science. All of the women who were interpreters with my mother earned a decent salary.

What about the 'double burden'?

I prefer the Soviet model: more or less women are educated the same as men and the same is expected. Yes, the double burden is awful, but that's just the way it is. My husband has a double burden: this evening he will come home and has to work in the garden for four hours to dispose of the old shed, while I'm cooking or doing a translation or resting. In a normal family everyone has a double burden, but it's not a burden if you like your work and you like your family. My mother would never agree to stay at home.

How do you picture the ideal woman in the Soviet Union?

What we aspired to and what we admired? I quite liked: the singers that we saw on TV; the figure skaters who were the champions were something that all the girls wanted to be; and the ballerinas. After the age of seven I realized that ballerinas had very little to do with me. I admired my teachers in art school. I thought they were excellent.

What did femininity mean?

Femininity meant having nice clothes which I didn't have, wearing high heels. My mother went to a tailor and when she travelled abroad she brought things from places like C and A. My first pair of jeans came from the black market and I completely wore them down. I shared things with my mom which she bought at work and in those toilets …. As for the shops, by the time you were served your size was gone but you bought whatever size was available, thinking of your friends. As for makeup, I only had whatever my mother had from abroad. From 1970 onwards my mother would go abroad once every five years and that was already something. She would buy nail varnish and mascara which was the only makeup I knew. She forbade me to wear lipstick.

Strong women in Russian culture

From literature, those amazing women, the Decembrists' wives, that followed their husbands to Siberia. And then there's the image of a woman who would stop a horse in full flight. Not all for the best but very strong women in Russia! And the woman we have to thank for most of Tchaikovsky's output (Nadezhda von Meck) and all our poetesses (Tsvetaeva, Akhmatova, Mandelstam). Not the women in the metro – I feel very sorry for them and this is why I say emancipation is not always welcome. Lots of women were very strong. The image of this enduring, hard-working mother -- Russia is a country of tragic history, every decade is a tragedy.

Was religion relevant for you?

Being Jewish, that's not religion. It's ethnic origin for the Russians. The fact that we were Jewish did not just play a part; it made us who we are and shaped our lives in a way that our lives have become. It's a crucial basic element in our fate. Two things I realized when I was small: that I was fat and that I was Jewish: they came to me at the same time! One I've been fighting all my life and the second one…

Validating some Western views about the past: children and older relatives

It's true that the children were the center of the universe as far as Russian Jewish families were concerned, much more than for an Edwardian English family. Modern, young educated English couples living here are fond of their children and don't send them away. But what is also important is that the children saw their parents work. Either there were grandparents to look after the children or the children would have to make do, alone, until the parents came home. Mum and dad would come home at six. So there were no mothers at home. Children grew up with the idea that everybody works and no matter how much they want to be the center of the universe, there is a limit. Also, almost every family was looking after aged or sick relatives; nobody would shove them off into old people's homes. So there was a very good balance and children in general were far less spoiled then here. It was much more a Spanish or Mediterranean approach to children, with an extended family. Of course my experience of living in a middle-class, Jewish educated family in the middle of Leningrad is very different from someone miles away where people are just drunk all the time.

Life in London

Why did you leave Soviet Union? Why did you come to London?

I came in 1982 once I married my husband. My husband originally worked in Surrey but when we were married he was transferred to Luton. After his divorce he bought a tiny house in a village in Bedfordshire. We had absolutely no money. Living there was absolutely awful after coming from Leningrad where I had loads of friends and my fantastic family. I ended up not even in a proper village -- four pubs, one post office and one church, totally uneducated and boring women whose biggest aspiration was to work in a restaurant. No books and the nearest library was in Luton. I felt like Chekov's three sisters. From the very first day I said we have to go to London (I said this continually) and then finally my husband didn't like his work anymore and he started to look for a job. Eventually he found one in

198

Greenwich in a sugar refinery as a maintenance engineer and that's how we finally got to London.

I worked in Luton in Woolworth's. My husband dropped me off every morning at 8 a.m. in the shopping center and I waited an hour until Woolworth's opened. Every day I went to every single shop with my pad, offering my services as anything and got a 'No'. I got an interview with Miss Selfridge and then they said I didn't fit the profile as I wasn't the right style of girl. I went to the only college they have in Luton and was told by a very nice gentleman that of course they don't need Russian teachers, but why don't I come and give some lectures about Soviet education to the students. All the time I was teaching myself to touch type in English and in Russian, and writing endless applications to work as a translator. I was beginning to get a few jobs teaching Russian and doing Russian translations, but it was awful in that village.

And then my life turned around again. My parents were friends with some refuseniks who probably mentioned that I ended up in this horrible little English village. (I never wrote bad letters home; I wrote every day and it's hard to hide facts if you write every day.) So they knew it wasn't great fun if I was looking for these jobs and if the only job I could find was stacking shelves in Woolworth's before Christmas. But I did learn about English money! So they mentioned this to Lynn and Mike Levy who were part of the refusenik movement here. One day the phone rang. 'My name is Lynn, and I know all about you. I'm friends of friends of your parents. Come and meet me in St. Albans; it's a beautiful place.' But I couldn't afford the train so she said she'd come and see me. She came the next day and she was just a wonderful woman! She and her husband sort of became my English parents. In St. Albans, walking on the high street, a bakery needed staff and I got the job immediately, washing floors, making sandwiches, washing up. I cried a lot initially in my greasy overall -- this was not what I envisaged my life in the West would be! But then I did really well. It was very difficult to get there (two or three buses and a train). My contact with the proletariat was salient, sort of sobering. The other workers were pretty horrible to me: they put acid in my gloves to destroy my lovely nails! They hated me because they thought I was posh and because of my English, which I had learned from tapes. Professor Higgins [*My Fair Lady*] had taught me! They thought I wanted to take their jobs. Then I was offered a career in catering by the manageress. 'No one makes such artistic salads and washes the floor so well!' ...I said I was really hoping to get to London, to do something with my languages....

Then I was offered a job as a receptionist/telephonist in Mike Levy's company. But I couldn't understand a word that the reps (who lived all over the country) were saying. But it was wonderful because I learned all the accents and dialects. I also learned that a man that makes a joke is not necessarily a male chauvinist pig because he's the one that takes you home and looks after you. Again difficult transport and very different from the United Nations/New York work that I had envisaged that was waiting for me ! And then we moved to London.

How difficult did you find it to adjust to:

Climate

I love it! It's a wonderful climate -- no problem at all. Mild and gorgeous.

People

I'm a terrible snob. In any country if you find people of your own kind, if they're educated people, with a slightly wider view of the world, then I love them and I have no problem and make friends. I have a terrific problem with the proletariat of all nations!

Language

When I first came, there was no problem. I thought that cockneys died with *Pygmalion,* that that was a fiction. I wasn't embarrassed with the way I was speaking because I spoke better than everyone else.

Property

When we first moved to London we had a tiny cottage in Greenwich where my first son was born. Mum and I lived in the park because but you couldn't even put the pram inside the house! It was absolutely tiny. We bought the present house in 1993/94 by a total fluke. Friends sold us the house they were planning on for their retirement. We were so lucky because this is the perfect house for us.

School system

This is such a pain! My children went to the local state primary school which is meant to be a good one but which I despise and detest. At 11 plus, my eldest son sat exams for five independent schools and got into all five of them; he was offered scholarships for two, and we chose Dulwich College. With my youngest son, I just couldn't tolerate it any longer and I took him out [of the state school] in year five. He did his last year in primary school in Dulwich Junior and then joined Dulwich Middle School with my eldest son.

I detest them [the state schools] and I despise them with all the support that they have from all these rich parents around here. They don't teach and they are mono-cultural, Essex estuary football playing, sort of strutting along. If you don't like football, your life is not worth living. It's another kind of discrimination. In Dulwich College there's room for everyone - you don't like football, then there's rugby or swimming. Everyone is noticed and encouraged in their strengths. Everybody has a space. If you're not a rugby captain, then be an academic genius; if you're not an academic genius, then be a charity leader.... there's room for everyone. But here in ....

Childcare issues

I had a nanny until my parents came in 2001. I travel for my work and half of the year I'm not here. Russian nannies weren't available then so I always had English nannies. They had to be able to drive and they were left in sole charge all day. For 17 years I was on my own. My parents came just in time to help my son with his 11 plus.

Transport

I've travelled all over the world for my work and London is a difficult city to live in. The transport system is very expensive and not very reliable. But nowhere else is it as extensive and nowhere else is as huge as London, so I understand the objective difficulty. (The Moscow metro is a monument to slave labor and thousands of deaths, so when I'm in the metro that's all I think about.)

Lack of family

I really missed having a family here; I missed them terribly. Every moment of my existence I wished my parents would be here. They would be very valuable members of this society as they are now. They earn their keep; they pay their taxes; they're very good citizens. They weren't allowed to leave the Soviet Union until 1989. And then the British wouldn't let them come until they became 65. That's the law: parents can join their children as dependents after the age of 65 when they are not eligible for pensions or anything, but they are allowed to work. They could come as my dependents. I signed papers that they will not claim any benefits. That was very sad and very unfair. Because we are law abiding, they couldn't come.

I felt lonely until my parents came. There's no need to hide it. The children have grown up a bit and I have become a bit more my own person. It took me a long time to become my own person.

With whom do you socialize?

I don't think it's the English. I think if you find the right kind of person for you, it doesn't matter if they're English or Spanish or anything else. I found it very difficult to penetrate the bastions of nonworking mothers married to millionaires at the school gates. On the one hand, they were jealous of my very interesting life because I'd be on the radio or on television. I just met Gorbachev; I just spoke with Clinton; I've just come from Tokyo or Venice; I've been to NATO, etc.., and they hear all of this (and I work in banks where their husbands work). On the other hand, I

202

was dependent and hostage to these wretched nannies with whom they would have to interact. My children were left out from all the activities that the mothers used to organize.

I understand them. They don't want to be friends with someone whose nearest port of call, if the nanny was ill, was their mother in St. Petersburg. They didn't want to be asked to take care of my children or to help because they knew I was all alone. My husband goes to work, come hell or high water being a man. And I have to go to work come hell or high water because I'm freelance and I've signed a contract. If you don't turn up, your career is finished. You can't let people down, and besides half the time I'm in Siberia anyway. So they didn't want to be responsible for my family. It's not very kind, but I can understand them. Therefore if I ring from hospital and I say, 'Can I give you the eldest one while I'm here with the youngest one?', the answer would be, 'Oh, I'm sorry we have a dinner party.' I find Russians would be more curious and have a bigger sense of drama. The Russians would come with their entire dinner party in tow! But I have found some wonderful friends -- one who is just English and the other is half Russian half English; another one from this circle is one who I've trained to be just a little bit more like us. I've also tempered/dampened my expectations.

Shopping

In the beginning I had no money so I looked and I looked and I looked and I walked the length of Oxford Street with a little notepad comparing prices in cheap shops to take presents home [to Russia] because that was a point of honor. We took lots of clothes to all my friends and my parents. Saving 10 p was a big deal. My husband bought me a pair of walking boots to walk over the fields and the mountains! At first I thought, what? But in retrospect it was a good thing. I was struck by how badly English girls were dressed given access to all the wonderful stuff that they could buy. I still am.

Russian food

Although everything was available and I didn't have to queue, food shopping was oh so boring and I couldn't get any ingredients. But now not only are there Russian and Lithuanian stores but in places like Sainsbury's you can buy harissa, coconut milk and thousands of ingredients from all over the world; it's changed and it's wonderful. The only nostalgia I have is for my stomach! I miss bread, all the dairy products which are made in a special way, some salamis, some sausages, sour cabbage, mushrooms, …. But now that my mother is here, we cook a lot of stuff ourselves. We have a Russian shop nearby.

Role of husband

My husband helps me to run the family. I would hate it if he was cooking or cleaning; he has more jobs than I have because he does all the DIY. That's how we paid off the mortgage because we can't afford any labor and he does it: he's forever fixing washing machines, dishwashers as such.

Are women's careers as important as men's?

Both jobs, that is, my husband's and my own, are sacred cows. My job earns around four times what he earns but it doesn't mean that he will take a day off.

Role of your parents

Now we rely on my parents for love, for being there, for being our family, for not being alone in this world with a husband being God knows where. I love the fact that every three seconds I could ring my mum or go and see her as my parents live two doors down from us.

What do equality and femininity mean?

I don't think that emancipation has necessarily been a fantastic thing for women. I also think that femininity is not an English woman's strong point. They despise me for the fact that I cook everything from scratch and take pleasure and pride in it and for the fact that my favorite

Christmas present is a cookbook. By not having a cleaner, I've saved the money for my opera tickets to go to Glynbourne in the summer. Femininity to me is looking after your family -- to be able to feed them nicely, to clothe them nicely, to be a friend to them, that's femininity. To look nice, to look presentable, to wear high heels, to have a nice haircut and a manicure! I do my own.

Does religion play any role for you?

It doesn't play any role here.

Are you going back to Russia?

To live there? God forbid!

What do you miss the most?

I miss my beautiful city. I never had anything against St. Petersburg. I love it. I go there at every opportunity and absolutely adore it. It's difficult to know really; things have changed. I miss the easier camaraderie between the Russians. We really had nothing and therefore there was more time to spend together. It's horrible to say that about a pauper society but now that I'm almost fifty it's easier for me to look back and to think that a less materialistic world (that our children all seem to be choosing) is maybe not so bad. When you have nothing, you really want it all. What I miss about Russia I also miss about my youth. But I think you can find it not necessarily in Russia. The way Mediterranean people live I would find more acceptable. They are more communal and easier to visit; there's more of a fluidity, doors are open. I miss the fact that here my children are like prisoners; in Russia we all go out and we'd all be together, never mind the climate. Everybody here has their own garden and they don't socialize; kids can't go out together because it's dangerous or deemed dangerous.... It's isolation and I miss the communality. London is huge and we all live so far away from each other. Everything is such a palaver. So St. Petersburg is a much more compact place. Maybe I idealize my parents' youth but when I was a child watching them live, they had huge parties and all their friends would come to them and then they would go to their friends and all the children would be there, etc.. That was a wonderful experience. I work very hard to do that now - I have huge parties and have twenty sitting here to dinner, etc.. There isn't this little core that in the summer would all go on holiday to Lithuania, all of us. Like a little colony. It's just a much more isolated society. English people are just not communal.

What do you value most and least about living in London?

I value most the opportunities for me to indulge my hobbies, my preferences. There are three opera houses, five symphony orchestras, something to do almost every night; all of my musical friends either pass through or perform here. London is a big hub for culture and for music in particular. I value the fact that I'm only 40 minutes away from one of the best opera houses in the world. Galleries, fantastic exhibitions come here. There is just so much variety -- wonderful restaurants, a vibrant place where modern architecture happens. You can keep discovering the world and never ever be bored, so much history and so much new.

As for least, it's obviously a difficult place to live. It's obviously expensive. The transport system is not easy and it doesn't work very well. I hate the fact that the airports are so far away and that it's so expensive to have a cup of coffee, so I gave it up. [Discussion about Geneva for its quality of life.] London is a hard city but it's so beautiful, with excellent parks. I hate all the Russians who just sit here and moan about the doctors, the food and the transport, etc.. So I say to them, go back to Russia. I'm a patriot.

For many years I taught English at Berlitz. When I first came to London there were fifteen people in the teachers' room with whom I became friends. They were supportive, interesting, inclusive. So London has so many communities. I wish sometimes I lived in a Jewish community and my children went to a Jewish school so that my children would belong to something. Then I think that my friends (who emigrated to America) belonged to a synagogue in order to belong but without believing in anything and now they say, 'What have I done, my son has gone to the rabbinate!' (You traded his soul for your comfort! What did you expect?)

How would you characterize British society?

A fair meritocracy. My father couldn't believe how hard we had to tutor the kids for these 11 plus exams, how hard we had to work with them and how hard the kids had to work. And he said, 'I don't understand you. Nothing to cover your ass with and you're an immigrant and you're working hard, but all these millionaires are all in the same boat: mothers are tearing their hair out whether or not their child will get into this school or that school.' But it's fair; we're all competing with each other on fair grounds. If the proletariat wanted to, they could do the same; they just don't want to. There is a system of assisted places where anyone could go to these schools and have it for free. And they didn't want to. But it's amazing and you can't 'buy' a paper at Imperial College in physics for example; again it's a meritocracy.

Nothing in Russia is on merit, nothing. Everything is bought, always has been, under the tsars, under the communists, and now under the capitalists. That country hasn't known one fair day and people don't know how to do things fairly and they feel uncomfortable when it's a fair competition. What I like most about the UK is that for the majority of people what they want to achieve they can achieve if either they work very hard or have the brains. In our family we work very hard and what we want to achieve we achieve, within limits. It is a total meritocracy. I haven't seen children of millionaires favored over mine in exams ….

Another thing which surprises me is the lack of desire of the British working classes to better themselves. I had all these nannies whom I offered [to pay for or sponsor] courses . *Tabula rasa* they arrived, and *tabula rasa* they left. I really feel strongly about meritocracy: it's a very fair country.

What I don't like about England is they despise intellectuals; it's a dirty word. Where I lived and where I grew up, intellectuals were admired and inspired others. Here people live quite happily without any books in their house or don't go out or go to plays or read books. They don't discuss the news. Football, television? England hasn't had a tragedy since World War II; they're not stoic, they're not heroic. They just are; they're mostly sloppy and I feel sorry for them.

ADDITIONS:

My life is much more complex than in this interview ! Life choices ....

The Anglo-Saxon life model is not for me. I have learned to value some of it; if you live somewhere for twenty six years it rubs off as well. The Russian life model is much more Mediterranean, much more open. The family is integrated (at least ours was) and so much more communal. I think we needed that to survive. Whereas here the notion that the Englishman's home is his castle is very true. You can't drop in on people without phoning them first. And now I'm trained to do the same thing -- no one can drop in on me because my husband wouldn't like it.

My life choices would have been totally different if Russia had been a free country and had I not been a discriminated minority within a dictatorship -- a totally different life experience. (For example, I never would've touched Spanish with a barge pole.) It is unpleasant as it creates a certain chip on your shoulder because I always felt myself anyone's intellectual equal, if not better. And at every stage over there, they put me down; at school they would mark me down and the boy who copied from me would get the top mark. When I said why, they said, 'We didn't like your punctuation' as if they were saying they didn't like the length of your nose. Anti-Semitic, horrible people! And I hated the waste of time at university. I needed top grades to get top money and prestige but it was such a waste of time. Boring subjects just driven by ideology and whipped by ideology, a waste of four years. ....

I meet all kinds of Russians and I feel we have come from different countries, from different universes. Our experiences are so different. My

208

mouth was ruined by Soviet dentists, yet I'm told that 'Russian dentists are the best in the world -- I went to a special clinic in Moscow.' Yet when I came here at the age of twenty one, my husband's dentist asked permission to show my mouth to his colleagues! He had never seen anything like it! So everybody's experience is so different. Mine as a child of technocratic intelligentsia -- penniless, but proud, Jewish – is a totally different experience from say a blond, blue eyed, Muscovite.

At the beginning of perestroika when I was translating at the Edinburgh Festival, people whom I respected, all kinds of dignitaries, the intellectual elite of Russia (poets, the filmmakers), said from the podium, 'Mr. Gorbachev opened my eyes. I have learned what has been going on.' Yet there wasn't a family that didn't have a member in the camps or in prison. How could they say that!

Natasha (47)

Life in Russia

In the Soviet Union, this [being a good parent] would include being understanding. I would say the biggest mistake was either being young or being under the impression of the traditions. Parents were sort of dictating to children and very much interfering in children's lives. This meant everyone -- parents, grandparents and everyone.... As children grew up, they rejected any advice of the parents.... So to be good parents meant to spend as much time as possible with your children, because many young parents could easily -- and with pleasure -- get rid of their children to the grandparents.

Natasha left the Soviet Union in 1990 and came to London in 1992 because of her husband's job. She has an undergraduate degree in applied mathematics and started to do a post graduate degree in Moscow. As well as bringing up her four children, she currently organizes large scale charity functions. Born in Kursk, her mother has a mathematics degree and like Natasha worked as an economist. Her father (who comes from Vladivostok) earned a master's degree in civil engineering and used to work in the Ministry as an agricultural engineer. Both of her parents, who are currently in Moscow, were in the Party but she wasn't. Like her father, her older sister in Moscow has a civil engineering degree.

Her grandparents

Both sets of grandparents played an important role in my childhood. Sometimes I lived with one set of grandparents and sometimes I lived with another although I grew up in Kursk. So, although my parents moved to Moscow, they were very busy with their occupations and childcare was not adequate at that time. So I stayed with my grandparents for quite a long time. I started school in Kursk while I was staying with my mother's mother.

Why did you choose to go to university in Moscow?

210

It was the only way to carry on with your life. I just couldn't even consider any other way to carry on with my education. I was very strong in mathematics but I wanted something more glamorous or prestigious, like being a doctor (of course, in the Soviet Union one had status as a doctor but it wasn't prestigious with money). But I had a very good physics teacher and he made up my mind. He showed me that science and physics played a very large role, even in surgery. I was going to go into the biological side but I met another tutor who helped me decide that applied mathematics would be most suitable.

University and after

When I was at university I lived for three or four years in a youth hostel. Our university was just outside of Moscow. So to avoid travelling I lived in a student hostel (*obshzhitie*). The university did sort of secretive projects but as the university grew, the projects became more civil. It was a network of academic institutes and scientific organizations which were carrying out investigations of academic research into quite abstract subjects, although some of the research was to be used by the military. I started working at the scientific institute in my third year at university, one day a week, then two days a week and so on. After university I had the ambition to become a scientist. I received my diploma after my sixth year at university.

Marriage

I was first married when I was 21.[She does not wish to discuss this marriage.] In 1989 I married my second Russian husband with whom after one and a half years I came to Britain.

Discussion of sex, sex education and birth control

No, there was no sex education. No, I never discussed sex with my mother. I guess I learned about sex from my friends which wasn't really the best way. Very occasionally I'd get information. Yes, I feared getting pregnant. It was hard to get contraceptives: as far as contraceptives were concerned, they were practically zero. So my first child was born because of that.

Abortion

I've had an abortion, but I try not to remember it. It wasn't that easy to organize it. Probably that emotional shock that you got was absolutely incomparable to the physical difficulties which you went through. I had an abortion after the birth of my first child.

Giving birth

My first child was born in 1985 in Moscow. I would say that I had all the medical support I needed and that birth compared very well with the birth of my second child in England. The only thing is they didn't give me an epidural or any relief at all. I don't remember how the hospital was chosen but I didn't have any connections [no *blat*]. I must've heard that one hospital was better. I came there and I said, 'I'm over my time.' They kept me for one week and induced the baby. So I don't have anything to complain about.

Being parents

In the Soviet Union, this would include being understanding. I would say the biggest mistake [for a parent] was either being young or being under the impression of the traditions. Parents were sort of dictating to children and very much interfering in children's lives. This meant everyone -- parents, grandparents and everyone. It was not probably the respect for freedom and independence as far as little children were concerned. There was a big gap then. As children grew up, they rejected any advice of the parents. Of course you can't say that was 100% the case. It was my impression that this was a general tendency. So to be good parents meant to spend as much time as possible with your children, because many young parents could easily -- and with pleasure -- get rid of their children to the grandparents. This was quite common. By giving the children to the grandparents, the parents could then carry on with their lives. Here [in the

212

UK] I think the younger generation cherish much more the time spent with the children. Of course the women were working, the women had to work. All the duties that you have to carry out, like coming back home and feeding your children (cooking, cleaning, all the domestic duties), all of this is exhausting. It's quite a deep issue; it's very much related to the culture of the spare time. People would like to do other things like read the newspaper, read a book, pursue their hobbies, meet with their friends or they would like to spend time with their children and enjoy what they were doing with them. I would say the second is much less popular in Russia. People were just getting tired and they wanted to relax that way. I now understand that the most effective way to relax is with your children; you just get much more energy to recover. Of course this understanding comes with age! A lot of us had children when we were very young and this makes a difference.

I guess I was lucky. I wasn't living with my parents and my father was working, so it wasn't easy for me to just drop my child off because I wasn't living so close to them. It took me several hours to organize this so it had to be special when I left my son with them. I spent most of my weekends with my son and I had to give up other pleasures, but now I understand how lucky I was. Because of the circumstances I was able to gain from that situation. I went back to work when he was fifteen months old, so he went to a crèche. But still I had to pick him up at five o'clock from the center of Moscow. This took about an hour and still I had to buy some food on the way, come home and then prepare some food. Time, time, time. My first husband didn't cook and he didn't help me at all not only with domestic life. He was also a scientist, also from the same community I mentioned, especially because it was a campus university. We had one hundred and twenty students on the course but there were only ten girls!

Were there any problems specific to women? What does equality mean?

Of course there were problems specific to women. You had to keep working as soon as you got home -- to sort out all the domestic things. It's hard to say about equality because I only worked for one year and then I

213

decided to take the full PhD course. Actually the grant I got for pursuing a PhD was higher than my salary in the scientific research institute. It gave me freedom so I could do all the shopping going between libraries. Traditionally males are supposed to earn more than females, but ideologically they are supposed to be equal: that's such a lie!

Party membership

Both of my parents were in the Party, but I was not. Belonging to the Party helped my father in his career a bit, but I like to think that he got his position because of his professional ability. I myself felt very much privileged at that time when I was younger.

Was religion important to you?

At that time in the Soviet Union religion didn't play any role in my life. Religion played no role in my parents' life either.

How do you picture the ideal woman in the Soviet Union?

You'd have to make a distinction between the 1970s and 1980s. In 1985 there was a break at the beginning of perestroika, in the thoughts and understanding of the situation. So for me the ideal woman would be a good housewife, everything should be perfect at home (I couldn't stand any untidiness), should be good at education, beautiful or sort of pleasant, that is, you must make some effort. Of course not everyone is beautiful but you could see when a woman makes some effort just to be pleasant, even to shake your hand. Mainly, of course, it's just to be able to support an intellectual conversation.

What did femininity mean?

Here I would include makeup and clothing. I knew how to sew and how to knit; a good part of my wardrobe was made up this way. The biggest problem was footwear. That's a complex I've carried with me and now I have hundreds of footwear! I was very lucky because my mother worked in connection with the trade, at least she helped me.

Validating some Western views about the Soviet past: degree of closeness to parents

I wasn't very close to my parents. I am ever so grateful to my parents because they gave me all sorts of possibilities -- to be educated, to go to the best university, to pursue my hobbies, whatever I wanted, but they never did a single homework with me. First of all, I didn't need it but still you could go deeper into it. My father went into school and he was very pleased to hear that I was doing very well, and there were a lot of jokes about that, but my parents did not have the ambition to carry on developing (my talent). I really regret that. For example, my musical education stopped at the age of ten and nobody encouraged me to carry on. I was not very good at that but I regret that. But I'm a very happy person because that's the only regret I have. Now all my children are doing music. You have to be supportive and push sometimes. You have to support the young.

Life in London

Why did you leave the Soviet Union and come to London ?

We left because of my husband's job. When we left the Soviet Union in 1990 we went to Londonderry [Northern Ireland] My husband was employed there in the research and development department of a large company. We came to London in December 1992.

How difficult did you find it to adjust to:

Climate

The climate was rather awful in Northern Ireland, and we also went to live in Malta and the climate there was awful as well. So after we experienced these two extremes (cold and damp, and hot and warm) we came here and we found the climate very good.

People

Of course we first went to Londonderry and because my husband was working for this large company, they really helped with the move. They arranged a car, a home, everything.

Language

I studied English at school and university. We had some difficulty understanding the English in Northern Ireland. But we were lucky enough to have some people from my husband's company who were considerate, including a lot of Americans who didn't speak very quickly and they were understandable. I took some lessons and I've carried on learning the language all the time. Of course I'm learning more as I do verbal reasoning with my children and it's fascinating. When I came here from Malta, I didn't have any problems. I tried one class. I used to write a lot of essays in the past. Although we now speak only Russian to our children, I enjoy their style of language, hearing my children speak English.

Property

Finding property was okay, it's just part of your life. Now you can laugh! First we rented in London and then we owned a house and now we're in this house.

Schooling

My children went to independent schools from the primary school level onwards. My oldest son switched from an independent school to a grammar school when he was twelve and then at sixteen he changed again; it was not demanding enough for him. (He's been at Eton for the last two years with a scholarship.) Now the others are at independent schools. I understand that the academic education in the grammar schools is great but you just can't compare the quality of student life in the school. School education is not enough. I don't want them to have a chip on their shoulder because still modern life demands a university education. You want to meet interesting enough people and you want to have your own sort of cut. People understand when you say you graduated from somewhere that you have done something and your intellectual level is good enough to deal with things. You have a particular amount of knowledge.

Transport

I haven't used the Moscow metro for about fifteen years. But I did spend quite a lot of time on the metro in Moscow because my parents lived in one section and I lived in another. They're always talking about improving the metro in Moscow but no one seems to know how to do that. Here it's quite irritating to wait for trains, like ten or fifteen minutes apart. But public transport is okay. I approve what they're doing with the Olympic Village transport; transport will be free but you can't drive. It's very clever if they supply free transport; public transport is great and I think we need as much public transport as possible. My husband travels by train to his office almost every day. I often drive into town because when I come back later I don't want to be mugged.

Was it a problem being a mother without your own mother or mother-in-law?

This was not a problem being without my mother or my mother-in-law, but I did miss my family.

Childcare issues

Finding help is always difficult. It's not as difficult as the Russian proverb about how difficult it is to 'unload a train with coal'.

Do you socialize with English people?

Socializing with the English has been different. It has to do with background. For me, still at present, it's difficult to carry on a conversation on modern issues like films, TV, celebrities, politicians. I'm still not the most easy person with these topics. I practically don't watch any British TV. I listen to the news in the morning and that's it; the rest isn't interesting for me from the political point of view. Somehow I'm not a political person. We socialize with English people through the schools but I know unfortunately that we don't share many issues in common. The children, of course, have friends at school.

Shopping

I wasn't shocked at the choices that were available to me with shopping but I certainly was pleased. In the Soviet Union we used to go into the *beriozka* stores and we travelled before coming here; we went to Austria, Czechoslovakia, that was the shock probably! I don't miss Russian **food**. You can really get everything here now. The only thing I really miss now is *kaffir* [sour milk]. Now in Moscow the bread is not so good as it used to be in my childhood, so I don't miss it.

What values do you instill from Russia?

Education! In this area a lot of people value education and a lot of people choose this area because of the education system (for the grammar schools) and the musical education. Still I'm not quite pleased with this system, but I've tried to instill education into my children. Values from home -- it's a little bit of everything, including Russian food. However I have changed my habit of eating for different reasons (health, etc.), although we still cook some Russian dishes.

Has your husband's role changed?

When we just came here, our social status changed quite greatly so that now I don't cook at all. We have staff who change all the time but if there's a new recipe I show them how to do it. Most of the staff are Russian from the Baltic republics; some are Latvians and Lithuanians. Last weekend my husband went to pick mushrooms and then he cleaned all of them. It's a little bit too much for the staff to do so he does it and sets a good example. He doesn't despise this type of work. He can change a bulb if necessary; he is a very adroit man as well.

I would like my husband to retain all the values that we always had. Sometimes I feel I just have to remind him of that. My husband now has a business career (not just sitting on an oil pipeline!!) and he's very creative. He is three years older than I am. We are the same generation, the same background, we have so much in common, and very much the same taste in art and culture for example.

Are women's careers as important as men's?

If I had a job now, my husband would say that his job took precedence over mine. He earns the money.

Concepts of equality

My ideas haven't radically changed. For me it's still strange when a woman is the main breadwinner. Among all of my friends the women are doing something, more like hobbies, but some of them are occupying themselves so much. For example, when I prepare an event (the last charity event was for 300 people), of course you spend quite a lot of time on it; of course I put aside some of my every day duties or just postpone them as much as possible. For these events, I like to do most of the work myself because I don't trust the companies that you can hire to do things very well. Food, flowers, etc.. I check everything. But still my children are my responsibility. I always encourage my husband to spend as much time with the children.

Does religion play any role in your life now?

Yes, because my life has changed quite a lot. Now you have to look at that development in the different scenarios from a different point of view. So trying to find a force or reason behind that, that's where religion comes into this, to explain these things . Still I haven't found the full answer to all of these questions, but I've chosen Judaism because my husband is a Jew by birth and for several events and circumstances I've chosen to be Jewish. I've converted into Reform Judaism, which wasn't difficult at all. It's very interesting and we were very lucky to have a very good rabbi in our synagogue. Somehow we came together to the conclusion that we would be able to give religious education to our children.

How do you spend free time?

I make my free time. The best way to recover is through sport, through tennis. Then there are concerts, opera, ballet, art exhibitions and reading. I don't read fiction during the day time because I think it's not right. I only read fiction before going to sleep and on holidays. I happily watch films and I would like to catch up with it. And I'm trying to learn languages, Italian and Hebrew.

Are you planning to go back to Russia?

No!

What do you miss the most?

The theaters. The theaters were a very big part of my life in the Soviet Union.

What do you value most and least about living in London?

What I value most about living here is the security, education and environment. What I value least is the food! What I mean is, the cuisine or the restaurants.

How would you characterize British society?

I would characterize British society as very positive. Positive, tolerant -- it's probably one of the great and immense features of this society. Although some individuals are trying to show their irritation with this fact, but it's not deep. Some individuals blame themselves for the imperial past. Another characteristic is being inquisitive, sort of that contradiction between appearance and inner feelings. There is a contradiction. On the surface they are very much uninterested and very unexcited about what's happening, but actually they feel very very deeply. Their inner life is very deep as well. Mainly because I don't know French society, in that sense of the philosophy based on their historical experience, I think that English people are much closer to Russians then to anybody else.

ADDITIONS

Role(s) of wives

Women have always had to be strong. And they have to carry out a lot of issues in modern life. They have to support the whole family. I think women have to be the leading core of family life in the sense of formulating and supporting their husband, giving him the motivation to achieve. The husband has to be an achiever, so you have to motivate him to achieve. And give him satisfaction when he reaches some position because they can go up the social and business ladder by jumps or they can fall and they have to have a very good *tyl* [the Russian means the rear in the military sense: the rest of the country supports the military]. In another sense, women sometimes have to restrict men from the negative influence from another society or from people surrounding them. When you're in business you are more or less exposed to everyone, not necessarily with the best attitudes. For example, you know the term 'new Russians'-- people without a strong cultural base. They are very adaptable, they can grasp new tendencies, like how to eat, how to behave themselves. But if they don't have the sensitivity and the moral fiber, they can bring into their lives and they can infect everyone around with the new style, and that degradation of the moral qualities is very much up to date nowadays in Russia.

Sophia (47)

Life in Russia

Our generation is suffering because we were brought up half of our life in the Soviet Union with communist/socialist ideology and the second part of our life is completely different, completely money market oriented. For example, now I am thinking about money. Since I am in London, every day I think money, money, I have to get money, I need it for this, to go there. I have to spend, I have to save…. in the Soviet Union it was a shame to speak about money. Now it's all changed.

Forty seven year old Sophia reluctantly left Russia in 2000 with her now twenty year old son and her second husband. She trained at a civil engineering institute in Moscow but in London she hasn't been able to utilize these skills. Her mother was born in Kiev but when she was twenty she went to Moscow where she trained as a dentist; she has lived there ever since. Her father grew up in Moscow and graduated from Moscow University where he became a tutor for fifteen years. Her parents are divorced. Her paternal grandmother played a major role in her upbringing as her mother was then a student. Her maternal grandmother died before she was born. Both of her grandfathers died in 1985 in spite of the fact that they had about 20 years difference between them; one was seventy something and one was ninety years old. She has no siblings.

Childhood

My childhood in Moscow was an ordinary childhood in the Soviet Union. When I was born we lived in a communal flat for ten years; we shared a kitchen, our family in one room, me, my mum and my dad, the three of us, and in another small room was a single woman who was a professor. In the other two rooms lived a nice family consisting of grandparents, parents and children. It was a relief to get along when we shared a toilet, a bathroom, and a kitchen. There were some problems or conflicts but that's just domestic and par for the course! When I was a baby, my mum left me with them all the time as my parents were students then.

222

University

When it was time to decide which education to get, it was a very serious question. We had to think about opportunities which I actually had. I had an idea to go to Moscow State University [MGU] , because my marks at school (although not perfect) were -- it was a medal -- good. The problem was my nationality as a Jew. MGU was completely banned at that time for Jewish people. I came for a consultation and some kind people told me not even to try because it was secret. They had some resolution: for example, if they had two Jews in a course, and if somebody comes and says, you are anti-Semitic and you don't allow Jews to go to university, they would say, 'No, we have two and these two were sent by the government. It was for special people, not from the mainstream.' So they told me that I would just waste my time. They said to go somewhere where it is real (and the technical university where I went was real.) My father worked in one of these places in civil engineering, and he, his friends, and his colleagues persuaded me to go there [to a technical university], because they promised to help me if there were some problems. I think it was my great mistake to go to a civil engineering university, because for some reason it's not for me; another reason was the five years of study. It was too hard because the university was located outside Moscow and it took us students a couple of hours to get there and back; when I came back home usually I was so tired, so exhausted. It was so hard to study there; it was a horrible five years. To get there was a permanent problem and there was a lot of home work. My university is my great regret in life.

When I finished university, I worked as an engineer. I was married in my third year of university and at university I was pregnant, so I worked for some months and then I had a baby. I had maternity leave for two and a half years. Then after maternity leave I worked only part-time as an engineer, but it was a good time. The work there was not interesting but it was not hard; I liked the work actually.

Marriage

My first husband was from Moscow. I was twenty when I married him; I was nineteen when we met and he was twenty one. We thought it was great love. We met on a long (thirty six hours) train trip. I was on holiday with my mum and my stepfather and we were on our way back from the Caucuses. When we met he was working in a factory as a technician. Although it was very important to get a higher education and very important to go to university, he didn't. He joined the evening course at university, but after we started dating he missed all the evening classes so he was expelled. The next year we married and he joined my university, my faculty in the evening. I helped him, but unfortunately when we divorced and when perestroika came and he started a commercial life, he had only one year to finish university, but he thought it was a good idea to earn money, to work and not to finish university. Unfortunately he still doesn't have an education and he definitely regrets this. He was very successful in business. As a couple we were like a model of somebody who graduated who has nothing and somebody who has not graduated .... It was strange because it was popular in our environment to have a higher education, to attend university. My husband, who was definitely different, started businesses at this time and it was maybe the beginning of our divorce. Sometimes in our life he was successful and sometimes not. But we didn't have money because when he earned something, he put this money into the development of this business. When I asked where is the money he would say, 'It will come'. He didn't spend it on himself, he never was interested in women or entertainment or going abroad. He was a workaholic; he liked only to work but not to do some stupid jobs for somebody. He liked to organize, to be the boss. It was absolutely horrible for me because we didn't have money.

Eventually he did very well in business. We were married maybe six years, the last two years we were fighting. I wanted to divorce, he didn't give me a divorce and it was absolutely horrible.

Living in Moscow as a married couple

Our situation was ordinary. We were young so we didn't have enough money. The problem in Moscow is accommodation. I am a typical model

224

of this because we didn't have our own accommodation, and we didn't have any prospects because I lived with my mum and he lived with his mum. We didn't have an opportunity to have our own place and it was absolutely horrible. I lived with my mum, my stepfather and my very old grandfather. For all of his life my grandfather had lived with my uncle, but my mum took him in to live us and we didn't have any space.

I was brought up in a family who divorced; my parents divorced after ten years of marriage. I was always in contact with my father and lived with my mother. Because I was brought up in a divorced family I never heard that family is important, that it is important to have a husband, children. My mum had boyfriends and a very active life. When I was watching the life of my parents compared to the life of a married couple, it seemed to me that married life was so boring and horrible. My mum's friends were engineers who didn't have money and had boring husbands; they never had the opportunity to go to resorts or somewhere. My mum was a dentist and she had more money. She was really beautiful, and had (and still has) great success among men (could you believe she is 67?). But she is so self-confident, and I was watching her and my father and I was sure it was much better not to have a big family. It seems to me now that when I was first married, I was sure that we would get divorced. My husband and I first lived with his mum and it didn't work; then we lived with my mum and it didn't work as well. Then we had a baby and were always fighting. Money was not a problem because my husband started his commercial life and we were maybe better off than somebody else at this time; my husband always liked to be a boss, liked to be different. We were fighting all the time, we were young, active, not very patient.

Discussion of sex, sex education and birth control

My mother never talked to me about sex. Never. Never, it was absolutely banned in the Soviet Union. We thought that sex was something that doesn't exist in the Soviet Union! This was done somewhere else maybe. We were absolutely not educated in terms of sex; we knew nothing. It was like a shame to speak about it, unless with female friends of course, but no education.

I did know about contraceptives before I got pregnant and I used them. In fact I didn't want to get pregnant when I was a student because I had a plan to start working, to have a career. And when it happened, I was absolutely unhappy because I wasn't about to become a mum so young. I never thought about an abortion at that point. If I were not married and didn't have somewhere to live or some different situation, maybe it would make sense to have an abortion, but I was married, I had somewhere to live, money and parents and it was crazy thing to think about.

Abortions

Abortions were popular, but it depended on the situation. I didn't want a baby so early, but it happens. I did have an abortion afterwards. It was in the same hospital from *blat*, and it was absolutely quick and easy and no feelings; you didn't feel anything -- it's like you sleep for fifteen minutes and go home the same day. It was very good medicine and the staff were very good because of this place.

Giving birth

My son was born in a Moscow maternity hospital which was the best in Moscow because my uncle and my mum were a popular doctor and dentist, respectively. He's a scientist and she is a dentist. And they had a lot of contacts. A lot of things were done only by recommendation, that is, we always visited a doctor or a teacher or somewhere else only by recommendation. We got the best, the most popular institute of maternity. I had to go there in advance, because when you have an emergency, the nurses aren't always there. It was an absolutely horrible experience because I spent a week waiting in this hospital where there were the most difficult illnesses (in maternity) in the Soviet Union. I heard so many horrible things, I was so scared because I had never thought about it before. There was young girls who were so ill, etc.., and the situation was so horrible. So I had a baby a week before I was due, because I was so worried. I was really there because of *blat*. My husband wasn't there for the birth; he was banned, he only saw the baby from the window! We couldn't even have flowers.

226

Did your in-laws and your parents play a role in bringing up your son?

His parents and my parents are very specific people. They definitely didn't plan to become grandparents. My mum was absolutely horrified to think that she could be a grandmother and do something. She is a very difficult character; she is heavy going, she can't say things, she pretends to show she is doing a lot but actually she didn't help. She only helped because we lived together. If she was at home, she could stay with my son and I could go to the cinema. She was working and a working mum is not a helper, even if she had a different character, so it was absolutely horrible that nobody could help me. My husband and I shared the hours and I managed to work two days a week. It was absolutely horrible, every day I worried that he wouldn't have an opportunity to be with the baby and I couldn't go to work. It was a worrying time and a lot of inconvenience.

Motherhood and perestroika

I felt the most important thing was to bring up a baby healthily. I decided it had happened that I am a mum and I have to do everything perfectly for my son. Yes, it was my preference, rather than a career. I was influenced by the times because when my baby was born perestroika came, and a lot of people who were specialists (like teachers or other specialists) were not paid and they had to go to the market to sell something just to live. Someone who is working as a doctor for twenty years had to sell something on the market, but I didn't have such a great experience. I had recently graduated from university; my thoughts were on different things, not on careers. So when perestroika came and I wasn't a specialist with twenty years' experience, so for me it was fine to sell. It was so enjoyable; it was easy money, it was fine.

Infidelity

Of course I thought a lot about this! Before nineteen, I was popular; a lot of boys wanted to marry me but this was before I was nineteen and I was too young. Afterwards I had a family, I had a baby, and when having

227

babies, I was at home preparing this porridge for the baby! I wanted to go see the theatres! Popular life was so important for me. Public opinion was very important and in our environment it was thought that my husband and I were different. It was thought that I could have married somebody better. I wanted to go and have other relations with men. But not my husband -- he is much better than me and he didn't have this in mind. He was not good looking, and women never liked him; it's not his cup of tea.

Communist ideology

I don't think there were some problems specifically for women, but I mean there were problems just from communist ideology. It was for people, for everybody. I think that communist ideology is a hard thing. I was brought up in communist ideology and this most influenced my life. Now we are too old to change, we live an absolutely different life. Russia now is a democratic country, like Britain or others; but communist ideology is so hard. In fact some people managed to change. For example my first husband managed to change, whereas me and a lot of my friends absolutely not. This is the reason of our 'unsuccess'. I blame this communist ideology on every hour of unhappiness, I blame this communist ideology because even now I am looking for a job, I go to interviews and I am so not confident. I have low self-esteem. It comes from years, decades, of our upbringing in a socialist or communist ideology.

How do you picture the ideal woman in the Soviet Union?

The ideal woman is hard working, who can do anything, who is the best at work, doing work for everyone, a great boss, helps everyone, who is great at home, cooks. We didn't have ready cooked food to eat, like the microwave. Everyone had to manage to buy food, and after work the woman went to one food shop, then another one to try to buy something or to queue to bring home some ingredients. Then she cooks, she looks after children, she helps with the homework, she does washing, ironing, everything and she is very hard working.

What did femininity mean?

Femininity may be for other women who are more interested in something, like fashion or clothes or something. I was never into things like fashion or clothes. In the Soviet Union it was very important that you show yourself equal, equal to men, and to show something feminine wasn't popular. So we are members of the community, members of our country, of Soviet Union, we have to work together; for example husbands and wives are friends, are colleagues first, afterwards women.

Women are portrayed as strong -- emotionally, psychologically. Does this have any resonance with you?

The problem was during the Soviet Union. This popular person whom we thought of as very strong, who sacrificed their life to the community, to their work -- this was not always the truth. Afterwards we found out it was not always the truth. In fact, it could be completely different. Our ideals completely changed, but some women even now are very strong. The images of those peasant women in the Moscow metro were important. They were symbols.

Life in London

Why did you leave Russia and come to London?

I never wanted to leave Russia because for all my life I lived only in Moscow and only went somewhere on holiday. I didn't have any idea to leave but my second husband wanted to leave, to live abroad. He didn't like a lot of things in democratic Russia because he is a bit different; he wanted to live in a normal quiet country, to work and to put money into the bank, which was completely impossible in Russia. He had some problems which everyone had I think; he didn't want to have them and he told me that he had enough strength to start a new life abroad in spite of the difficulties. He worked as a managing director of a company, and he made good money. I didn't work at all for three years, because it didn't make sense for me. We lived much better than our friends, for example, and I was absolutely happy with this; we had our own flat eventually. We were together since 1994.

Why did you come to London?

My second husband wanted to go abroad and I didn't and we were fighting a bit because he told me, 'I want to go' and I told him, 'So go. We will divorce.' I told him that I don't want to go abroad because I can't see myself living somewhere abroad; I can only live in Moscow. I can't even speak with foreigners; their mentality is different, the languages are different. I can't live in a different society at all, but it's only about me. 'You go, no one dies about this.' My husband didn't convince me but he didn't go himself. I told him, 'Go, please go and start your new life. I don't keep you, I never keep somebody else, I keep only myself, I don't have the right to keep somebody.' We were arguing and his boss knew that my husband wanted to go abroad and he offered him some places when they opened a new office in other countries. We were offered San Paulo, Toronto, Prague, Rome, Australia. My husband was scared because he had to be on his own in a new office and I refused everything. I didn't want what he wanted, and this lasted for some time. But he wanted to go to America; he thought about America a lot. I was in America and it definitely is not my country at all! Europe is closer to me than America, so never America. But mostly he was offered some opportunities in America. Then we received the offer to go to London, but conditions were horrible, because the business in London was in decline. So my husband had to decide what to do: to believe his boss and try to do something here or to close the business. We accepted the offer although we didn't know what the prospects were. That is, we had an offer to go to London to try and save a declining business, which was a loss for the company. When I heard about the offer to go to London (a place I'd never been before), I was told by my ex-husband that it's the best place in the world to live. My aunt, who as a guide worked everywhere in the world for more than twenty years, also told me it was the best place in the world to live; it's the most interesting city, the most cultural, it's a fantastic opportunity. And I decided that other offers would be worse than London.

My husband would always want to go abroad. I figured that the others would be worse than London, so we decided to go: we didn't know the process, maybe it would be for four months, depending on the success of the business. I decided if this happens, if we were only there for some months, we can go and learn English. We cannot miss this opportunity. My husband came first for four months and in four months he realized that it's possible to make a profit. He made not a big but some profit and he found it's possible to keep going, yes and to live in London. I came here in 2000 with my son and we had so many difficulties. Actually I regret coming here because I was not ready to have such difficulty.

How difficult was it to adjust to:

Climate

I think that the climate is definitely good compared to Moscow. But I miss the snow. I like to ski, I like a lot of snow but not the low temperatures: for example -6° it's a rare thing, sometimes -30° when you can't ski, you can't go with your car. It's full of snow, you have to clear away the car every morning and the most of the year the climate in Moscow is absolutely horrible. And here it's easier -- you just go. The climate is easier.

Language

Speaking English is horrible. Although I studied English in high school, English for me is absolutely horrible and difficult. I am imperfect with English in spite of attending college here for about a year, a very good college but bad time, but it doesn't help but still my English isn't perfect and unfortunately this is the reason why I can't make any career, find a job and do anything. Maybe this is it and maybe not, I don't know [as dictated, this gives an impression of her English.]

Property

My husband found a one-bedroom flat before I came. We were very short of money and it was a nice flat, just a new development. But the area was not very good. I think it's very important in London what area you live in. We now live in a good area but we are still in a flat. Our flat is in a very green area, the greenest because Epping Forest is nearby. We are tenants, we can't afford to buy, we can have a mortgage, but we can't afford something, because we are still on my husband's salary, only one salary.

Role of husband

He is doing much better than me. My husband is a very good person actually! He does everything like he did before in Russia. He used to clean everything, he likes shopping, shopping for food; he can spend hours buying this beef, he knows every price, what is fresh, etc.. He likes to do this and he used to do that in Russia. He does cook but now he doesn't cook much because I cook a lot since I am at home. So it doesn't make sense for him to cook now, so he doesn't cook anymore. I think that we are the same here as we were there. It is absolutely the same because I think in our situation we are not so young to be influenced.

Schools

We had a horrible experience in London when my son was thirteen. I went to the local authorities and they told me, 'It's no problem. Don't worry, you have to choose three schools and the one that you choose you will get into. I visited all the schools in our area and we chose three. And when I received the notice it was not my choice but was absolutely different. All the teachers were from Africa; all the children were from Pakistan. I decided that I had come to London to bring up my son and to learn British English; I don't need African English or other accents. Also the area was a bit criminal. I went to the authorities and told them you promised me three schools that I chose. And they said that they are the best, they have long waiting lists. They told me I have to refuse this one and will receive one of the three which was absolutely the wrong piece of advice because I refused and then I didn't have any school at all. This lasted five months; for five months my son didn't go to school. So every morning I packed my things, said I was going to Moscow because in Moscow the director of schools kept a place for my son. Every morning

232

when I said was going to Moscow, my son told me, 'Mum, you're going on your own; I'm not going.' I said I was going because of him. He told me, 'Mum, here there are new opportunities, eventually we will get it, let's try.' But for me this five months was absolutely horrible. We had some hearings at the local authorities. My son went to a special place where children who don't go to school attend, whether they are foreign or not foreign. He just attended, and they told me to put him into school, any school; then when you receive a good place you will just put him anywhere. I didn't and I was told at one hearing that I could be taken to prison because I kept him out of school. So I banned him from going to school; it's my fault, so I could go to prison. In five months we received a place in one of the schools of my choice, but we had already chosen another one actually. It was an absolutely horrible experience.

I always wanted him to get an education here and I am now very happy that he is at university.

Transport

I don't like the transport system because it's very expensive and it doesn't work well. Something happens all the time. I commute a lot and I am suffering with strikes, delays, everything. I was so worried about these because, for example, I had an important appointment at school and there was a strike.

Do you miss your mum?

I miss my life in Moscow. My mum and I have a difficult relationship. We don't get on and never did. My relationship with my parents unfortunately is not good at all but when we lived in the same city it was easier. My father came to visit but my mum has not. She wants to but we're always fighting so she didn't.

Last April my first mother-in-law died, absolutely unexpectedly; it was the first death in our parents' lives and it was so horrible. She was pushing seventy. She always worked. I didn't have very good relations with her but maybe it was because I was very young; she was a very important person in my life. She always was in our lives in spite of the fact that my parents and she didn't get on. She always loved me and in spite of the fact that my divorce was so many years ago, she always called me. And we were in contact .

Whom do you socialize with?

Most of my friends are the same; they are in Russia and all over the world like it was before. I feel close to them and I can spend a lot of time on the phone with them (using Skype)

Do you have English friends? I am not adapted in this society. I have some friends here, but not many. Mostly the English friends are the husbands of my friends, that is, they are Russian women and their husbands are English. After their marriage to English men, their English is much better than mine!

I did mix at my son's school with some of the parents. Maybe because of my age, I actually don't want to make new friends. I am a very good friend, and the friends I have I am deeply involved with their situation and I am very helpful. I just can't say, 'How are you doing, okay, bye.' I can't do this because if I know you, I know your problems, I want to help and I definitely worry about this. I don't feel myself that at my age (forty something), I can put more people into my life. It's not because they are English or Russian or some other nationality; it's only because my relationships are so involved. Here some people want to be my friends, but I'm not very much interested in them. I have some friends here, but I am not too close to them actually -- I am not very much involved.

But in any way English people are much better than Russians. In my opinion life is great for English people, maybe due to they're great conservatism. It's a very convenient society and relationships are very convenient. For example, you have a family and you have a friend, but they have their own life. It doesn't impinge on your life. You can be with your family, with your problems and you can help others. In Russia it's a very inconvenient society and [there are] inconvenient relationships. For example, if something happens to your friend's family you don't leave it, your family doesn't leave it at all, you are all deeply involved in situations [in Russia]. You are not only helping, you are the main person there. It is impossible to keep your family life separate. So everyone is involved with everyone else in my group. For example, if you are single in Russia, you are so popular in work; you don't feel lonely. Here if you are single you are lonely, because at Christmas and other holidays everyone keeps with their own family and you are not needed. If you are single in Russia, you are needed everywhere because you are not so involved in family life.

Shopping

I don't like shopping. I hate shopping. I cannot buy clothes at all, because when I see something I like I have to try it on and that's horrible for me. So I go shopping only when I go to Russia because I have to buy presents first and then clothes for myself. In Russia everyone is wearing such rich, such expensive clothes, clothes which look so great. I have to have not the clothes that I allow myself to wear here, some jeans for example. I have to buy good things to go to Russia to show them that I am not too much lower than them. If I'm not going to Russia I don't go shopping at all, never. In Russia now there is everything from every country. I prefer to buy shoes in Russia because shoes here are absolutely horrible. They look horrible and are uncomfortable, but in Russia I can buy Austrian or German shoes. In Russia everything is much more expensive than here now, but it' s better for a lot of things.

Food

Every Saturday, me and my husband go to the supermarket and buy food for the week, mostly. But it's absolutely horrible here. You are used to these tastes, we are used to different tastes. Everyone likes what he is used to eating, from your childhood. So maybe here the food is much more healthy, but I miss things such as foods which I used to have. Bread, even white bread, is different --everything, cheese, etc.. I cook a lot at home, just to prepare food like in Russia. So when we go to Russia we put on weight. We just eat, eat, eat.

How do you spend your free time?

In London there are so many things to visit and it depends on money, because I am not working; all the time I am very short of money. If I had more money I would visit exhibitions, theatres, cinemas and cultural events which I definitely want to see. I meet with some friends. For example I have a friend and once in two weeks we meet here. Then sometimes we have a lot of visitors from Russia or from America or from somewhere else. When we have guests we are like a guide to London, to go everywhere and spend all our time going to museums. We don't do it ourselves just with the guests, but it's a good time.

Femininity and equality

When you asked about femininity, I should have said that it was feminine to look after children, to cook, to go shopping in the Soviet Union. Men only worked. But now in democratic Russia everyone is doing everything differently. Men are equal to women. Men are helping more in the home, absolutely. In the Soviet Union it could be that men can't wash dishes, can't iron at all, etc.. Now it's supposed to be that every man can do these things.

Has religion played any role here for you?

No, we are not religious. You know that in the Soviet Union religion was banned. I joined a synagogue here. I used to work there as an administrator, but I am not working there anymore. I joined this community, and I go for some services, some festivals and I meet a lot of good people and their families. I don't feel so lonely as some of my friends are from the synagogue.

Would you want to go back to live in Russia?

I want to go back to live in Russia, but I am not going because in Russia now it's a very expensive life. I have the same situation there; I don't have work there. So we are thinking of staying here, but if, for example, something happens and I have an opportunity to have a good job there, I go.

What are your hopes for the future?

My future is to get some job, to have some income, to rely on that in the future because this will be the main thing. Our life would definitely change if we could get a second salary! If I don't have it I have to go to Russia, but in Russia because of *blat* I find something, not a big salary. But now the most important thing for me is to find a job which is stable, which I can develop myself somehow. Life is not like that here. (My son's school mates will help with this *blat*, in the future.) No one helps like in Russia. There everyone tries to help. It's different. For example I had a job in Moscow and a secretary was leaving on maternity leave. My boss wondered what should he do because his secretary was leaving. In the evening I found him a secretary, because this friend of mine came and told me she was so depressed, her mum died, she is not working. She was thinking about maybe doing some part-time job, and I asked her, 'Would you like to be a secretary?' and she said yes. It saved my boss, it saved her and my recommendation was enough for my boss because I said that she is reliable, she's honest, she's hard working, she's fine. This was possible in Russia, but here it's impossible. Here you need work experience as a secretary for twenty years, some agency, some procedure -- you don't get a job because I tell you that someone is hard working, that she is an absolutely nice person, honest, etc.. It's not enough, it doesn't work here!

What do you miss most?

I already had my life organized. When you're young, your life is absolutely crazy and you can change, but when you are thirty something, life is organized. My place is very important in Russia. Here you can buy, sell, but in Russia everything…. we suffered a long time from not having accommodation. I lived with my mum when my stepfather died. I had my

237

own flat which was so important for me. I loved my flat so much, and everyone who comes thinks this flat is lovely. I still own that flat. My flat, my friends, even some aspects of our life there ... I loved one theatre in Moscow; it's not big, it's small like a studio but this theatre is like part of my life. For all of my life I have been going there from when they started. The organizers I think made it the best theatre in the world, but a small one and its name was *Yugozapadny* theatre (like the theatre in the south west). It's my favorite theatre -- it's a part of my life, this theatre. I also miss some aspects of our lives, how we spent time with my friends.

What do you value most about living here in London?

More quiet! It may sound strange because people who live in London think that London is an absolutely crazy, great capital, but not compared to Moscow, where life is really very stressful-- stress is in the air and you feel stressed all the time. Here in spite of the fact that this city is bigger than Moscow (twice as big by square) this is a quiet environment. I think the rest of the people around are absolutely calm. Life is not so stressful; it is much quieter than in Russia, in Moscow.

How would you characterize British society now that you have lived here for six years?

I like British society and I like British people in spite of the fact that they don't like me and don't give me work. They like me as a person. Yesterday I had a call from this company which sells magazines and they asked me to come back because when I work with somebody, they love me because I am easy going, of good character. So I agree to stay. But I can't find a job, nobody wants me; I don't know why, maybe there is something wrong. I like British society, I think it is a very clever society, all old conservative and traditional society. Sometimes I realize that the problems that I have are one hundred or two hundred years of history; I am not the only one, everyone has this [problems] for centuries. I like British society, I like British people. I think they are clever, intelligent, most are polite. They have high priorities, they manage to have high priorities.

ADDITIONS:

Russia before and after 1991

Everyone had pensions. People could live on pensions, so pensioners could live normally, not like now here where it' s impossible. There were some positive things in the Soviet Union. In the Soviet Union everyone had somewhere to sleep, everyone had somewhere to have a bathroom or toilet, or something to eat. So people could be poor, for example be a single mum, have no money, but no one died from poverty. Everyone, even five people in a room like this [indicates my small office], can sleep and they have heat, a toilet (toilet could be one for ten families), a kitchen and some food, maybe a very simple food, but no one, no child died.

People then were much happier than now because they were sure about their future. It was not necessary to think about pensions, about money in the future. Everyone was stable more or less; everyone could predict their future. When my son now watches Soviet films, I tell him, 'Look, nothing in the shops, no food, just three things, just only one type of banana, only one type of bread, only one type of sausage, one type of shoes! Look, it's horrible.' When he's watching the films he says, 'Mum, look, people look much happier. They didn't know what was going on around in this capitalist world, with horrible mafia crimes, etc.., but they are safe, they are perfect, There are no tramps, no homeless people!' Our parents' generation regrets so much of this communist time. They were safe, they felt much better, they were happier.

Our generation is suffering because we were brought up half of our life in the Soviet Union with communist/socialist ideology and the second part of our life is completely different, completely money market oriented. For example, now I am thinking about money. Since I am in London, every day I think money, money, I have to get money, I need it for this, to go there. I have to spend, I have to save. Before I didn't know this word. In the Soviet Union it was a shame to speak about money. Now it's all changed. *Blat* is important. When my dad came here, and we were out, I told him, 'Dad, money is everything. Why didn't you tell me, you never told me this!' He said because money was nothing.

Natalia (46)

Life in Russia

The mentality of the society was -- and still is -- against women. When people ask me if Russia is European or Asian, I think the mentality is pure Asian because the man is everything there and the woman will follow. In general, if everything good in family life happens, it is his achievement. If something's wrong, she is the one to blame. And it was always like this.

Natalia grew up in Baku but went to study political economy [similar to PPE at Oxford] at Moscow State University. Married, with one daughter, she left in 1993 and is currently an interior designer in London although she was a lecturer in the Soviet Union. Her 77 year old mother spent her childhood in a tiny village in the Ukraine and then studied hydro-meteorology (weather and agriculture) at the beginning of the 1950s in Odessa where she currently resides. Her now deceased father, also born in a small Ukrainian city, studied in Odessa and worked at organizing the Odessa seaport and dealing with the environment. She had one older brother who, aged 47, died of pneumonia which was only diagnosed at a very late stage. He trained at the Institute for Sea Engineers in Odessa and worked at the seaport in a similar management job as her father.

Role of grandparents

I don't remember my father's side because they had died by the time I was born; I was named after my paternal grandmother. My father was the youngest of six children and my mother was the oldest of six children. So there was a big age gap. **How did you chose where and what to study at university?**

As a teenager, I was mainly interested in books. My first choice for university was to study history, but with a lot of effort my teacher and my parents persuaded me that it wouldn't be that interesting to do history because after university history meant either teaching at school or doing some research and spending a lot of time in archives. It took me two attempts to get to Moscow State University because of my exam marks (no *blat*).

I wanted to leave Baku because that was always a temporary place for our family. In Soviet times there was a system of compulsory sending of graduates to remote places and that's what happened with my parents. My father was the first one to finish his education and he was sent to Baku; my mother followed him one year later. We felt we had no family in Baku; we had friends but not family. So to see family we had to travel 24 hours by train to the Ukraine. My parents always thought it was temporary, but they stayed for thirty years. My father was Russian and my mother was Ukrainian. The adopted nationality of the family was Russian. I think they would've liked me to go to university in Odessa as that's where my brother had settled. But there was no PPE there so I went to Moscow. When I graduated, my diploma said 'teacher for the university' in economics. I went to Odessa. Unfortunately my father died when I was in my last year at university and my mother was alone, so somehow we decided we would go and live with her.

Living accommodations at university

I only lived for a couple of months in student accommodation because my brother really insisted that I shouldn't do that [live in a student dormitory] and persuaded my parents that I should not live there. In general my department had luxurious accommodation. Let's compare it to where my daughter lived when she went to Oxford! Oxford was like the Middle Ages compared to what we had. But she did have a room to herself, whereas I had to share a room with two or three other girls.

Marriage

I was twenty one when I got married in 1983 and my husband was twenty six. He was born in Irkutsk [in Siberia] and when he was twelve his family moved to Krasnodar. My husband went to the university in Moscow

242

(where we met and married) and he graduated one year before I did; he studied mathematics and economics. He worked during my last year at university but when I graduated we decided to go [to Odessa]. And we never regretted it.

When we got married we moved to Odessa and my husband was working for a Soviet company which provides a maritime satellite communication system. All the international maritime companies had to join to supply the support, equipment and the base stations all over the globe which the sailors needed. We were living with my mother in her apartment which consisted of three rooms, a kitchen and a bathroom in a nice old building.

Sex, sex education and birth control

I had no sex education in school. And my mother never spoke to me about sex! Condoms were available and some contraceptives for women, like the coil, as well. For us, before our daughter's birth, we were cautious because we didn't want to have a baby straightaway. I wanted to finish my degree, so we were careful. There were a lot of possibilities to prevent pregnancy (like taking your temperature). The pill was not popular because we always thought it would interfere with our hormones. Even now when I decided to stop using the coil, doctors in Moscow advised me to take the pill; I was very reluctant to do so. The doctor took a long time persuading me, saying that our generation was always very cautious, whereas the younger girls now just go for it. The pill now is much safer.

Abortions

I did have some abortions and they were not difficult to get. They didn't really affect me because they were at a very early stage. After giving birth, I had two abortions two years apart basically on Women's Day, March the eighth. When I realized I was pregnant I went straight to the doctor. Before I gave birth, I was very cautious, but perhaps after that I was a bit to blame. Basically there was no financial base to bring up more children at that stage. For me, it was much better than for my mother who had quite a few abortions. The first one was during Stalin's time and she did it

243

illegally. There are lots of stories of women who had abortions who then couldn't have children or who themselves died. It was even worse for my grandmother who was doing abortions to herself and terminated pregnancies. She had six children already and it was straight after the war and it was very tough, so she did it herself. There was no doctor even to do it illegally.

Giving birth

My daughter was born in 1986 in Odessa. My mother heard a lot of stories about childbirth, bad experiences of childbirth. So when my turn came it was all bribed and *blat*! My daughter was born in a good maternity hospital; there was *blat* there. Although it [*blat*] wasn't needed to get into the hospital, it was needed to get the head of the hospital present at the birth. I think that made a difference. I was very weak after giving birth. During the pregnancy they discovered that I had an irregular heartbeat and I was put in hospital three weeks before the birth. Normally a woman stayed in hospital for five days after the birth and if there were complications, for seven days. But even after seven days they didn't want me to go home. But I insisted I wanted to go home. I was in hospital, sharing a room with eight other women.

My daughter's upbringing

My mother did take part in the upbringing of my daughter. She is quite a confident cook and loves to spend the whole day in the kitchen. I'm quite a decent cook and my aim is always to spend as little time in the kitchen as possible! My mother stopped working when she was sixty three. We lived with her until my daughter was five, so for the first five years I did have some help. My daughter went to kindergarten when we lived in Odessa. I worked at the university and I had quite a lot of free time, so I did as much as I could with my daughter. I never wanted grandparents to bring up my daughter. I always thought, if you have children they are there for yourself. My husband's parents lived in Krasnodar so they really didn't help but they visited several times and my daughter spent two summers with them.

I'm quite different from my mother. In some ways it's good and in some ways it's bad. For example, I always felt very safe when I was a child around my mother and if I had any problems in my life I was 100% sure that my mother would do everything right; everything would be all right after her involvement. With my daughter I was never involved with her problems. My position was that I will talk to her and I will tell her what to do and how to do it, but she will do it herself. So everything she did at school, before school or out of school -- that was her doing. We discussed everything, but the doing was hers, always. I never went to her school. Well, I went to school once when there was a major conflict with the headmistress [in London] but otherwise no.

Were there any problems specific to women? What does equality mean?

The mentality of the society was -- and still is -- against women. When people ask me if Russia is European or Asian, I think the mentality is pure Asian because the man is everything there and the woman will follow. In general, if everything good in family life happens, it is his achievement. If something's wrong, she is the one to blame. And it was always like this. In the case of divorces they were always talking about women who couldn't keep the family together, who couldn't save the family. In terms of the workplace, there was no discrimination. On the manual level I don't really know but with higher education we had equal salaries to begin with (120 roubles). After that of course if women got pregnant, men would advance more. Women couldn't stay at home. Hardly anyone could afford not to work, so both parents had to work. But in terms of bringing up children, for example, I had three years of paid leave. When my mother had me, she had two months of paid leave. It changed just before I gave birth to my daughter; before that it was one year.

Was religion any relevance for you?

Religion didn't play any role in my life.

Were you a member of the Party?

I belonged to the Komsomol but not to the Party. Everybody belonged to the Komsomol; that's the thing we did. Before that it was the Pioneers, the young Octobrists. I never questioned it. The things, for example, we questioned in our family (which was not popular in the 1970s) were mainly about the Revolution and the things that happened after the Revolution. We never questioned these sorts of political instruments. For example, my father never joined the Party because he thought that was his principle not to join the Party. It didn't help him with his career because at some stage he just stopped at a certain level of a management position, and that was it. This happened because he wasn't a member of the Party. That's why, for example, my husband joined the Party when he was in the army before going to university because everyone knew it would be easier for his career. It actually was very difficult to join the Party. For him it was easy because he was in the army and they invited him. For me, with my sort of specialization, it would be very good to be a member of the Party because my course was very political. There was a lot of propaganda in it. But I had no choice and I wasn't even given this opportunity. I don't know if I would've taken it or refused it. I always knew that my father thought it was against his principles to join the Party. It wasn't important for my mother and she never joined. She was on the middle level of management in a big organization and she was very involved with the bringing up of her family. She never wanted a huge career.

How do you picture the ideal woman in the Soviet Union?

I always thought that the ideal woman has to look presentable, be a good mother, be a good wife, have a lot of friends and enjoy herself. I never thought about a big career; I'm not ambitious. In the end, my husband left Odessa two years before me because he went to study at the American College, a private college in Moscow; he was studying management and insurance. I was still working in Odessa with my daughter. He visited us and we visited him regularly. But when he decided to stay in Moscow when he found a job, I left Odessa and we moved to Moscow. So I just parted with my job and my university and I went to Moscow, not to work.

Was there an idealized image of femininity?

No, I wouldn't go along with this. Basically the propaganda was that women are very strong, opinionated, ambitious and they have to be this way. They have to be like a superwoman, balancing family, balancing work, being good at everything. Basically women were under a lot of pressure. For example my father dreamt about my mother working part-time (at least not the whole day); he thought that would be best for family life, best for him and for her. But it wasn't possible.

What did femininity mean?

Clothing was always a problem. You always had to hunt for clothing in the Soviet Union: boots, shoes, clothes, everything. It was difficult but in Moscow there were things to find. All over the Soviet Union there was nothing to hunt for. In Odessa, because it was a seaport, there were lots of things from the West that were brought in. Neither I nor my mother sewed, but we used tailors. I wasn't into makeup at all. I hardly used any makeup before I was thirty. I've had the same hairstyle, for example, for seven years; before that I had the same style for ten years! I'm not into appearances, that's just too much. There's more to life than just a pretty face!

Myths about the Soviet Union

There are a lot of myths around life in Soviet times in the 1970s and 1980s. Of course there are good days and bad days. It's not black and white always. For my generation, even Stalin's time, we think about it as black-and-white but people who lived through it don't see it like this. For example my mother hates Stalin but her understanding is and her understanding was that she was in a small village and they were deprived; they didn't have passports in Stalin's time. So as peasants, they couldn't move at all. That was one myth. Another myth was (even when I was at school in history lessons) all this stuff about the kulaks and the bad people. My father used to say that the kulaks were the most capable of working; they were the hard workers in the village basically. So it's not always right to think in book categories; it's better to talk to people.

247

Life in London

Why did you leave Russia?

We left because of my husband's work in 1993. After he finished at the American College, he went into an insurance company in Moscow. Then we found a small advertisement in a newspaper about an exchange (introduced by Norman Lamont) for young professionals (qualified specialists) from Russia to go for two, three or six months to have work experience in England; this was to support the new [Russian] regime. After my husband's interview, he was accepted to work for a firm in Brighton. He was there for two months when my daughter and I joined him.

Why did you come to London?

After six months at the job in Brighton, we had to leave England and work at least one year in Russia. But while doing some projects my husband was introduced to some people from the Isle of Man because the legislation there was different. They were prepared to take him straightaway. So we went to live in the Isle of Man for five years. I think we were very lucky that we went to the Isle of Man rather than coming straight to London. In 1998 we came to London, again because of his job.

How difficult did you find it to adjust to:

Climate

Climate was no problem for me. I think it's a beautiful climate, the most gentle and body friendly climate you can imagine. I've been in Baku, I've been in Moscow and I've been in Odessa. I think not to have that hot a summer and to have a mild winter is perfect.

Language

I studied English at school and at university. But when I came here, I had a lot of words but it was difficult to talk properly. So I studied here. I think I make a lot of silly mistakes but I'm not really self-conscious speaking English. I always thought, especially on the Isle of Man and Brighton, when the life is quiet there and I had a lot of friends there, they never corrected my mistakes. I would very much have liked them to correct my mistakes. That would have helped me. ... they're very different in their attitude towards language compared to Russians or the French, for example. Their position was that as long as they understood me, it was okay.

Property

It took time. We had a house in the Isle of Man and we have an apartment in London. In the Isle of Man it took us six to eight months and in London about a year to find property.

School system

My daughter started at the state school in the Isle of Man. She went to the nearest school. The Manx are very proud of their health system and their education system and in a way it's much better than here [in London]. It was very comfortable and friendly and I think that your schools are friendlier than the Russian schools. The attitudes towards children and towards newcomers are much kinder. (You can't even compare them.) In our Russian system, when there is a class of twenty five or thirty youngsters and a new boy or girl comes into the class in any year, it doesn't matter which year, they always greet them with suspicion, asking who are they. My daughter started school in Brighton for just three or four weeks, then she moved to the Isle of Man, then she moved to another school, etc.. She changed schools a lot, but it wasn't stressful for her. She always had a group of children waiting for her there, friendly, helpful and welcoming. I didn't find this for myself in London but I did find it in the Isle of Man. In the provinces, in the countryside, it's an absolutely different mentality compared to London, like in any country. In London my daughter went to an independent school.

249

My daughter is a proper bilingual girl. (I don't miss being a lecturer because I spent all that time with my daughter.) For 10 years she learned Russian at home: Russian language, Russian literature, history and maths, according to the Russian system in the Russian manuals. I think this helped her. The history course is very poor here and maths went up to O levels. I think education here should be broader and more intense at the same time.

Transport

I find the transport system in London appalling because of the price and because it's really not efficient, especially the underground. I'm quite familiar with the Moscow underground system and it was wonderful. In the rush hour one train is leaving and you can see the next one approaching. When it wasn't the rush-hour the trains came at one or two minute intervals, not like the ten or fifteen minutes wait here. I was very disappointed here.

Lack of family

I do miss not having a family here. But my mother visits every summer and stays for about two months. I go back once a year to visit her for a week and we've been to Moscow many times.

Whom do you socialize with?

My neighbors are English. Here it's like in Moscow. You can live for ten years without knowing each other. In a way I like it. For us as a family to come and live in a foreign country, it was very good that we started in Brighton. We don't socialize with our neighbors but we have a lot of Russian families living around (in north London) and normally during the week I socialize with Russian women. But when we're having a party or something, English people are always present.

Shopping

When I first came to England, shopping was exciting but we couldn't afford it basically. It was exciting to go window shopping. Now, I don't really like shopping although I have to do it for the interior design work. As for **Russian food**, I only go to Russian food stores very occasionally. It's just when I need some sort of pickled herring.

Has your husband's role(s) changed here?

He was never involved with cooking and he's still not involved with cooking. And I would hate him to be involved because when I'm doing it myself, I can do it very quickly. Only two years ago we got a cleaner who comes once a week. Before that we cleaned every Saturday together. He was basically a very caring father. He loved to play with our daughter and we did a lot of games, table games, as a family. This is why I think life at a very slow pace is very good kind of life. It brought some sort of quality to the time we spent together.

I don't think his role has changed since he's been in the West. It's more or less the same. Of course it's different now because my daughter is twenty one. It's different for the last four or five years because she's a grown up now and before that he didn't have patience to deal with her.

Different types of Russian women living here

Basically I've come across two groups of Russian women or Russian speaking women. One group is well off. The moment they came to London they started having cleaners. These people are here not because of career choice or on account of their job. It's just their style of living. They follow their husbands, although some are living without husbands. The standard of living is very attractive here. Even now people who live in Moscow who are very wealthy still have restrictions. They live in closed gated communities and they go into streets in Moscow very occasionally. They hate to go there because they feel the hostility. So to have standards of living they all come to London; they're looking for this.

251

The other group of Russians is very hard working, without hardly any means to live here but they still live here because they think it's comfortable. A lot of them are struggling. But emotionally they feel the future for them and their children is here.

Are women's careers as important as men's?

Normally a man's job is more important than a woman's job in Russian culture. It's the Asian thing again.

Concepts of femininity today

When they write about binge drinking, I don't think it's very feminine. At my daughter's school, some of the girls drank vodka when they were twelve! I also don't think femininity means being involved too much with your own appearance which is part of this culture. I also don't like all the reality TV programs (like Big Brother). We never had Russian TV here and we never spoke to our daughter in English, not to spoil her English and not to embarrass ourselves.

Do you have any thoughts about going back to Russia?

No. My daughter thinks of herself as Russian, but that's her thinking. Her mentality is English and for her it would be very difficult to live back in Russia. I think that the fact that we came to live in England was a great thing we did for my daughter.

What do you miss the most?

I especially miss friends and the cultural environment in Moscow. Odessa is still provincial, but the multicultural life in Moscow is different. But being in London I'm not that disappointed I think of all the possibilities that I could enjoy life here, but they are still not in the Russian language. For example, we go to the Barbican twice a year to see Russian theatrical troupes performing and I enjoy it immensely, but this is not on a regular basis. Russian films are readily available on DVD now and modern

Russian films are not my favorite media. Theater is a different story. As for concerts, you have to go to the Royal Festival Hall for world class Russian performers or to Covent Garden.

What do you value most and least about living in London?

I value cultural life the most. As a city, as the capital, London has a lot of museums, concert halls and there's always something going on. What I value least is I don't like what's going on politically. It all started with the bombing of Belgrade which I was very much against. Then it carried on to Iraq and Kosovo. I mean Britain's involvement. It's very good to be tolerant and hypocritical but political correctness has to stop somewhere because sometimes it is too politically correct as a society. Sometimes when things are not right in the government, especially foreign policy, I don't see all the groups and representatives on television and the media. I think it is very controlled, and getting worse.

How would you characterize British society?

Being very tolerant is the most important thing about British society. Hypocritical which is very good for daily life because I spent my first eighteen years in a very hypocritical society in Baku and I think on a daily basis you do not need to hear all the rude things about yourself even if they are right or true. Normally Russians are intolerant of each other and cruel to each other in Moscow. They are very good at empathy but only if you are very down, very sad and very upset and very unsuccessful: everything is wrong in your life. If you bare your soul (*dusha*), then you share it with everyone and you'll get a lot of empathy. If you are confident, successful, strong enough, there will be no good feelings towards you.

ADDITIONS:

Changing ideas about women in Russia

Unfortunately when perestroika started, all the things that were first brought from the West were the bad things. Now Russia is a very money

253

oriented society and unfortunately not like in the West where they [women] go to school and from that moment they learn that they have to earn a living. In Russia, this mentality prevails: get rich quickly. For women who can't compete with men as great managers, they all decide that they will marry quickly; that is, they'll marry very rich guys. A lot of girls now think not that they'll do something interesting with their lives or have a family, they all think about life styles, just because they will marry quite young, very rich, no matter how old the guys are. This all started about fifteen years ago and it is still there. The real ambition is to go to work as a secretary and get married eventually (to a rich man).

Brainwashing

Compared to Russian society, for example, even in Brezhnev's time, when I first came here I met a female Cuban exile who went to live in America and she greeted me with open arms and she told me welcome. She thought we were some sort of political dissidents or exiles. She pitied us in the Soviet Union because we were so brain washed. At that stage I just thought inside my head that that wasn't correct because we were not brainwashed. In our family we are always discussed all situations in our kitchen and we knew everything about governmental policy, things that were not said on TV or in the newspaper. In our family we spent a lot of time talking about politics. We listened to the BBC and the Voice of America, samizdat, all of this literature which was not printed by the normal publishing houses. So in no way did I think of myself or my close friends as being brainwashed.

A couple of years later when everything started in Belgrade, I thought that teachers at my daughter's school (the politics and history teachers) were talking about this situation as something normal and ordinary because they believed everything they saw and heard on the television and in the newspapers. We never did that. We questioned everything. And people here normally don't tend to question things. I don't think that's because I came from an educated family. I think that that's an attitude of people in a society with a lot of problems under the carpet, but people saw things in the shops and the lack of things and all the problems. All the people knew that it wasn't right the way we lived. I came across some well educated people and some uneducated people. Russian people are very well read; no matter what sort of education you had, you could be a factory worker and be broadly read. It came as a surprise that people here are not like that. As far as the Soviet poetry readings are concerned, I now think that the society was very closed and there was no freedom to travel to the West. We could occasionally -- with a lot of effort --get out to the West. For example, my father went on a Mediterranean cruise (and to Egypt) and my mother went to Austria, but that was few and far between. Reading books, watching movies and looking at albums with all these famous artists-- it was an escape. It was something to look at which we couldn't get or see with our own eyes in real life. I think that was the main attraction of reading.

I hope your book will be balanced because with my daughter for example the newspaper always looks for the negative. So I'm always disappointed.

Marina (46)

Life in Russia

I heard about contraceptives from my girlfriends but I didn't use pills. For me this is a very difficult question because all my proper adult life I have had a problem with this subject. I'm scared of men because men didn't think about this question, especially Russian men -- about getting pregnant, that is. I reduced my sexual life because I didn't want to risk it.

Marina left Russia in 1992 to join her artist husband, whom she had originally divorced but later remarried. They studied at the famous Academy of Arts in Leningrad. She has two teenage children. Her mother was born in Leningrad and her Russian father in Abkhazia, a small republic near the Black Sea where, during the war, her mother was evacuated. Both of her parents became architects. Both parents are deceased: her mother died at the age of 58 of stomach cancer and her father, who died at 65, didn't want to go to a doctor and, according to her, stayed in his flat and waited until death, probably from a heart attack. Her paternal grandmother died when she was four years old at the same age and of the same disease as her father; she doesn't remember her paternal grandfather. Her grandparents were really strong Party members: her grandmother was a salesperson and her grandfather made furniture. They were, she indicates, 'real workers.' Neither of her parents were in the Party.

Main Interests and the Academy of Arts

All I was interested in as a teenager was art. I was crazy about it. I went to a special secondary school, specializing in art. I really chose my profession around the age of eleven—oil painting. I tried three times to get into the Academy of Art and on the third try I was accepted in 1982. No *blat*!! It was a six-year course, five years of education and the sixth year for a diploma.

I spent six days a week from nine o'clock until six at the Academy. I was painting, drawing, painting, studying history of art. Around forty students were studying oil painting with me. But in the auditorium where all the students came (painters, sculptors, etc..), there were around a hundred students.

The Academy of Arts had a really strong traditional education; we kept this style until we got a diploma. Afterwards a lot of my friends went another way, maybe abstract, maybe decadent, it didn't matter. We had a great deal of knowledge and so we could do anything because it was easy for us. The educational level was really very high. As students we weren't interested in politics.

Marriage

I married my husband twice! My first marriage was in 1985 or 1986. After about three or five months we separated. My husband is from St. Petersburg and we met at the Academy of Arts. We were educated together. The first time we were married we lived with my parents and maybe that's the reason that the marriage fell apart. He didn't want to live in my flat with my parents and I didn't want to live with his parents. It was a problem with property. My parents didn't have a communal flat; it was a separate flat. My second marriage -- to the same man -- was in 1993. When we were married the second time, we lived in London where we bought a house and a car, and now we have a studio.

Discussion of sex and sex education

I learned nothing about sex in school. Nothing! I learned nothing from my mother either.

Contraceptives and the fear of pregnancy

I heard about contraceptives from my girlfriends but I didn't use pills. For me this is a very difficult question because all my proper adult life I have had a problem with this subject. I'm scared of men because men didn't think about this question, especially Russian men -- about getting pregnant, that is. I reduced my sexual life because I didn't want to risk it. Now I'll risk it because I've had a hysterectomy three or four years ago. Now I am so happy about it. It's changed my life!

Abortions -- Have things changed?

I've had two or three abortions. They were not horrendous. I was a lucky woman. My parents were working in a rich company and they used really good and rich clinics, and so I went there as their daughter. This clinic had a really good service. I had an anesthetic. My mother and my grandmother had totally different experiences. In Stalin's time, abortion was illegal. My mother had two abortions in a normal clinic which she didn't tell me about. My mother and I are not really very close, especially about these topics.

Did religion have any relevance for you in the Soviet Union?

I'm a Christian, a Russian Orthodox. (I was Christian in my free soul.) Before perestroika I didn't go to church, but now sometimes I go. I wasn't baptized.

Were there any problems specific to women?

The problems faced by men and women were totally different. In Russia women are working at home, are working in a company, have problems with their children, with the house. Men have problems with themselves: like not feeling good, feeling miserable, feeling not like a man. (This 'male' problem may have an influence on women.) Of course I would support the use of the term **'double burden'** which women have and men don't. Women in Russia are working hard like horses. Women in Russia have a double pressure--from housework, from their job, from their children. Men, on the other hand, don't think about food, lifestyle, everything to do with health. I hope this is changing because now there are programs on Russian television about a healthy lifestyle and health.

How do you picture the ideal woman in the Soviet Union?

From my earliest youth, the ideal woman was a businesswoman. She must own her business; it didn't matter what kind of business. She must be working for herself and realize her brains, her education.

Strong woman in Russian culture

If a woman is strong and a professional woman, she doesn't have a family or maybe she doesn't have children. It's strange but it's true. Russian society is not feminine, it's mostly masculine. Men will be at the top of society. It's really a difficult style for women, this patriarchy. Maybe this is an influence from the East because we are in the middle between the East and the West. We're like a Turkish country; in St. Petersburg there is Turkish clothing, Turkish style. Men are wearing black leather coats; women are wearing a lot of makeup all the time on their faces. It doesn't matter if she is going to work or to the theatre, it's just a lot of makeup.

Life in London

Why did you leave Russia and come to London?

I don't know. After four years of being here, my (former) husband called for me and asked, 'Do you want to come to London and see how people live here, in this particular country?' And I said 'Why not!' And I came. In Russia in1992 it was such a bad time. I felt so miserable in 1992, so poor. Everything was in a black, black hole. I was working in a school of art and earning just this money from teaching. Sometimes I could sell a copy of a picture on commission.

How difficult was it to adjust to:

Climate

The climate here is much better than in St. Petersburg. But there is one problem. There aren't changing seasons and changing colors; here there are just two seasons, and mostly no change. I like the snow and I like the freezing weather. The air is fresher than when it's damp and wet.

Language

I studied English at school and at university and had lessons in English. But I never tried to properly think about English. I just translated texts with help from my friends. One of my friends helped me translate a text because she was studying English and German. The first five years were a nightmare because I was with my children and I wasn't able to go to school and practice with other people. My understanding now is much better because I listen to the radio and watch English television, especially the educational programs like those about geography, English or European history. We learned history from a Russian perspective.

Property

My husband and I went together to look for property. We went to a lot of places. We spent two months without a car looking for property and it's really hard work.

Transport

Now in St. Petersburg the underground is full of dust and I really don't like it. In Soviet times, the underground was much cleaner and there weren't as many people. There are other forms of transport as well, like trams and buses. But now it's like a nightmare with just little buses everywhere; the quality is bad. In my opinion transport in London is working well but I don't use it all the time. I've now been driving for three years. There's lots of traffic and long queues. East London needs more bridges and/or tunnels.

Was it a problem being a mother without your own mother or mother-in-law?

My mother-in-law comes to us once a year. In the past my mother came three or four times but she died in 1997. When my children were younger, my mother and mother-in-law came and helped me. They stayed in my house and it was a problem: two generations in the same house --that's a problem! Now my mother-in-law's eighty three and she stays in our house; sometimes there's a problem with her health. She stays two or three months with us and then goes back to Russia. In my own family -- that is, my husband and children -- we are really close as a family and we stay like a little part of Russia!

In bringing up your children, do you apply different gender roles?

My children were born in Britain. Yes I relate to my children differently because of their different genders. But my daughter and my son are really different persons [personalities]. It would have been better if my daughter had been born a boy; she is a really strong person, a really strong character. My son is stubborn and wants what he wants. He doesn't want to prepare for his exams next year. It is a nightmare for my husband and myself because we are really very well educated and we want to educate our children to the same level.

My husband says about his own childhood that he just went onto the street and didn't think about anything. His education really started when he was 16. But now life is totally changed, especially here, and this style is not useful.

Childcare issues and schooling

I wasn't working when my children were young. I sometimes did my pictures. Both my children went to independent schools at the primary level. Now my daughter goes to grammar school in Kent. I would like to send my son to the same school, but.... Tutoring isn't working for him. He's at a preparatory school now.

Socializing with whom?

At the children's school, I socialize with English people just a little bit. I'm a little bit shy and I don't go and introduce myself. As for my neighbors, I do talk with them sometimes. The area I'm living in now has changed. Before our neighbors were old people. And now the neighborhood is changing with people like barristers who are buying property. Now the people are really quiet, really polite, no problems. My family might not be really quiet!

Shopping

The first time shopping here was a shock for me because I came from a poor country. The quality was really bad in Russia. My future husband introduced me to Chelsea [in London]. The first time I came we lived for a couple of months in Chelsea and it was beautiful. I stayed in the historical part of central London rather than in the suburbs -- and it was my natural style! I really stayed in a in a rich style. My husband was really smart; he knew how to get me to come here! Chelsea was especially nice in spring.

Russian food

In the beginning I missed Russian food. But now I find the same style of food, a little bit maybe, in English food shops.

Role of husband

He is a typical Russian husband. He doesn't do any shopping or cooking or cleaning or gardening!

But now he's starting to work with his son, starting to work more like a tutor with him than before.

Do women still have a 'double burden'?

So basically the woman still has the double burden. If I start working properly, if I start painting, I have the double burden. But when I'm not working and staying at home and taking care of the children, it's really boring for me. It's a routine. Now I have a lady cleaner and I'm so proud of that and life is much easier. **Are women's careers as important as men's or whose career takes precedence?** Artists are a special style!

Concepts of femininity

Before I had children, I never thought about this. Now that my children are older, I started working in the studio [as an artist] and try to do something myself, some independent thinking. I'm thinking about me, not about all women. My ideal feminine woman is really strong, really independent because I'm dreaming about it from an early age, from about fourteen years old when I chose my profession. I'm dreaming about my success in art. And success means independence. Clothing and makeup are part of it. I started going to a gym and now I'm thinking about improving my figure. When I came from Russia, my weight was 55 kg. I was really beautiful, a really cool woman. But now I'm different and I want to get back, to get back my self-confidence. With the extra weight my self-confidence was gone. But it's not only the extra weight. It's my not really good mood as well because life has changed for me totally. I'm separated from my parents, from my family. I want to make changes. I personally feel better than I did a while back when my mood was so terrible about everything. Maybe it's because my children are older and I have much more free time for myself. My husband is a little bit distanced because before my husband controlled my time and everything. Now I have a little more freedom.

Not everything has changed in Russia since I've been there but femininity has now changed. The sexual revolution came to Russia but not really in a very good way. Now I see what's happening in the streets. In St. Petersburg, a lot of really beautiful women, wearing really good clothes, are selling themselves. Everything is on show. It's not good for the next generation. (Although some women are going to university, some are having a really good job in making a lot of money.) I've seen on Russian television that every second girl wants to be a prostitute. And every second young man wants to be a 'bandit' [gangster, thug] because it's a lot of money and a lot of freedom. Maybe women need twenty or thirty years more to think about themselves as women.

Is religion important?

Sometimes we go to a Russian church. Sometimes we go to the one in Chiswick. We go to Russia two or three times a year and it's much easier to go to a Russian church there.

Do you want to go back to Russia?

Now that we have property here it's much easier and better. Before our children go to university we wouldn't want to go back. But you never know. It depends on our work. My husband would like to get into the Russian art market in Moscow; there are a lot of rich people in Moscow.

What do you miss the most?

Maybe just my old friends. It would be better if they were living closer. Most of my friends are living in St. Petersburg and we just talk on the phone. I have a lot of Russian friends living in London, especially Russian artists because there are a lot of them around.

What do you value most and least about living in London?

For me normal life is much easier here, like driving a car, like food shopping, and an easy daily life. In Russia there was no car, no proper food. The other thing I really like are the art exhibitions, really good quality art exhibitions (like the Velasquez, the Renoir exhibitions).

My negative views about London: now I have changed. It's not politically correct to say, but I don't like a lot of black people. For a lot of people it doesn't matter the color of your skin, but in my thirty years of living in Russia I had never seen black people, maybe just a few. But in my borough when I use the bus to go from my studio to my home, I'm the only white person on the bus. It makes me a little nervous. (They're really very noisy, especially the teenagers.)

How would you characterize British society?

I mostly meet nice people. But it takes a long time for people to open up, say ten years! For example, we spend our holidays in Cornwall in one place where we rent just one flat. And only on our eleventh visit did local people start to really communicate with us! Now I feel much better because I'm feeling part of this society.

Nadezhda (44)

Life in Russia

This is a joke I tell. I started to consider myself 'settling down' when I stopped waiting for the rain to stop. The first year I used to think, 'It's raining now, I'm not going out. I'll wait until it stops.' Then one day I said, 'It's raining now, but I am going out. It's okay'. I don't miss the snow because I don't like the cold.

Nadezhda grew up in Siberia but went to university in St Petersburg where she studied metallurgy in the faculty of economics. She was employed in the Soviet Union in an aluminum factory but since coming to London she has started a jewelry business. She and her husband have three sons, aged ten to nineteen. Her seventy one years old mother was born in Barnaul in Siberia and trained as a doctor. Her now deceased father also grew up in Siberia. Educated in Moscow at the Prikhanov Institute, he became a director of a restaurant and worked as head of food supply. Her older sister studied technology there in Siberia and now works as a head of accounting. Neither of her grandmothers were educated women. Her maternal grandmother had six children; she knows little about her maternal grandfather (wounded in World War II) except for the fact that he and his wife lived in a small village in Siberia. Her paternal grandfather was a teacher and then became an accountant. Nadezhda emigrated in 1995/1996.

University

I grew up in Barnaul (in Siberia). I finished secondary school with a gold medal and I decided to go and study somewhere else. I was ambitious. I was very interested in mathematics but I also liked to write. I thought of being a journalist but to be a journalist in the Soviet Union you really have to prepare yourself, that is, you have to get published in newspapers. Nobody told me about that. At seventeen in 1981 I left and chose to go to Leningrad because I loved Leningrad, probably because of the books of Dostoevsky, my favorite author. A friend of mine went to Moscow and

266

she never regretted that. I didn't want to go to Moscow at that time and I still don't like it now!

After university?

When I finished university I was sent north to Karelia as an economist in an aluminum plant. Because my education was free, I had no choice but to go where I was sent for the next three years. So I chose a very small town in Karelia, a town of 10,000 people. I went there, I was working there in 1986, I got married, I had my children.

Marriage

My husband studied in Moscow and he has the same type of education as I have; he studied economics and metallurgy. I met my husband in the little town in Karelia as we worked in the same plant. There were four young people working in that plant after university. One person was already married and another one left the plant. My husband is from Grozny. We were both twenty three when we got married; we are both Russian.

Discussion of sex, sex education and birth control

I wasn't afraid of getting pregnant. I had my first child when I was just about twenty four. There really was no real discussion about birth control or sex education and I never really discussed it with my mother. I knew about contraceptives, that is, condoms, and they were available, but I was too shy to buy them. If you weren't married, it was out of the question to buy them in the shops.

Abortions

I did have one abortion between my first and second child. I didn't know that I was pregnant. While I was working, because of tuberculosis, everyone had to have x-rays. I didn't know that I was pregnant when I had the x-ray and after that I was advised to have an abortion because the x-ray would have affected the fetus. That abortion was not difficult to obtain and abortion is easy to get in Russia. When I had that abortion, the Russian system was becoming more Europeanized and enlightened, and we were allowed to have a general anesthetic. When I was giving birth to one of my children, I actually heard other women screaming who were having abortions.

Giving birth

My first two children were born in Karelia and the third child was born in London. The hospital in Karelia was certainly not great but the doctor was very good. For my first child, the hospital was full of a lot of ladies giving birth at the same time. There was one room for all of us, that is, there were fifteen mothers all in one room. You had to stay in hospital for six days; there was no way you could leave earlier. The husbands weren't allowed in the hospital and the babies were taken away from the mothers. The babies were brought to the mothers just to be fed. The babies were shown to the husbands from the window. Finally they are changing -- at least I hope they are changing -- this practice.

Living accommodations

We didn't live with either set of parents as we were living in Karelia. In the beginning we had a one-room flat, a state flat, but that became a two room flat with kitchen and bath. The first child lived with us in the one-room flat but we had a two room flat when we had our second child.

Role of grandparents

When I had my children in the Soviet Union, my mother (who is a doctor) was still working and she lived quite far away so she couldn't spend a lot of time with us or rather she couldn't help us out very much. However, she did spend two or three months with me when the first two children were born. Once, my husband's mother took my eldest child for a summer.

How did you spend your free time?

I was working for just one year before the birth of my first child and then one year after his birth. I didn't have to work after that. With two small children some of our free time was spent visiting with friends of the same age. There were several women who had young children and we got together. There weren't many cultural things to do in this small town!

What did equality mean?

It's probably getting a job and the same pay. Even when we came to the plant at the same time with the same qualifications, my husband was given a flat straightaway and his salary was higher than mine. Both of us had the same education, the same qualifications, and were doing the same job, but we were actually paid different salaries. I earned 115 roubles per month and he earned 130 roubles per month; it wasn't much, but still …. and of course he had the flat. I wasn't offered a flat at the beginning. When you finish university and you go somewhere as a specialist, you have the right to get a flat. So my husband had a flat straightaway whereas I had to wait one year! I had to go into a dormitory when I arrived.

How do you picture the ideal woman in the Soviet Union?

Somehow I think about a doctor who cares about patients and at the same time has a family. Probably it's my mother. She has her job, a family, and she has to be 100% when she spends time with her family and she has to be 100% when she is a doctor in hospital with her patients.

What did femininity mean?

I remember from those years that if you are feminine, if you wear feminine clothes and have a feminine hair style, everyone thinks that you are a prostitute. It was not in fashion to be feminine.

Were clothes important to you?

We didn't have much money so I survived on what I had and what I was able to get. My mother told us that for the New Year you had to have a new dress all the time, no matter what happens. New Year, new dress. What I remember from childhood is that I was told to keep the dress for the good times, for the special times, for celebrations or something like that. And it is still with me. If I buy something nice, I put it in the wardrobe and wait for the time to come when I can wear the dress. I have a sister but she very rarely let me borrow any of her clothes (we weren't the same size of course). She did like clothes. She had a pair of jeans and they cost 200 rubles at that time; my parents bought her those jeans. And they were like, wow! My father died at the age of fifty three of a heart attack when I was 19. My mother alone had to support me. That's why I never asked for extra money for clothes.

Strong woman in Russian culture

I'm a strong woman I think. I think Raisa Gorbachev was a very strong woman, whereas Anna Karenina was not a very strong woman.

Was religion important to you?

I was in the Komsomol, not in the Party, but still I did visit the church and if I was ever caught I would have been in trouble. My parents weren't religious and I wasn't baptized. My grandparents were religious but not my parents.

Life in London

Why did you leave Russia and come to London?

After living in Karelia, we went to Moscow for one year and in 1995/96 there was a lot of crime in Moscow. The education system had collapsed. So we had an opportunity to come to London and we took the chance. I didn't want to leave Russia at all. But my husband said it was London and so we came. He's a business consultant between Russia and the United Kingdom.

How difficult was it to adjust to:

Climate

This is the joke I tell. I started to consider myself 'settling down' when I stopped waiting for the rain to stop. The first year I used to think, 'It's raining now, I'm not going out. I'll wait until it stops.' Then one day I said, 'It's raining now, but I am going out. It's okay'. I don't miss the snow because I don't like the cold.

People

I love the English. I've never met anyone who upset me. Touch wood. Even in the school system!

Language

Neither of us knew English, but my husband's was a bit better than mine. We both had studied English at school which meant that I could read children's books and write, but I couldn't speak the language. It really was very difficult for me. On top of that I was pregnant and for me it was very difficult with young children, trying to understand the new system, the educational system for the children.

Property

One of your other respondents really told us where to live. We met her when we came to London as visitors and she gave us a guided tour. We saw a lot of houses, but it was difficult. I presume it was a bit better for me than for the older generation. When we came from Karelia to Moscow, we already had a big flat and for me that was wow. My parents had a very small flat with a kitchen half the size of your office [where the interview took place, not a very large space]!

School system

We always thought of sending all three of our sons to an independent school. These schools were very different from ones that I knew. At the beginning I didn't really agree with these schools but now I think maybe it's right. I studied a lot of subjects but the concentration was really on maths. And now where do I use my maths? Really just for Sudoku! I would rather have studied and spent more time on history and literature. I think in England the education is more balanced. They do not concentrate on just one subject now.

How do you find socializing with the parents of these children in the schools?

It's still a problem for me. At the beginning my English was not good. I didn't speak at all; I did understand but I didn't speak at all. So they must've thought that I was a Russian who didn't speak English. Now I don't have time to go to school. Since I started my business I don't have time to go to school and I think they think I'm posh or something. They think I don't want to be with them, but honestly I just don't have time. I started a jewelry business, design and production. I took a course at the Institute so I was studying from four to five o'clock. There was no time for me to go to the school that year.

Transport system

I didn't drive in Moscow but I did drive in the small village in Karelia, but we didn't have much traffic there. But I don't like the tube in London. I find it dirty.

Is it a problem being without your own mother or mother-in-law?

My parents used to visit us here in London every winter. They and my in-laws used to spend every winter, that is three months, with us. There was a sort of competition between them. It's now more difficult for all of them to travel: my mother-in-law has difficulty walking and in February my mother was in a coma following a stroke. I would like to get my husband's parents here next year for a visit. They are near the Black Sea, not far from Sochi.

Childcare issues

I didn't need a nanny when we came because I wasn't working. I had a housekeeper to help me clean the house. This was the first time I had a housekeeper; in fact, I used to clean the house before she came.

Whom do you socialize with?

My neighbors aren't British. One side is Greek and the other is Saudi Arabian. But we do have British friends. I like them: they always leave at 11 o'clock and they never come unannounced. If a lot of Russians get together and I don't know if it's only my family or not, the women have separate conversations from the men and the men have separate conversations from the women. With my British friends, somehow we talk altogether and I like it. In Russia, the men would have 'clever' talks and the women would have 'silly' talks!

Shopping

At the beginning, I was very calm about shopping. But then I had a friend and it became like a nightmare almost every day. Shopping, shopping, shopping, buy this, buy that. With the ability to buy if you have the money and the amount of goods in the shop, I went crazy. So I said to myself, 'No, no more, enough.' I would say it was like an illness. Like an addiction. It was crazy. I stopped because I just thought I was wasting my time and I decided that there are other things to do. At the beginning it was the same for my children, not for clothes but for games and toys; after all they are boys. Now it has calmed down. In fact, I've given up shopping! I used to miss **Russian food**, but now there are Russian shops here with Russian food.

Styles and femininity

Now that I'm here in London I try to follow the styles. Now I like to be feminine. In the Soviet Union maybe I didn't think about it. I didn't have any money. Maybe if I had money I would have thought about being feminine or about new dresses. Once when we were in Moscow (although we still lived in Karelia), there was a huge queue. We didn't know what the queue was for but we joined the queue (we are Russian, after all). And then my husband went and checked what the queue was for. It was for a purple lipstick and it didn't suit me at all, but I bought it anyway as it was in fashion. So maybe then I was thinking about being feminine.

Has your husband's role(s) changed since being in London?

My husband is not more helpful in the house nor does he do any cooking. Shopping, yes, if we go together. He really hasn't changed that much. When we came to London, I had a housekeeper so there was no need for me to clean. And then when my son was one year old we had a nanny, so there was no need for my husband to be involved in childcare. As he put it, 'I bring money.' Very Russian!

Are women's careers as important as men's?

His career would take precedence over mine.

Are there gender differences in bringing up children?

Of course, if I had a daughter I would teach her how to cook, how to clean, how to look after herself. I would talk to her about sex and the boys as well. The boys say, 'Mama, come on, I don't want to hear it from you.' My husband would also talk with them, but I do tell them all the time about these issues.

What does equality mean here?

I think in this country it's more or less the same. But I really don't know. I know that in all of the British families I know the husbands really do help the wives. Sometimes they cook, sometimes they do shopping, they can stay with the children. But also I read in my newspapers and I know the other side.

Does religion play any role for you?

Now that I'm here I'm Russian Orthodox and so are my children. I don't go to church very often. If I went I would go to a church not far from Hyde Park; it's a Greek Church but it's also a Russian church. My husband doesn't go to church. We celebrate some Russian Orthodox holidays like Christmas and Easter and my namesake's day. It's the day for all students because Moscow University was opened that day.

Do you want to go back to Russia?

No, not to live.

What do you miss the most?

If I miss anything, I would buy myself a ticket and go and visit. The first generation of people who left the country were not allowed to go back. That's why they missed various things. But we know that we can buy tickets and go back at any time. So there's no pressure that you'll never see the country again.

How would you characterize British society?

It's too patient. What's happened in the last ten years, I think British society is too patient. We came to live in one country and now it's completely different, for example, in the way of crime. We've been robbed twice but the police really didn't care. But once when I stopped on two yellow lines, two police cars surrounded me and made a big fuss of it. They are patient because they allowed it to happen. I think it's up to British people to make the changes. I think if the government would change, it would change everything. To be honest, we need British people in London. Now in order to meet real British people you need to go to the countryside.

What do you value most and least about living in London?

I found freedom in London for myself, that's what I value most. Not freedom from government. I found freedom within myself. Maybe what I value least about living in London is crime. I don't feel comfortable after seven o'clock in the evening outside. And now some of my children are teenagers, if they go out, I jump. Of course once my children learn to drive I'll be even more nervous.

ADDITIONS:

Last year I had to decide what to do next and I decided to get another degree since economics wasn't my favorite subject. So I went to the Gemological Institute of America. It was a one year degree with exams every Friday, a very intensive course. I used to cry every Thursday because I was so afraid of making mistakes with my English presentations. When I finished the Institute, I still was thinking what to do next. I wanted to work in the lab but I developed an allergy to one of the chemicals, so the lab was out of the question. Slowly, slowly, slowly I came to the conclusion that I would open my own business, a jewelry business. I went to China, I found someone who would produce my designs, I designed the jewelry, and then I have an invention which is patented. I'm really very excited about this.

I would like to say that I think my children are quite happy here. And I'm very happy here. It was a good move for us to move to London. I don't like what is happening in Russia at the moment, with the young generation, with education. It is getting better but still.... My eldest son is studying genetics [at Nottingham University] and I think with the choice of subjects such as genetics there's not a lot of availability in Russia, not a lot of choice. Of course we had Lysenko [controversial Soviet biologist and agronomist]! And the middle child wants to study at the LSE. His favorite subject is history and I push him to learn history. I'd like him to learn what I didn't. The youngest says he'll be a lawyer or a doctor, whoever is paid more!

Larissa (42)

Life in Russia

At the time an unmarried woman at 25 would be considered a spinster, so you had to kind of rush into marriage and make sure that you have a husband and kids by the time you are 25. Otherwise you are an outcast, so that was on the agenda. And a good education was very much on the agenda for women, much more than for men because again, you had to make sure that you've got something to sell. It's not just your body but your mind as well.

Larissa was very insistent to emphasize that she and her husband left the Soviet Union and not Russia in 1991. She attended Moscow State Pedagogical Institute and studied English and foreign languages. She also did a course in London called Women in Management and is a business woman. She has one daughter. Born in a tiny little village in the Nizhny Novgorod region, her grandmother was the daughter of kulaks. Her grandfather died at the front in the first week of World War II. So her mother grew up in the village with her grandmother and two other children. Her father came from the same type of peasant family who always worked hard as laborers, factory workers, drivers. [So they were working-class]. Both parents, currently 69 years old and living in a small town on the Volga. went to the *uchilishche* [a school, training or technical college, between O and A levels]. Her older sister has two university degrees, one in accounting and finance and the other in economics. She lives in the same small town on the Volga with her family and is the chief accountant in a consumer goods firm.

Role of grandparents and childhood

Both of my grandfathers died during World War II so I never saw them. I do remember my grandmothers very well as they were the main figures throughout my childhood. I spent summers especially with one of them,

277

whereas the other one was living close by as well. I grew up in a very small industrial town where the main structure of the town is the plant producing engines for Volga cars. About 90% of the population of the town worked in this factory.

As a teenager, I was mainly interested in sports; I did sports throughout my school years. I was also the head Pioneer of my entire school. I was always the leader, I was always the top of the class and I was very pleased about that. I was very involved in the activities of the school and I was always organizing things, including Saturday work [for students] and the summer camps. I was a wonderful example of a Pioneer, very typical and very happy about it until I was eighteen. In fact I went through all the stages [of the youth organizations] and I became a member of the Komsomol. But when I was leaving the Komsomol, I was refused at the very last minute to participate on an exchange with the University of Surrey (which consisted of a three months stay in London), on the grounds that I had not been politically educated. I was becoming a bit of a rebel!

What were your living conditions like when you were with your family?

Truly awful! We had a one bed roomed flat (that is, two rooms) and my parents are still living in that flat. When I go there now I don't see how they managed. The bathroom was separate and we had our own everything, but it is just that it was so tiny. **When did they get a car?** We had a car because my father was a driver, a truck driver. He couldn't really live without a car and he made good money; he was earning a lot of money because he was always doing business trips and doing overtime and was very hardworking. He was also a member of the Party. My mother wasn't a member of the Party: she didn't have very good health although she was working very hard and always doing shifts. She was working for the *vrednost'* [unhealthy conditions of work], that is, when you give pensioners extra money because the conditions in the factory were so awful that they got an extra premium (it was an official term). So she was supposed to get a higher pension at 55 and retire earlier, 5 years earlier, but because of all the changes....

University

I studied English because I think it was like a trampoline to the world for me really. I thought of it as a step I could take to be able to travel and see the world. My parents never had any influence over me; they would probably have wanted me to stay in my home town and my mother was hoping I would stay at home. I kind of defected to Moscow. English was okay but still it wasn't viewed as a proper profession. Teaching was okay but I didn't want to be a teacher; I wanted to be an interpreter or a translator or something like that. I didn't tell them that that was what I wanted to do; I told them I wanted to be a teacher and finally that was okay with them.

At university I met very interesting people. Why did I choose to go to Moscow? Well, the closest university to us was in Nizhny Novgorod, about 40 kilometers away; the town was called Gorky and it was a closed city. I hated it and never wanted to live there. I wanted to meet people, I wanted to speak English, and I knew I would never be able to speak English and meet foreigners in Gorky. I wanted to be in the center of things. **Did you ever meet Sakharov** [the famous dissident physicist who was exiled to Gorky]? My friend was actually working in the hospital where he was kept, but I never would have met him as I wouldn't have known that he was kept there at the time.

Marriage

My husband was studying physics and astronomy at the same university but obviously in a different department. We met when we were both in our 3rd year. We got married in 1988 when we were both 21. His parents were divorced (so he's got only one parent) and his mother was very against our wedding; at the time I didn't have anything to do with her. I didn't have any support, maybe a little bit of help from his gran. But my parents were still at hand; it took me six hours on the train to get to my parents, so I visited them frequently as well.

In the first two and one half years of our marriage we didn't live together, and I was visiting him a few times in St Petersburg as he was sent there [to the armed forces]. We saw each other occasionally but I was still living in the university hostel and he was away so no, we weren't living together. We knew we would get married because, although he is Russian, his family emigrated from the Ukraine to Baku in Azerbaijan. So they [the authorities] would have sent us there after university. There was still this two year placement after university to do, and they would have sent us to different places. That was also part of the reason why we were rushing to get married when we were still at university. Initially he was going to be a teacher. But in spite of the fact that we got married, he was sent to the armed forces and he had to do almost three years in the navy. And when he came out, he decided he didn't want to live in Russia anymore, let alone be a teacher there!

Discussion of sex, sex education and birth control

I had no sex education in school. My mother did not teach me anything. I was afraid of getting pregnant, but I didn't find it difficult to find basic condoms. But other than that we didn't consider anything more serious at the time because we were kind of taught that you couldn't have the coil. That was the alternative, the coil -- that's it, so we couldn't have used a coil legally because it wasn't used for unmarried women or women who hadn't given birth. That was it, so that was a no no really, so we didn't seriously consider it at the time, so condoms were okay.

Abortions

My friends did talk about abortions. We had somebody in my class at fifteen who had had an abortion. So that was talked about and widely discussed. I knew about abortions but we didn't have any proper education; it was all either reading through *samizdat* books or talking to peers or maybe your sister, but not your parents.

280

I had an abortion. It wasn't difficult at the time to get an abortion because I had the money to pay for it. It was a mutual decision with my husband; we were already married and we were just about to go to London on holiday. I think we had tickets, if not tickets, then the visas. It happened there and then and in fact that was the reason why he came here [to London] first, although we were meant to go together but he had to come first. I joined him later because I had an abortion in Russia.

It was really horrific for some of the girls who went through it and I knew about it very well. But I made sure that I went to a private clinic. It was done with *blat*. I knew I would be taken care of; I would be given an anesthetic or something like that, so it was not as scary and I was hoping that I wouldn't feel anything. I didn't feel anything but the whole scenario and the whole attitude of the doctors and this kind of conveyer belt industry (which it was) were still very horrific and it was very traumatizing nonetheless. I don't have first-hand knowledge but one of my friends was put through it by her mother to give her a lesson not to ever have sex! It was done without any anesthetic and it was a really horrific experience.

Were there any problems specific to women?

Well, first of all I am sure you have already heard this a hundred times! At the time an unmarried woman at twenty five would be considered a spinster, so you had to kind of rush into marriage and make sure that you have a husband and kids by the time you are twenty five. Otherwise you are an outcast, so that was on the agenda. And a good education was very much on the agenda for women, much more than for men because again, you had to make sure that you've got something to sell. It's not just your body but your mind as well! But I think a more kind of liberated stage was coming. In the late 1980's perestroika was everywhere. It was felt everywhere so I didn't really feel that I was under any pressure to be any different from any men that I knew. We had the same problems, the same aspirations, the same ambitions.

Would you have been paid the same as men if you got the job?

I would make sure that I would be paid more! But probably not, I know what you're asking so probably not, it's still the same. When I was growing up there were so many strong women around me, especially in our school. I know it's part of the actual social structure at the time, but I don't think that I can give you good examples of what I saw, because in my surroundings, in my childhood and university years, I didn't feel that pressure that women were discriminated against that much. I didn't. But you won't be able to validate that through me because my perception of the times then was totally different as I only realized what sort of culture I was living in after I left it. In fact, at the university all the top professors and lecturers were women. Men were in fact (maybe because it was a pedagogical environment) always kind of on the back benches

Did religion play any role in your life?

My grandmother was very religious and she was teaching me how to pray and how to say my prayers. But no, religion wasn't really relevant. I mean I was baptized and it was something that was done just because I think my parents come from religious backgrounds. They are Russian Orthodox. I think I went to church a couple of times but I didn't take much part in the church. The churches around where I lived were destroyed anyway, so it was a very atheistic society which was a shame.

What did you do at the end of the1980s?

At the time of perestroika I joined two companies, mainly working as an interpreter and a teacher of English at the co-operative, teaching adults English. During the day I would do some interpreting or translating or something like that. It was mainly freelance. I would take on any project -- be a guide, a Moscow guide, a city guide, I would take a group of tourists to the Caucasus for two weeks. So whenever there was a group of foreigners I would take it. Teaching was needed to pay the bills, as it was good money, and every evening I had three hours of teaching adults.

How did you picture the ideal Soviet woman?

One of the rare examples of an Oscar (film) winner in Russia was about a woman who was head of the factory. She had a great sense of humor, she was very stylish, she was very unauthoritative, she was respected by everyone and at the same time she was fun loving. She liked to be with her friends, to have a bit of passion, to do a little bit of gossiping, etc.. That would be my ideal woman, from that character. The only problem was that she was divorced and was very lonely, but at the end of the film she found her true love and they lived happily ever after.

What did femininity mean?

I always thought that children were important and I didn't like women who were only career oriented. I couldn't understand that that would be fulfilling for me. It probably wouldn't be anyway, although I was very career oriented and I wanted to achieve some kind of status. I was very fashion conscious, still am, and I wouldn't leave the house without full make up if I were in Russia. I read a lot and at times we did have intellectual discussions on whoever read what. We were kind of going with the fashion as well, because if I didn't know, it would be so-and-so or some dissident material at the time, we would discuss the book, even if it was some 'chick lit' (I don't know whatever you call it).

Who would be a strong women in Russian culture?

I'd say my form/class teacher throughout my school years from year three to year ten. She was a woman who didn't really have anything else in her life but the school; that's her life. She's always with the kids, even on her birthday. She doesn't really have kids of her own but she loves the children. She's not married. To me 'strong' is somebody who is strong in spite of all the shortcomings, of all the disadvantages, of all the problems she has to face.

Validating the prime emphasis on children and degree of closeness to parents in the Soviet Union

I have to say that my childhood was quite happy. I never had a babysitter in my life, ever. The only people that I would have been left with (apart from my parents) would have been my grandparents. I don't remember a neighbor or anyone coming to my house while my parents were out. We were always travelling together; we travelled around Russia in our car, around the Baltic republics. We were a very nice family.

You know I look at my friends now and they are talking about their children who are eighteen or twenty even. They are scared of sending them to live in a different town or university campus. I don't understand why they don't let these children go their way and stop being so overprotective. I think it's not going to do them any good. So I am more probably an advocate of giving more freedom to the children than trying to stay with the parents.

Life in London

Why did you leave the Soviet Union?

It was our mutual decision that we couldn't live in Russia anymore. We had to go somewhere in 1991. We had some friends who could organize an invitation for us. Throughout my university years I met some people who could help me with that. We were considering England as one of the countries we could go to. We were also considering Germany but neither of us was able to speak German. So England became the only possible country for us to try and go to. Also my husband had just done three years in the armed forces and then there was a war between Azerbaijan and Armenia. And he would again be called up to fight for the Azeris in that conflict and I couldn't possibly let that happen.

How difficult did you find it to adjust to:

Climate

10 out of 10! No adjustment needed, it's my type of climate.

People

This is one of the questions I am always asked: why England, why London? Now I think I know why: I just absolutely love English people. I don't find it difficult to communicate, I don't find the English reserved or hypocritical or arrogant or whatever else. I really find the English friendly and I socialize with the kind of people I am meeting through my work, although I have to say that 90% of my social life is still with Russian people.

Property

It wasn't difficult to find property. But obviously it was very difficult to raise the first couple of thousand or whatever we needed; I think we needed more than that in order for us to get a mortgage. We bought our first house in 1994 and we were just lucky. We felt we should do it otherwise we would not be able to get property. It was a bit of a struggle. I remember we had to borrow from my friends to buy our first washing machine as the bank wouldn't lend us any more money. It was tough for the first few months but only because we were just starting our own business at the time and money was very difficult to come by.

I live in a tiny village in Hertfordshire which is just on the borders of the M25. My neighbors are not particularly English. It is a very cosmopolitan little village so foreigners are not looked upon as aliens. They are very friendly, very nice people around me. I have never felt any kind of suspicious attitude. We talk to each other when I walk my dog and I see my neighbors every day and we say hello; we have parties and barbecues. I think we are just lucky because it is such a wonderful area. I am sure it is not the case everywhere else. I have been lucky throughout my life but when we were buying houses we were very careful about the area we were buying in. So depending on money it [the area we chose to live in] grew and grew to be a better and better area from my point of view. I made it a point that I would rather have a smaller house in a better area than a bigger house in a bad one.

Transport

It's very expensive. At the time I thought I would rather walk from one tube station to the other rather than spend 80p. Of course it was 80p then and now it is £3.

Language

I still find it difficult although I learnt English, studied it and I can understand everything. I still search for words, and obviously I will never lose my accent. So yes, it is constant awareness.

Birth and childcare issues

I loved the way I was treated in the maternity unit in the Surrey hospital (in 1995). I didn't pay a penny for anything. It was on the NHS and it was absolutely wonderful: everyone was helpful and friendly. Also my daughter had to stay in the intensive care unit for two weeks and I had to stay with her. It was quite a difficult period but everyone was doing their best to help. At the beginning my husband and I were coping, just the two of us, as we were working from home, so it was possible. Then once my daughter was one year old we sent her to a child minder and then to a proper new private nursery in a house in the countryside.

School system

Now she is at an independent school. I think the school is wonderful but it is a girls only school and although it is a very international school, sometimes she gets a bit lonely. I wanted to make sure that she would not feel a complete foreigner, different, because her parents are immigrants. So I sent her to that school so it's not that bad. Sometimes it surfaces that she feels a bit different, such as the way other children relate to their parents, the way other children are at home and how they discuss things. She will come back home to me and says, 'Because we are Russians and we do this and that, we are totally different, it's not the way things are done.' She speaks English as her first language and she struggles with Russian, but she'll get there.

Shopping and Food

Oh shopping was my hobby for a long time! I would just go into the supermarkets or the grocery shops, it was an excellent pastime. Now I don't miss Russian food. There are so many Eastern European shops that you can buy your herrings or whatever, but I still miss the gherkins, the cucumbers, the proper ones, but I grow them now. I haven't got as far as to pickle them yet. I don't miss mushrooms; I have a field where I go with my dog. I pick my mushrooms, I bring them home and I cook them.

Has your husband's role changed here?

He's totally not Russian; in fact he doesn't like much about Russia. He would probably be considered a foreign body, even now in Russia. First of all he grew up in the Caucasus where they are very gentlemanly to women. Men treasure women, they respect their mothers. So he was not Russian in the proper sense of the word. But now he is more English than many English people. He has his English hobbies. He is very English in his way of thinking, in his dress sense or his political views. No, he is totally different from the typical Russian men that I know. We go out together, we garden together, we travel together -- that's my family life for you. And I work a lot, sometimes in the evenings, and he stays with my daughter more than I do.

Does his job take precedence over yours?

We work together, we have done until recently. It was always 50/50 and we would be very diplomatic. So women's careers would be as important as men's.

Do you miss your parents?

Yes of course I miss my mother. But because I have lived without my parents since I was sixteen, I wouldn't want to live in the same house with my parents, even though I love them a lot. About five streets away would be wonderful; that would just be a perfect arrangement, but unfortunately that is not possible so it is best to live separately. I think that we have very good relations because we live so far away; and we would be more, you know, quarrelling. **Does your daughter know her grandmothers?** Until she was six she never knew the grandmothers because we couldn't travel or visit Russia for twelve years. She actually met them because they visited for a short time, but she couldn't really communicate with them and she didn't realize that they were her family. So it only happened when we started going there regularly.

What does equality mean now?

If anything, I think we have probably gone too far with equality. I don't like the fact that there are all these lawsuits from women who are (supposedly) harassed by their male colleagues. I think it is blown out of proportion. I think the fact that it is possible - legally - that women, thank God, can be natural and have normal office relations, they try to be so artificial in their behavior just not to attract any kind of lawsuit.

Has religion become part of your life at all?

Well, my daughter has been to a church school and she is teaching me. It's a Church of England school. I do respect it, and I do follow what is happening to the Russian [Orthodox] church here. I have supported the church, I have been writing about it. But personally, no, I am still not involved but I am sure it will change. I think I find it, that is, the religion itself, good for making us better people. I don't necessarily believe in God but observing all the traditions and the rules, including the ten commandments and the moral values, etc.., I respect that a lot. Having said that, if you look at what all the religious wars have done, it is unbelievable. I suppose I am still drifting; I don't know exactly what my views on religion really are.

Do you want to go back to Russia?

Not if I can help it! Although I do not even have Russian citizenship anymore and I am only a British citizen.

What do you miss the most?

Friends. It has nothing to do with Russia. It's just missing your younger self.

What do you value most about living in London?

I love the fact that you can be in London and still be in a village. You can still be five minutes from the next tube station by car and at the same time you can walk for an hour and not meet a single person. It is such a diverse city that you can find areas to suit your different moods, twenty four hours a day throughout the year. You want urban --there is your city; you want shopping -- there is Bond Street; you want relief from stress -- you go to a meadow just across the street from me where I can walk my dog. That is one of the best moments in my day. I think past the age of forty I am becoming more kind of in search of not loneliness but space to myself. Yes, I don't want to do any more social occasions, or as many as I used to do, although last week I didn't see my daughter for the whole week, not a single evening. So I still do it [social occasions] but I prefer not to.

What do you least like about London?

The traffic jams and probably the fact that it is not as friendly to walkers and cyclists as other European cities. So I think that could be developed.

How would you characterize British society?

Well, I think it is one of the best democratic models that exists. I like the fact that the people are law abiding citizens. I like the fact that there is so little inequality, that there is a benefit system. It is probably too much actually, it has to be reformed, socially, the infrastructure. I think that the press is free. I really love this about this country, the fact that a politician can't ignore what is written in the papers. A politician can go down by something …. Also I find that the British people in general are very decent and very kind, generous people. I have met different nationalities, different people. I would love to live in France but I would like France to be populated by the British.

Women in their thirties

The four women in this final group are the most recent arrivals in the UK. One came to earn money, another was sent as a seventeen year old to study at an international college in Oxford, one came to do graduate work and married a Russian already resident in London, and the fourth met her British husband in Russia and came to live with him in this country. The last two women are the second wives of their respective husbands.

What do they share in common? All four were born in the Soviet period but were educated after the fall of the Soviet Union. Three have university degrees; the fourth went to university but changed courses. All value education very highly. All four speak positively of their mothers who had a university education and who were or are gainfully (and professionally) employed. As educated women who had careers and also raised their children, these mothers are role models for their daughters. Three of the respondents had siblings in their families, one of them having step-siblings whom she considered to be her brothers. In most cases their grandparents played a formative and loving role in their childhoods.

Two of the women divorced their first Russian husbands but did so for quite different reasons. Both of them were married at an early age, twenty and twenty one, respectively, although as has become clear, many Russian women marry young. Both sets of parents were not happy with their daughters' choice of partner. (See the texts).

Unlike the older respondents, this group of women are the first to indicate that they had some – if very minimum – sex education in school. As **Irina** says, '[it] was something like a fairy tale -- not meaning everything, trying to conceal a lot of things. So basically the education was absolutely not very good. It was as if, "Children, be careful about sex because it can lead to pregnancy and remember, you will not find small children in a Cabbage Patch."' **Luba**'s mother, who was a 'good Russian woman,' didn't talk about sex with her daughter, whereas **Tanya**'s mum also didn't speak about sex but did give her daughter a book about the 'facts of life'. Three of the women discuss different maternity conditions in Russia as well as

291

maternity conditions in their mothers' time. All knew about abortions although they hadn't had any.

The question regarding the 'ideal woman' evoked some differing answers. **Luba**'s remarks are specific to Uzbekistan and to her understanding of the local Moslem women and their role vis-à-vis their husbands. All, however, discuss the roles that women could or should play regarding careers, children, families, etc..

What about their ability to adjust to the UK? For three of them, the easiest thing to adjust to was the climate, but this wasn't the case for **Yevgenia**. The transport system was deemed very expensive. All found that speaking English had its problems even though they had previously studied English in Russia. Not surprisingly they found the lack of family in the UK the biggest obstacle to overcome, especially since two of them have very young families and little familial support. Both of them, however, see their husbands as being more helpful both in the home and with childcare than they assume they were with their first wives; both of these husbands are now 'a fair bit older'– and wiser?

They all speak about conditions and difficulties of living in Russia in the 1990s and offer some insights about the future for Russia, including the increasing separation of rich and poor. They note the changing maternity provisions and equally the altering role of the 'strong' woman today. **Yevgenia** specifically contrasts what being a woman is like in Russia today with what she sees as the norm in London.

Two offer quite specific comments which we might deem, if not racist, then at the very least, pejorative. **Luba**, for example, indicates that Moslem women in Uzbekistan are subjected to and are themselves influenced by very different social expectations than in Russia, especially those expectations imposed by the men in their communities. She states that their main role is 'to please the men'. **Irina** takes up the question of the position immigrants can adopt, especially immigrants from Afro-Asian countries. She is upset at what she perceives is their (mis)use of the benefit system as well as being concerned about what is taught in the school system, especially about the role that explaining Islamic culture is playing at the expense of other (in her case, Christian) religious awareness. All four women profess to be Russian Orthodox Christians.

As with most of the other women interviewed, these four have an interesting 'take' on how they would characterize the British, a fact in their case which is mostly positive. **Luba** criticizes parents' inability to say 'no' to their children and also youngsters' attitudes towards older people. **Tanya** comments on and criticizes the British reaction to death.

Luba (34)

Life in Russia

I prefer a proper husband, a husband who earns money and has a proper job. I don't want to just sit at home. I would like a job but not just any job to earn money as I do now. I would also like to have children. And many Russian women want the same as I do.

Luba is a 34-year-old Russian woman who was born and brought up in Uzbekistan, a fact which becomes very important for her future. Her grandparents were, respectively, Russian and Russian/Ukrainian who left Moscow in the 1930s to live in Tashkent. Her father's father was from the Russian republic and his mother was from Uzbekistan. Her maternal grandmother was a doctor from Odessa (Ukraine) whose brother eventually worked in construction in Tashkent. Her mother liked the climate in Tashkent so much so that she moved there; that is, as Luba says, the climate was better and the food was better! Both of her parents went to university. Her mother studied economics in Moscow and her father studied at the University in Tashkent and, unlike her mother, was a member of the Party. Her older sister also went to university and is currently living in Tashkent. She herself is a university graduate in English who became an English teacher in Russia, but after leaving in 2003 she is working in a fast food shop as well as being a student in London. She has left her ten year old son with her mother in Tashkent.

University

I didn't know exactly what to do. My father wanted me to be a fashion designer but I wasn't very good at drawing. My mother wanted me to go into economics. My sister followed my mother's advice much more than I did. There really wasn't any reason why I chose English but it suddenly came to my mum that I could be an English teacher. I wanted to learn English but I wasn't sure that I wanted to be a teacher. I wanted to work in an office where English and Russian were used. After university, I worked in a office/association of Uzbek teachers of English which had a library and I did research. I organized seminars and invited speakers from Britain and the USA. I was enjoying that job and speaking English as well.

Marriage.

I met my husband at a friend's birthday party. We were both twenty one. We actually met during our last course at university where he studied transport and communications. We got married at the age of twenty one. He was a lazy guy; he didn't want to do anything. That's why I tried living with him for two years with my parents in their home. My parents always supported us financially. My husband was always trying to find something to do, but I think that he was always looking for an excuse. He didn't want to do anything. My father had a small enterprise and he wanted to involve my husband. My husband and I are now divorced.

Living arrangements

We lived with my parents in their house. My mother wasn't very happy with the marriage; neither was my father. My sister now has two children and since I am away in London, she and her husband live with my parents. Her children and my son go to the same school. They live in the flat where my sister and I were born. Then my father bought this house and we moved; the flat stayed with my sister.

Sex, sex education and birth control

No, my mother never spoke about sex. She is a good Russian woman, a very proud person so she could never speak about sex. She is a very, very strict person. It depends on personality. But my friends' mothers could speak easily about sex. My mum was afraid that something would happen to me and my sister and she didn't like to talk about these things. Actually, I don't think I ever asked her about these things.

I think there was some sex education in the schools, but I don't exactly remember the name under what subject it was taught. I think I remember the main teacher speaking separately to the boys and the girls. I don't think contraceptives were easily available for my mother; condoms, yes. For me, you could get some tablets from the doctor, and they were free.

Abortion

Abortions certainly were a means of contraception. If you have money, it isn't difficult to get an abortion. If you're sixteen, you must ask your parents' permission

Birth experience

My son was born in a maternity ward in Tashkent. In the UK, some of my friends gave birth in the morning and were sent home in the late afternoon. That would never happen in our country. Women have to stay ten days in hospital after the birth of the child, until everything was checked out and the umbilical cord had healed and the placenta and the uterus were examined. The doctors always controlled when you were ready to leave. Medical treatment was given and the baby looked after. Now the rules have changed. When I gave birth [ten and a half years ago], mothers and children were separated. Babies were brought to the mothers to feed (I had stitches and couldn't move around very easily). Now, the child usually sleeps with the mother but if you have stitches they will help to keep mother and child together. Also the baby will be brought every 4 hours to feed.

My husband was not there at the birth because we had already parted. Now in some private clinics fathers are allowed to come for the birth. But in the main, fathers are not there, primarily for hygienic reasons; they [maternity hospitals] don't want any infections. I don't think Russian husbands actually want to be there in the first place – in any case!! I just wanted my baby to be okay. *When asked to comment about how poor giving birth in Russia was,* Luba said that wasn't true in her case.

Infidelity, Uzbek women and divorce

I think it's more acceptable for men, especially due to the Muslim religion where men are able to have more than one wife. Actually many Muslim women have to accept this as they really don't have any choice. They have three or four children and they know their husband is going out with the other wife or wives who also have children. It's now becoming more normal for a man to have another woman who is not one of his other wives. So they just have to accept this. Muslim women living in Uzbekistan are more polite and know their main role is in pleasing men. For Russian women, it's totally different. As for real Russian women (who are in Russia), the ones who are more powerful try to keep their husbands very very close to them.

Uzbek women are different in that they are not working; they are just housewives. But now I think it is changing as they are trying to get careers and become educated.... They get married and they try to keep this marriage because of the children, even if they don't like sex or the husband. My generation is different now. *If you don't like him anymore, divorce!* I was married for two years and I wanted to get divorced. **Was he unhappy about that?** Who cares? Now that I am divorced, he doesn't see our child. He even was saying that it wasn't his child.

How do you picture the ideal woman in the Soviet Union? What did femininity mean?

The main idea in the country was that the woman has to get married, to have children, to be a good wife. For example, my mum was a good mum; she was very well educated and a very smart person. She was working all of her life. My father actually didn't want her to sit at home or something, but she worked for herself, not for earning money. I believe in two things: one is that women believe that women want to work or have to work, and the other thing is that they think their daughters have to get married, sit at home, look after the children, look after the husband, and cook for the family. A woman doesn't have to have a higher education or something else because she has a husband who has to earn the money. The wife's

297

responsibility is to look after the children and the house. **Do you think this will change with the demise of the Soviet Union?** No response...

I prefer a proper husband, a husband who earns money and has a proper job. I don't want to just sit at home. I would like a job but not just any job to earn money as I do now. I would also like to have children. And many Russian women want the same as I do.

Life in London

Why did you come to London?

I came to earn some money. When my father was alive, I was supported all the time -- financially, emotionally, every way -- so I never thought about money. He did everything for us. He gave us an education, he gave us stability, he gave us everything. He created small machines, for example, for producing flour and/or ice cream. He was an engineer who had his own business.

Before I came to London I tried to move to Russia. I was there for four months but without papers, you just can't get a job. I tried to go to Moscow. I was trying to find some employment that was similar to what I had in Uzbekistan, like an office job that dealt with English or with education. But I couldn't get a job because everyone was asking for my papers. Although I am Russian, the minute people heard I was from Tashkent, I couldn't get a job. So I came to London.

How difficult did you find it to adjust to:

In the beginning it was very difficult to adjust to London. I couldn't find a job and I didn't have any money. I really wanted to go back home. You don't know how to do everything. I couldn't find a job for three months. But I wanted to study and come here. And then I found a job. I was living in Wimbledon (south London) but I got a job in Brent Cross (north London).

Climate

I used to have lots of headaches back home because of the heat. It's much better here where it's not so humid (wet heat). In the summer time when it is very hot it isn't very moist.

People

I don't communicate very much with English people. I have one very nice friend who is English who actually is a friend of my boyfriend. That's all: I don't know any others [friends] who are English. All the people I know come from other countries.

Language

I did find it difficult in the beginning. When I came to London, I felt I knew nothing in English. I was much better at writing English than speaking English. The college where I am studying helped me because I started speaking and communicating with other students.

Property

In Uzbekistan, my husband and I only shared a house with my parents or my parents-in-law. This is normal for our country. After I got divorced, my father bought me a flat. I moved in with my son and we were living alone for three or four years. Here I have lived in shared accommodation and I find it quite difficult to get used to living with other people, especially with people I don't know.

Transport

I found the underground very expensive and that's why I have had to travel all over London by bus. Now that I am a student I can get a discount. Of course it is very different in my country: for every underground, every bus, and every station – the fare is the same because the system is not subdivided like it is London.

Lack of family

Not having a family is very hard. But now it is better for me because I have a boyfriend. I am no longer totally alone and therefore it is easier. I met someone here who is from Tashkent. All the people in the new place I moved to were from the former Soviet Union: Uzbekistan, Latvia, Lithuania. They all speak Russian rather than English. My boyfriend and I became 'acquainted' after a year in the house. He is much younger than I am, but we have now been together for over two years. He actually is ten years younger than I am which in England isn't so bad but it is back in Uzbekistan.

Do you feel part of this country now?

I think I am becoming more English. In fact when I go on holiday I feel very strange in Russia/Uzbekistan; I am a stranger there.

I have applied for an extension of my visa. [If you stay as a student for ten years, then you can apply for residence.] There are too many reasons why I am doing this. I'm afraid of what I can do back home. For me it will be very difficult to go back. All of my friends can't find appropriate jobs. I could work at the university but my salary wouldn't even be enough to pay my bills, my transport. There are lots of jobs but they don't pay enough money. Another reason which is keeping me here is my boyfriend.

Waiting to hear about the extension of my visa is indeed quite unnerving, but since they [the Immigration office] have all of my documents I can't do anything until I hear from them. I can't leave until I hear from them, even if my visa expires.

What do you miss most?

Sometimes I want to go home because I miss my family and friends. I feel I already have quite a distance between myself and my son. We were much closer before than we are now, mainly because he is growing up and has different interests. My mother is very strict with him. I miss my relationships with my family and friends most.

If there were better jobs in Tashkent, you would be happier to go back?

Probably yes because I have family there. It is very difficult to live without family and it is very difficult to bring my family here. My mother has never visited me in London. No one has visited me in London. I go to Tashkent every year for four weeks and I phone home three or four times a week. To invite someone here for a week is too expensive and to invite someone for a month is really too long. I couldn't find housing for visitors; it's just too expensive.

Are you depressed about going back to Uzbekistan?

Yes, because of the national problems. I am Russian and not an Uzbek. The main language is Uzbek and if you go somewhere to work all the documents are in Uzbek. So, in a job, even if you know your job, they prefer people who are Uzbek. I think it would be better to go to Russia for my son. I don't see any future there [in Uzbekistan]. My boyfriend is Uzbek but even he doesn't speak Uzbek; Russian is his language too. His parents are very educated people and he also has a university education. He doesn't want to go back home. He wants to try as much as he can to stay here. He is younger and has many more possibilities than I have. Since he has no family besides his parents, he doesn't have to think whether he wants to or has to go back (like I do).

How do you spend your free time here?

I do have free time and I usually spend it with my boyfriend. We go for dinner; we don't go much to clubs. Most of the time we are at home. The year before I didn't have a day off. **Is that legal?** Everything isn't legal. I can't work more than 20 hours with my visa, but of course I have to. Most of the women who come from Russia are working more than 20 hours.

Has religion any relevance for you ?

Yes, I am an Orthodox Christian --and was so in Uzbekistan-- and I think I believe in Jesus Christ and I don't want to change my religion to become Muslim. But I respect any religion.In London I've been to the Russian Orthodox Church in Knightsbridge three or four times. My friend goes to a Baptist church here and she has invited me to join her., but I am not that keen. When I was working in the center of town, it was much easier to go to Knightsbridge. Now it is very complicated.

What don't you like about London?

The only thing I don't like in London concerns how youngsters grow up. Their attitude towards older people makes me really mad. They are very rude; they never stand for an older person on the bus. I wouldn't want my son to behave like this and I wouldn't want him to come here.

I'm not saying that all of them are bad, but if you see a busload of children, it can be a nightmare. The children are so horrible. I think it depends on their financial situation. The same as in the Soviet Union. Intelligent people and non-intelligent people may be the same. School children from private [independent] schools are more educated. Normal school children can do whatever they want. For example, this friend of mine has a sixteen year old daughter and she - and all the other students - doesn't have any interest in music except for rap or pop.

In Western countries, I know that the child is allowed to do whatever he/she wants, up to the age of five or six. The parents never say 'No'. They think this is very important for his/her development. But after six it is too late to say No.

Some thoughts about Uzbekistan and changes since 1991

It is getting worse and worse. When I entered university in the 1990s, many professional teachers who were Jewish tried to go to Israel or America, wherever they could go. Too many really educated people left.

302

They went to Russia [as opposed to staying in Uzbekistan] as well. So now we don't have any teachers. Therefore students on the last course were teaching arts to students on the first course. What kind of education can they get? You can pay for all of your exams and get good marks. For example, now I don't trust any medical doctors because all of them just pay for their diplomas. Most of the people now go to private clinics; the clinics are more trusted. In the Soviet Union, education was good; health care was good – much stronger than today.

In the past, when we were children, we could travel and go to the seaside. Now I can't afford to travel and most of the population in Russia can't afford it. Even my son and my nephews can't afford to go somewhere all together; it's too expensive. People are just thinking about how to earn money to keep their children. People don't have enough money to buy new clothes for their children or for themselves,. This is really horrible as we never used to have to buy these things. Many second hand shops are now opening. I never used to buy second hand clothing. I used to sew some of my clothing.

For some people the changes since 1991 are better. But when it was the Soviet Union there wasn't too much difference between rich people and poor people. Everyone was middle class. Now there are the very rich; I don't know how they earned their money. I think that 60 -70% of people are middle class. When my mother was a student at the university she used to be paid a stipend which allowed her to go to and from Tashkent to Moscow for her holidays. Now on her salary she can't even take a taxi home from the university! The situation now is very serious, especially for the educated. My mum wants to live in Russia. I believe that living in Russia would be better than living in Uzbekistan.

Since this interview Luba has returned, reluctantly, to Tashkent

Yevgenia (31)

Life in Russia

The majority of Russian women really do take care of themselves. And I found quite a few English women who really don't care -- it doesn't bother them at all. So in that sense, femininity is a bit different. A friend of mine said she could tell who is Russian and who was not by the way the women dress. For Russians, image is so important.

Up to the age of seventeen Yevgenia lived in Moscow. After secondary school in 1994, her parents sent her to study in Oxford for the International Baccalaureate at a private college. After several forays into different avenues of study, she enrolled in acting school in London and has become an actress and a model, working in London and in Moscow. She is single, living with her boyfriend. Her mother was born near the Sea of Azov and went to Moscow to study linguistics. She taught English and German as well as working as an interpreter in Moscow where she now lives and runs her own business. Her father was born in the Caucuses and studied mathematics and computer sciences in Moscow. He is currently in London. Her maternal grandparents live in Moscow where they were forced to move when the civil war in the Caucuses began at the end of the 1980s. Her grandfather was a military officer. Yevgenia spent whole summers in the Caucuses with these grandparents.

Life as a teenager in Moscow

As a teenager, I did lots of sports, figure skating (very Russian!), but I had a concussion so I had to be very cautious with falling and I was not relaxed (I wish I had done it professionally). I was not really into drama when I was young.

I finished secondary school in Moscow and then I went to study for the International Baccalaureate at a private college in Oxford. This was my parents' decision, namely, to send me away. I was planning to go to university in Moscow, to study international relations or something like that. In 1994 when I finished my school, Moscow was very unstable. My parents were separated. My mother's second husband was the second person to open a private restaurant in Moscow at the end of the 1980s and the beginning of the 1990s. It was tough in the beginning because there was no structure for opening a business. He really had to take so many risks. He managed to get a loan and was a pioneer. Eventually he opened several restaurants and it went very well. But in the beginning because of unorganized [sic] crime there was just so much risk for the family. I was a teenager and I wanted to go out, I wanted freedom, I wanted many things. They were so concerned for me, so afraid, that they decided to send me away to a stable environment, to get a good education. A friend told us so many good things about this college in Oxford; he came and introduced me to the principal. I had an interview and they took me on. In the beginning it was exciting and scary to go to another country, especially since I was quite sheltered. I am an only child.

Discussion of sex, sex education and birth control

I didn't learn about sex at school, not at all. As for my parents, I don't think I ever had a proper chat with them. Whatever I learned, for example, about condoms, I learned from my friends.

Abortions

I learned about abortions from my friends. A girl at school had had one and a friend of hers told me about it. She tried to hide it from everyone. She went secretly and I heard this awful story about it. It scared me for life!

Was there equality for women?

When I lived in Moscow I was still a teenager. You think differently then and you act differently. I never encountered inequality. Everyone seemed to work and to be busy. I never felt any sense of inequality between the sexes.

How do you picture the ideal woman in the Soviet Union?

Sporty, healthy, women working, working mothers: positive, happy, energetic! I remember the Pioneer period -- healthy, sporty, young -- not the real Soviet ideal as it was disintegrating in my time.

What did femininity mean?

Being quite young, I would say that 'femininity' was quite strong from a very young age. I started putting on makeup from a young age, maybe thirteen or even earlier. My mother kept saying it wasn't good for me and asked me to stop putting on all that stuff. But my friends at school were putting on makeup and making themselves pretty, wearing jewelry, etc.. Eventually the school uniform was abandoned as many girls started to rebel against it. Then whoever could get hold of fashionable clothes, they did their best. In that sense it was a very mature way of portraying your femininity and sexuality. My mother had a tailor (using *Burda,* the magazine) for herself and for me as well.

Strong woman in Russian culture

I have an image of a woman who takes care of everything [it is from a poem]: she's the breadwinner, looks after children, looks after her husband, works in the garden, does everything. For the nineteenth century it's Chekhov – sense of aristocracy, decadence and wanting to be strong; the women wanted to do all of it, but they never did. Aristocratic women would be quite spoiled and leisurely. The ideas [of strong women] are more kind of associated with the Revolution and Soviet ideas about being strong: women who wanted to be equal to the men who lost their lives to the ideals and went to fight. So the image of a strong woman for me is associated with the Soviet period.

Was religion any relevance to you?

306

Until about the end of the 1980s, I was a Pioneer, preparing to become a Komsomol member (I never did become one). I never had any sense of religion then, although a few times I went to a Russian Orthodox Church with my parents. But later in the 1990s, my mother became more religious and went to church more. I started to learn more about religion, not in depth. But I started to learn about confession, what it means, certain things, but not enough. When I came to England I learned more. Now I have faith and go to church.

My grandparents weren't religious and being brought up in the Soviet regime with those ideals, religion didn't have a chance. Now, my grandmother goes to church with us in Moscow and my grandfather, at age eighty, got baptized for my mother's sake and for the family as well, although religion isn't for him.

Life in London

Why did you leave Russia?

My parents were concerned about Moscow, especially unorganized [sic] crime. I came to England in 1994.

Why did you come to London?

I moved to London in 1997.

How difficult was it to adjust to:

Climate

I didn't have time to understand about the climate but I know that it affected me a lot. I started to have hay fever (which I never had before) and I had colds all the time. So the climate affected my health quite badly. Since I lived on the campus of the college, often you would just run out without any outer garments: it looked sunny and warm but it became windy and wet and humid. I could never judge the weather properly. My mother was very concerned about my health. The weather was quite a drastic change for me. But it was so difficult for me at the beginning -- so many new things -- that I didn't have time to think about it.

People

At the very beginning I found it quite difficult to adjust. The college was so mixed that I don't think I had a very clear picture of who was English and who wasn't. There were English tutors and of course people outside [of the college]. The language barrier was the main thing. I never had a chance to mix with foreigners before, so I think the mentality is quite different as well. I found lots of English people almost a bit Bohemian, kind of too easy going, don't give a damn. I couldn't quite connect with their state of mind; I couldn't make friendships with them at the beginning. They were too laid back and I was concentrating and trying to impress people. This was the younger people. The older people at college were so caring, so considerate, so helpful. So on the other side I got this sense of a very warm hearted people who really helped me as well.

English men were a completely different story. Coming from Moscow, even if a teenage boy invites you somewhere, he pays everything, everywhere; he tries to give you presents. He tries to impress you. With English guys I never had this sense – you had to impress them rather than the other way round. In that sense I felt like the relationship was very different. More democratic, more equal. I felt I had to work harder in a way because in Moscow just being a girl was enough. Guys had to take care of things. Here I had to prove myself; you had at least to offer to pay for things, or share, be polite. I learned this quite quickly. I had an experience quite soon in which I was almost quite shamed for not offering to pay. It never even crossed my mind! A German man, actually, said, 'Why don't you even offer to pay? I'm a student like you, I get money from my parents, don't you think you should be more considerate?' He really gave me a lecture and I just sat there getting more red and thought, okay – I'm really embarrassed.

Language

308

My English was pretty basic. I could express myself but understanding native speakers was really tough. I never had a chance to speak to a native speaker properly, so hearing fluent English was tough. I came to the college and literally the day after I started classes including going to lectures. It was too much and I was struggling to understand. But they were quite gentle; there were tutors and counsellors, and they were well organized. I was an only child and quite closed and internal. I guess I should have asked for more help. But it only took a few months. After Christmas, I started to answer back -- there was a breakthrough after the first three months. My Moscow school was a normal school (not a specialized school) and English was really awful there -- teachers kept coming and going. I had a private tutor at home but I never had a chance to practice my English. I also had to take Russian literature as part of the International Baccalaureate and speaking with a Russian teacher was really comforting.

Property

At the moment I'm living near Tower Hill with my Italian boyfriend. In Moscow we had a two-bedroom flat, quite central. It was a nice flat, close to my school.

School and universities

In the very beginning it was pretty difficult to adjust to the school system. The thing that really helped is that the college is international and there were lots of foreign students from around the world. After this I went for one year to do a business degree but found it wasn't for me. By chance I then applied for and was accepted for a four year Italian and design university degree. At the same time, I kept being asked on the street, 'Are you a model? Are you a model?' Then after my first year at this course, I went to Milan where I brought some of the [modelling] photos taken of me; I called some modelling agencies and they took me on. Although I didn't get any jobs, I did have some great photo tests because Italian photographers are really fantastic. And with those photos, I went back to London and was taken on straight away by top modelling agencies. Then I took a year out so that I could do the modelling jobs I was being offered. Although I enjoyed the experience, now I wish I hadn't taken the year out. Then I went back for my second year at university and carried on with my modelling. After the second year, I was supposed to go to study in Milan. But that's when I encountered Italian bureaucracy! I was then searching for a solution to escape. And that's how I came across acting, by chance - it just came along! This happened in Moscow when an actress friend of my mother's bumped into her. She needed someone who looked physically like myself and she asked my mother if I'd be interested to take part in her production. When I met her, I told her I had done some modelling but not any acting. She was a very good actress herself and she tutored me for the part. And I really liked acting!

And, to make a long story short, I eventually went to drama school after I did a foundation course. (It's a long, long story of how I entered the foundation course – knowing various contacts who did lots of tutoring.) And now I really want to be an actress and that's what I am doing.

Transport

Once you know how to use the underground, it is easy, but it is too expensive. Moscow underground is much bigger and more complicated.

Lack of family

My parents are divorced. My father came to London a year or two after I came. My mother almost moved to London. When I was in Oxford, almost every weekend I would come to London to see my mother; my mother was around quite a lot in the beginning. Now she visits London but she doesn't have the same need as she did when I was much younger. She fell in love with London and she wanted to move to London at some point. My stepfather passed away over two years ago and my mother is alone now. But she's quite happy in Moscow. We see each other quite a lot as I also go to Moscow to work. I was always very close to both of my parents so I never really felt that I had a lack of parents.

Socializing with whom?

Now most of my friends are very mixed. I have a few English friends, not that many Russian friends. I haven't kept very much to Russian people. Italians, Americans, French – it's a mix.

Shopping

I'm a shopaholic. Before I came to England, I had already travelled so I was already used to the variety of things that I could afford. So it wasn't that overwhelming for me. But the idea that I could go and independently have my money and buy something for myself without the guidance of my mother was really exciting.

Russian food

I miss homemade Russian food. Nothing can compare to homemade Russian food, especially what my grandmother cooks. I miss it most when I come back and see that I haven't eaten it for such a long time. It's so yummy, so tasty. I love borscht, pancakes, *glubtsy* [meatballs in cabbage], *pel'meni* [kind of ravioli] – and everything. I do go to Russian stores but I haven't found a really good Russian restaurant.

Concepts of femininity

Overall I'm very happy that I moved here because I can see the difference now. I think it's important to keep your feminine side. It's important to stay a woman, but the fact is that you can't just rely on that and think that the man has to do the rest. I think that's quite different here. You feel you have to make something of your own. Russian women are quite educated and they really have great potential, but many women just decide that the main goal of their life is just to find a man. That is important but if you just concentrate on that you go crazy. I really feel it when I go back because I'm much more open-minded and much more democratic in that I try to be part of things, I try to participate. I often see girls of my age who just try to be cool and make men work, make men pay and buy. I love being spoiled and when I go back I have this treatment and it is great, but that's all it's about. I'm not saying that the whole generation in Moscow is like this. Friends who actually studied here and got this 'influence' and then went back to Moscow are very successful. They work, they're very busy, but because they studied here they got this 'influence' and they went back. So I would say that the equality side is quite different. I especially see this in the area where my mother bought a house with my stepfather. It's quite an elite area and all you see are these pampered and spoiled women, rich, so much shopping, going on holidays. You can't make a decent conversation with them!

Now I've lived in England and have seen such a variety of people. In the beginning I felt women weren't looking after themselves properly -- not dressed elegantly, not looking after their hair properly or make up. Especially at college the students were wearing dirty jeans and had unwashed hair. I always was washing my hair and making myself pretty, especially after coming from school in Moscow where everyone was wearing makeup and high heels. I saw all these scruffy students and I thought, 'They're girls, don't they want to take care of themselves?' The majority of Russian women really do take care of themselves. And I found quite a few English women who really don't care -- it doesn't bother them at all. So in that sense, femininity is a bit different. A friend of mine said she could tell who is Russian and who was not by the way the women dress. For Russians, image is so important.

I've taken on English styles now and when I go to Moscow they all say how English I look! I think it's the behavior I've adopted, like being extra polite and saying things like, 'thank you' 'excuse me' and 'sorry'. In Moscow people look at you as if ....of course London isn't so English anymore, so it's changing ....

Does religion play any role in your life?

I've had a very strong influence from my mother actually. I don't think it is because I am here. She never kind of forced me into it, but she told me so much from a spiritual point. Being here was so difficult from the

312

beginning. I was a bit lost and confused, isolated at times. Whenever I had a chat with my mum her solution was spiritual. (Not from my father, however, because he's a scientist; and my father is quite atheist.) There was so much new information and when I didn't feel well, being alone so much, and dealing with so many things myself, although it was exciting psychologically it was difficult. Also in Oxford I was put in this room with a girl who was very troubled (doing drugs, on antidepressants, and alcohol). I'd seen so many awful things and this scared me to death because I've never seen anything like it in my life. She was so emotionally out of control and unbalanced that it got to me and I started feeling unstable myself. Although I didn't really share much with my mother about these things, at some point I did have some anxieties and her solution was not to see a doctor but to offer a spiritual solution: go to church and find your peace there, and pray. This didn't start during the Soviet period (when I was growing up) but it came to her later on. The initial trigger was that she had some issues with her health and after some bad luck with doctors, I think that brought her to church and to religion. She shared those experiences with me and persuaded me to try it, to go to church, to try to confess, things like this. And so step-by-step, slowly slowly -- but at the same time I was thinking, do I believe or do I not believe, why are things like this, why are things like that. Step-by-step I wanted to go by myself. I go to the Russian Orthodox Church in Ennismore Gardens. I love this church, it's a fantastic church. It's really warm, it's a great atmosphere. It's quite relaxed as well.

Do you want to go back to live in Russia?

At this moment, no. I love working in Moscow and I love going back and spending time there, but I just feel living there is so different. It's not an easy city; it's quite an aggressive city. London is a pretty aggressive city but Moscow is more so. In a way it's very good; it's ambitious, it's very dynamic but it's constant pressure, constant stress. I don't like it but I like to get an injection of it for a certain time, but then come back to London and relax a bit.

What do you miss the most?

313

I miss my family, I miss my grandparents, I miss my dogs. I never had very strong or close friendships. Unfortunately I haven't kept in touch with my friends in school. I'm dying to know what happened to some of those people because we came through mayhem, through such a turbulent time. To look back at my school time, as much as there were great happy moments there, it was a tough time. It affected people so much. The extreme side of it was girls becoming prostitutes, guys dealing in foreign currency, carrying guns, stealing cars. I just look back and it's like a movie. I wouldn't believe that some of my friends at school were doing this. So my generation grew up so fast. It was tough. I was really sheltered from this but still I went to school and had friends. It's really unbelievable what some of them went through. After I came to England, I felt the friends I had were so different from me. I didn't know how to maintain a conversation with them after a few years. So I've sort of given up.

What do you value most and least about living in London compared to Moscow?

Most definitely I like the fact that London is a cosmopolitan city. I love mixing with people, I like the tempo. It's quite a transient city compared to Moscow; Moscow is huge, but you go to the same places and you meet the same group of people; it almost makes you feel (not now but before) a bit claustrophobic (like going to the same clubs, for example). In London you never feel this. In London you always feel people come and go, come and go. You don't have the feeling that you are being watched. It's a city of so many chances, so many opportunities. So is Moscow nowadays but before I never felt that. In Moscow, you always needed to know somebody to get somewhere, you always needed contacts -- *blat!* You still need to know somebody; it's still the same. In London it's good if you know people but you can make your way around without the contacts. You can still make something of yourself.

Comparing London to Moscow, Moscow is a nightmare, so huge, so crowded, so much traffic, it's polluted. Moscow is not very green whereas London is beautiful. You can escape in the center of the city to some beautiful parks and it's so green. Getting around London is much easier; I can't stand the tube, even though I mainly use it. People are quite polite even if it gets quite busy, you still can feel kind of relaxed. In Moscow the tube is like a troop of elephants running through it! It makes you feel that people are stressed and unhappy.

London is expensive. You realize how much money you need to make in order to live and maintain a certain quality of life. Now I prefer English winters to long Russian winters which are so tough; it gets a bit miserable sometimes. But I love the snow.

How would you characterize British society?

I always get the sense of certain traditions and values. It's almost like: it's been here and it always will be here. In a way I still think English people are quite laid-back. You don't feel the aggressiveness or ambition I sense from other nationalities, for example, Russians or Americans. On the one hand, British families - not many stick together; the institution of the family is not as strong here. I know young people who haven't been in touch with their parents or grandparents for ages. I found at boarding schools and colleges that children have been pushed out quite quickly and the children start living independently at quite an early age. On the one hand, this is quite good, but on the other hand they lose this sense of the family as a unit. On the other hand, it's quite a stable environment, I mean, overall. I guess it's not such a volatile environment. People are much more relaxed. They don't have to push and prove something. You have a job, you have your routine, your bath, your holidays. So why do you have to push or try to achieve anything more because you're already happy, you have a mortgage, etc.. Of course it's changing a lot now. I've always found, why try harder here?

But of course London is an expensive city and to make your living and to survive here, people are still like: okay, I'll be okay, I'll get a part-time job, I'll get a job, it's fine. It kind of relaxes you. When you go to Moscow, you feel you could do so much more, you could do so much better, you could make so much more money, it's much more competitive. In some ways it's good because you feel so energized and you have so many ideas. My

315

contemporaries in Moscow are so advanced; they have businesses, they have children, etc.. Here I think, if I have one child, how am I going to manage? Overall people get married younger in Moscow and start families younger; it's not normal if you don't get married! If you're not married by the age of thirty, there's something wrong. If you're divorced with a child, that's fine.

ADDITIONS:

My changed life

Overall, being a 1990s child, I think it has been such a turbulent and exciting time. I feel very privileged to go through this and to catch one life and one set of rules, and then go through this huge change and come to a different country and experience all this. At times I wonder where I belong. I know I'm Russian, I'm proud to be Russian, I always will be. Sometimes it makes me think: I look at my parents and they are quite specific in the way they are. My grandparents are even more specific -- their mindset, their ideals, what they think. I sometimes feel that I've had a taste of this and I've been through all this and now I'm here and there have been so many influences. In a way it's a bit strange.

I feel quite European, quite cosmopolitan, but at the same time Russian. The Russians I meet here sometimes are still quite Russian in their mindset. Sometimes it's even difficult to learn a language, to mix with people. But overall I've been quite privileged through the times I've been through, what I've seen and the opportunities my parents gave me to come here, to build my life here. It broadened my mind so much coming here. I go back and I understand so much that they gave me. The fact is I've changed so much, so many degrees. My parents had to pay for it and they were so loyal to me. If years ago someone had said to me you're going to be living in England, you're going to be an actress, you are going to be acting in English and Russian, living in London and Moscow, I would've thought it would be virtually impossible. I'm really grateful. I wish I had a brother [to share her life]!

Tanya (31)

Life in Russia

A massive, huge, huge woman in orange overalls became a symbolic figure of the equality I think from the good side in Soviet times. That statue or icon is a woman working on the railway with a massive spanner in her hand, in the orange overall. But in the everyday culture in my mum's eyes, for example, that was the ultimate awful, awful thing about the Soviet woman. There was always the ideal that in the West women can actually say, 'I don't want to work, I want to look after children.' That was considered a wonderful and great option to have.

Thirty one year old Tanya graduated from Moscow State University in Russian language and literature. She left Russia in 2000 when she married her second husband, a British academic. She is currently raising their two sons, aged 4 ½ and 6 weeks. She is also a journalist on a Russian newspaper, a business development manager for a consultancy firm, and as a hobby writes espresso stories (stories consisting of twenty five words). Her mother, who was born in the Tula region fifty five years ago, received her degree at the Tula Polytechnic Institute in IT. Her father is the same age as her mother and graduated from the same university, the same department. Her parents started working together for a big optical glass factory in the same town just outside Moscow where they live, but fifteen years ago her mother became an IT school teacher. Her dad also left the factory and is now an independent consultant, training people in using financial systems. Her younger sister went to the same university as Tanya in Moscow and earned her degree in applied linguistics. She now works for an advertising agency in Moscow as an accounts manager.

Grandparents and parents

My maternal grandparents, especially my grandmother, played a massive role in my childhood. There was lots of love, lots of attention. I spent all of the three month summer vacations with them in the Tula region. My grandma died soon after my first husband died in 1999 and that was a massive, massive loss for me; my granddad followed her in 2003. My grandmother, born in 1929, didn't have a higher education degree, but she worked all her life in sort of accountancy, the financial field. (I'm not 100% sure what exactly.) My grandfather was born in 1923; he entered World War II as a seventeen year old. After he came back, he met my grandmother and they got married. Then he went on to get a degree at the same time roughly as my mum. He got a degree in architectural design and designed pig sties, exciting things like that, but anyway agricultural things.

The other side of my family is a bit more hazy. I don't remember my paternal granddad who died when I was just ten, but I think his death was related to alcohol and I think my grandmother also had a drink problem. None of them had degrees. When I was a kid I saw them occasionally. My dad had two brothers who were both younger than him, but they have both died now. His youngest brother died of a heart attack; his little brother (who was a year or two years younger) died of alcohol disease. They had to sell the flat in the town where they lived and move out to the country, partly because of the money (I think someone conned them into selling their flat) and partly because I think of all the community there - it was a stigma. You know Russians, they were ashamed to keep going like that so they moved out into the country. My mum and dad visited them there and were horrified to see the state that they lived in. And then my grandmother died in 2002, just when I got pregnant with my first child.

The Soviet system wanted to encourage the working class (and the peasants) into the education system. So now it's gone full circle. My parents actually never became communists. My dad, for his career, wanted to but he was told that because he was part of the intelligentsia, he had to bring working-class guys with him. And that's where he stumbled.

Family accommodation

It was a flat, it's a Khrushchev era flat; by saying a two bed roomed flat we mean two rooms, a big and a small room. We shared a kitchen. In fact, we shared everything. I shared a bedroom with my sister. We lived in one of these flats until I was six. When my mum was expecting or just about to have my sister, we moved into this flat. Before that we lived in what was called an *obshezhitie*, a communal dormitory, a family dormitory. There we had one room and we had a long corridor. We had a communal kitchen, communal showers and communal loos -- all that stuff. I was pretty happy there as I had friends and all the rest of it, so I was fine for a while. My mum tells me now that I had lots of tantrums when we moved to the new flat because of being isolated. She on the other hand was ecstatic. Only now I have realized the degree to which she was so happy to have her own kitchen, to have our own loo!

What were you like as a teenager?

I was a very quiet girl until I changed school for the last two years. That's where I met my first husband. Before that I went to school where I was the odd one out because I did well academically and it was an environment in which it was not very popular to do well. I desperately wanted to blend in and I wasn't blending in. I hated the way I looked and all this teenage stuff ! My escape was reading. One of the books which probably stands out for me was *Jane Eyre* which I read in Russian. I just read, read and read certain bits again, and even now it holds some sort of special place. But I was interested in other things such as music. I played the violin and the piano a little bit. We had a piano in the flat.

University

I loved reading, I loved literature -- all our literature classes. I learnt to love writing essays, which was part of the way we did literature at school. I was pretty good at maths too. My mum, when I was about fourteen, just quite bluntly said you're either going into maths and follow our footsteps or you go into the humanities area. I think that my mum secretly, deeply down, wanted me to become a doctor, like many women. (Like I would like one of my sons to become doctors!) But I couldn't stand chemistry so becoming a doctor wouldn't happen. But then my mum found this wonderful thing to do called a speech doctor. In order to do this, you have to do humanities and it's part of the teacher training university, part of the

319

pedagogical institute and you had to do biology as an entrance exam and literature in the Russian bit, so we set our eyes on that. I even started to go to the preparatory course for that university. There was a massive gap between what you leave the school with in Russia (there still is now) and what you have to show when you enter university, especially a good university. So in the last couple of years you end up having to have private tuition in various things. I ended up having private tuition in literature and in the Russian language from two teachers from Moscow State University [MGU]. They said to me, ' Okay we know you want to do the speech therapy at university, but why don't you have a go at MGU.' So I did try and I did get in, apart from the fact that I had to do English and I was rubbish at English. I had school level English and that's why I could only get into the evening department. I spent my first year [1993] going to the evening department and having private classes in English at the same time. I managed to catch up and from the second year I worked hard. Thinking back, I probably never worked as hard in my life as I did then. So from the second year I switched to the normal full time department and I stayed there for two years. My private English classes over the two years cost a lot and I still think I owe it to my parents because back then, they paid for these two years more or less with about 90% of what my mum earned. I lived with my parents then until I got married.

Marriage

I met my first husband at school and we got married in 1996 when both of us were twenty. I was with my first husband four out of the five years of my university years. He went to teacher training (not MGU) but he fell ill the summer before going to university, so all of the years he was supposed to be there, he was off for a long time to have his treatments [before he died].He was very ill, so those were quite sad years for me.

How did you live when you were married?

When I was married I lived with my husband for six to eight months. We rented a flat and that was a big bone of contention, one of the things we should probably not have done. He was very influenced by his mum and his family. They saw the fact that we rented a flat as a big waste of money. They thought that we should live with them as they had a big enough flat by Russian standards for me to move in. I just couldn't even start thinking about that and I was very firm about that idea.

Do you think that your parents or his parents played a destructive role in this marriage? Yes, but also I was so young. It was like inertia or like you're slowing down but you're still moving. We were at that stage, at least I was in my kind of relationship with him, when we got married. We should never have married, if I were honest with myself. If I looked at myself in the mirror and asked, 'Do you see yourself spending your life with this young man?' --no way! But we were under pressure to get married because we were at that stage in the relationship. We went through his illness and it was a perfectly normal age to get married. We were both twenty and we had been together for four years; it just happened. But both sets of parents thought we were still kids and financially we were totally dependent on them. My mum fell out big time with his mum over the wedding, over petty things like who pays for the food, etc.. The whole philosophy, the mentality, was different in the two families. It was very difficult. The illness made it difficult. I also fell in love with another man while I was married, and probably that was when it was the point of no return for me. But my parents helped even though my mum didn't want me to get married. The fact that my mum was so unhappy about the marriage -- because we were told we couldn't have children, for example, because of his treatment – was a massive thing for me.

Discussion of sex, sex education and birth control

I didn't have any sex education at school. My mum did talk to me about periods and stuff when they started. But she still wouldn't discuss sex with me. My mum claims (and I believe her and I don't see any reason why not) that she hadn't had sex until she was married. She married my dad when she was 24 and you know that 'moral high ground' is still there in her head. I had sex with my first husband before we were married, but my mum and I never discussed that. She probably knew I did but she pretended she didn't know anything about it. She gave me a book when I was fifteen or fourteen about this sort of stuff.

I don't remember any problems getting contraceptives. We just used condoms. I never tried to get the pill, the one that you take every day, but I knew I could get one (the same one as I can use here). I knew I could get it in Russia at that time, but I remember being scared to death of taking the pill because it was deemed very harmful for the body. Definitely, I felt very awful about this several times. I have had to take the morning after pill and it makes you bleed for three days, and you are thinking, god what am I doing to my body?

Abortions

I didn't have any abortions but my girlfriends did. One of my closest girlfriends, who is now pregnant with her third child, had one in the university clinic when we were at university. She just said, 'Don't ask me about it. It was pretty grim as grim goes but yes better than many.' You have to remember that Moscow was probably better than the rest of the country. My mum had one but she didn't describe it to me. I don't think she was that traumatized by the procedure itself, maybe she was. But I know that she was deeply traumatized by the fact that she had done it. Nowadays one of my friends had one because she was pregnant and she already had a very young little boy. She had an injection, there in Russia.

What does equality mean?

Equality, I tell you what, it makes me laugh a lot! When I came here and was really learning about feminism, I thought, 'crikey we had all that in the Soviet Union and Russia!' We had that much equality in the Soviet Union and in Russia subsequently. I remember when my mum had my sister, her dream was to be at home, to stay at home. But she couldn't financially afford it and secondly it wasn't in the culture. The culture was to work, so is that equality? Women worked. She had pretty good maternity leave probably for a couple of years, but she still wanted to stay home; she wanted to look after me and to come to school, to music school, and take care of my sister, but she had to work. I think she started working part-time and then she changed to full time.

Now another thing -- equality in the house doesn't exist. My dad is an exception and I think my mum was very lucky and we are very lucky with my dad. He can't cook but he can do the washing up and he helped my mum a lot, looked after us when we were tiny. That was not very fashionable. It had not reached Russia yet, the new man and all that -- you know, man who looks after children and helps a lot in the house. I remember when I was at university, my dad always did breakfast for us. One of my friends at university was saying to me, 'Don't you ever think that, be realistic, be real, don't ever think that you will come across a man who'll be as good as your dad. Prepare yourself, men are not like that, they don't do breakfast!' I have to say my husband does, my second husband does do a lot of that; he does breakfast yes, he does ironing and stuff like my dad does!

What did femininity mean?

Femininity meant having to look after yourself. I suppose how I saw it back then was you have to let a man give you your coat, help you put your coat on, give you a hand as you step out of the bus, be a gentlemen and you a lady, as opposed to something else. The opposite of femininity was feminism: we loathed it, because we thought that feminists are women who don't like men giving them a hand when they get out of a car or out of a bus.

What about clothes?

When I suppose my mum was young, there was this deficit when you were happy to snatch a pair of boots regardless of the color and you could queue up for hours. When I was at university in the early nineties, there were lots of cheap stuff sold on the market. We had this flooding of all the crap which they bought in Turkey and China by the kilo and by weight. But there was loads of it. We had choice.

323

My mother didn't sew, but lots of her age group did. My grandmother always had things made for her in an atelier. She had a tailor and my granddad would always buy her material as a present for the 8th of March (International Women's Day) and for her birthday. So she would have a piece of cloth, she would take it and she would have things made for her. I remember loads of these clothes because I remember going to fittings with her; they were always the same design but different colors. It didn't happen for me. I bought things in the market, including the wedding dress for my first wedding that was bought in the market, and then I moved on to shops.

Strong woman in Russian culture

A massive, huge, huge woman in orange overalls became a symbolic figure of equality I think from the good side in Soviet times. That statue or icon is a woman working on the railway with a massive spanner in her hand, in the orange overall. But in the everyday culture in my mum's eyes, for example, that was the ultimate awful, awful thing about the Soviet woman. There was always the ideal that in the West women can actually say, 'I don't want to work, I want to look after children.' That was considered a wonderful and great option to have. But also a strong woman through literature is someone who is very feminine on the outside and tough on the inside, being able to face all sorts of challenges. Yes, I think that basically for men and women life in Russia is more challenging; it makes them tougher.

Did religion play any part in your life?

I wouldn't say my mum is religious, that would be an exaggeration, but she goes to the Russian Orthodox church. She tries to keep to the teachings of the church, and she was always quite keen on all these things. We were baptized when my sister was one and I was eight. The funny thing is that whole church going thing was part of my mum' s life, because my mum spent her childhood with my maternal great grandmother. The icons were always there in that house and in the village where my mum grew up. My maternal grandparents were very anti-religion because obviously a major part of their lives took place in the Soviet era. For example, their big passion in life was their allotment and their dacha; the dacha was a sort of massive tent. It was a lot [grounds] and they had bees and chickens, and all that. I remember my mum had a massive argument with my maternal grandmother about working over Easter and my babushka was saying 'Get in, it's rubbish. You have to dig, here is your spade, go on' and my mum was saying, 'We're not supposed to, it's Easter.'

So she learnt from her grandmother and I sort of learnt from my grandmother. Well I wouldn't call myself an atheist, but I wouldn't call myself a deeply religious person. I don't think I have been influenced by either grandparents or my parents. I think I have been influenced by literature, by poetry. I took a lot from Yesenin, Bloch and other silver age poets in the 1920's. It struck me that I read somewhere in some literary criticism that people like Yesenin and definitely all the others (Bloch, Akhmatova and others), who are supposed to be deeply religious from within, were more taken by the whole symbolic side of things -- the icons, the music, that side of things, the ornamental. Don't get me wrong. I go to church every now and again, but I haven't been for about a year. But before I was pregnant I would make a point of going there quite regularly.

Life in London

Why did you leave Russia?

I left Russia because I met my second husband. I was working on a summer job in the small town where my parents live, in the same optical plant where my parents started their careers. I was working as an interpreter for someone else and he came. There was a contract for large optical mirrors and he came for an acceptance test or something like that. I was interpreting for him and I was also asked to show him the Kremlin. He's an optical scientist now and works at the university, but back then he worked for a company. We got married in Moscow in June 2000 and I moved here in September.

How difficult was it to adjust to:

Climate

Can I say I didn't have any problems with the climate? Lots of people here say that you must miss the snow, whereas I say that after seven years, I still don't miss the snow! If I go to Russia in the winter -- and I love going to Russia in winter -- I have, let us say, ten days there and that's enough snow for me.

Language

I spoke English okay when I moved here. But certainly there was a degree of shock about the accents. In fact the people who lived in this house before us were on all the lists for cold calling and sales. The phone kept ringing, we kept answering it, and I just couldn't understand a word sometimes. But I could understand talking to people in person. I got a job about six months after I got here and that's when I think I kind of rapidly caught up. If you want to say I was completely okay, that would be wrong: to say that it was a massive shock and massive problem for me would be wrong. I was somewhere in the middle. When I first moved here I was very aware that when I went to the supermarket, I could communicate perfectly well. But at the same time I was aware of what people were thinking, such as, 'Oh god, she's foreign!' Now I am kind of proud of being foreign and having an accent and thinking, 'Yeah right, I am foreign, any problems with that?'

Property

When I first moved to the UK we were still renting, but two months later we moved into this house which my husband had already found. We now have a joint mortgage, so my husband took me to the building society and the bloke said, 'I have to talk you through what a mortgage is' and he did; he showed me the graphs, the interest going up, the set rate, etc.., and then I got home and said, 'Talk me through it again.' Then several months later I asked him to talk me through it again; it had to sink in gradually.

Lack of family

It was pretty tough without my family and I still miss them all. It's a new dimension with the children, when I know that my friends in Russia drop their children off every weekend and have a good life and I can't do that! My husband's father died but his mum lives in Brighton, but it's a totally different sort of relationship between him and his mum. She phones up every week and we talk, we go to see her but it's not the same. When I first came here I had academic aspirations and was planning to do my PhD in Moscow University and I actually did two out of three years, that is, I did the two years postgraduate course of *aspirantura* and I did all the exams that one had to have before you are qualified to write and defend your PhD. My first year here I was going back and forth to Moscow to take exams. That eased the transition.

Childcare issues

My oldest son is at nursery, an independent nursery; he's being going since the age of 8 months when I worked part-time. He is four and a half now and he will be going to a state school in September. I put him in the nursery at the age of 8 months, much to the disgust of my mum! But she realized that she never actually had aspirations for me to be a full time mum; I think she would hate that actually as she put a lot of effort into us excelling ourselves in various fields. Anyway I went back to work, three days a week, and my son went for two days a week at first to the nursery. My husband did one day of childcare and I did two days, and then we changed so that my son would go three days to nursery while I looked after him for two days. With my second child I am allowed a year off; I am planning to go back to work when he goes to nursery. My eldest will go to the state school as we cannot afford private school.

My parents and education

My mum' s view (and she doesn't say it)--because children are the center of the universe in Russia-- is that she is obsessed with private education in this country. She spent 90% of her salary when I was already eighteen, maybe nineteen. Basically over the four years my parents were spending loads of money on trying to get me the best education; I did get the best education I could in Russia which is all thanks to them. Then they spent loads of money on my sister who didn't have enough points from her entrance exams at university so we had to pay for her education. Her university (my university!) was really cheap -- fifteen hundred dollars a year -- but my second husband and I paid because I felt I had to pay something back. So for a couple of years we paid for my sister's education. Then my parents, my dad, was earning more reasonable money and they paid for her.

Have you found the British friendly?

Wonderful! It's partly because of my husband's relationships, partly just because it's complicated. Still the degree of close, close, close, closeness I have with my Russian friends and my family, I probably don't have with any British friends. But I have one very close girlfriend who is from Yorkshire. My husband is a fair bit older than I am and he's got a daughter who is only a couple of years younger than me; we are pretty close as friends, so I would say she is a friend as well. I socialize with loads of British people and I'm very happy to spend time with them. If you dig really deeply I think there is warmth in British people and they are sociable.

Status matters

I have worked as a journalist and I interview people and it's much easier often to interview Brits than when you step into the world of Russian people who have done well for themselves (and all these very rich Russians). I have been to parties and to posh do's and I have enough brains to understand that having a Chloe bag on your shoulder doesn't prove you are a good person! But at the same time I know that I'll be assessed on the type of handbag that I carry and I can't afford. I would love to be able to afford a Chloe bag. I was interviewing one of these ladies who has a big flat in Knightsbridge and she was saying, 'Yes, I can afford whatever I fancy, I can afford a Birkin bag.' She said what she hates is the whole status and the importance of having 'that' bag on your hand,

and she said whenever you walk into a restaurant in Moscow, they check you out -- they check what you are wearing, whom you're with, your age.

I kind of find now with Russian people that the way you dress, what car you drive-- all these sorts of things matter much more than to the Brits. I mean people in the public eye, such as footballers and pop stars, and others you come across who have done well for themselves, money wise, in Russian people the degree of arrogance is much higher. I just think with the British, basically it's common knowledge, that the better your upbringing, the better you are with people, that is, have good manners.

Shopping

I loved it in the beginning and still do. I'm getting over it a bit, and getting a bit more jaundiced. It totally went to my head when I came here, the fact that there were sales, for example, the whole concept of sales. We have loads of sales here now so I don't feel I have to buy all this stuff just because it's half price or whatever. But when I first got here, I couldn't get enough of it!

In Moscow back in the nineties GUM [the State General Store] was full of pretty obscure makes and things. I think it is better now. I mean they don't just have Gucci and Prada. If you go to GUM now thank god they have Monsoon, Next, Zara and Mango, things which are okay. I wouldn't say they were affordable for the whole country but they are affordable for my sister and I don't think my sister is extremely rich. There things are evening out, some sort of middle class thing is going on.

Russian food

I miss it! I see chocolate bars from Russia, caviar --things I miss and things I can get now in the Russian shop are things like tomatoes in the jar, pickled tomatoes, fish like smoked mackerel (the smoked mackerel you buy here is a different type of smoking). The one in Russia is much greasier. Actually I thought I was craving it, I thought I was missing it. Then I went to the Russian shop and bought some. I had one piece and

329

thought I can't eat that, I am not used to that anymore. Waitrose sells great Russian bread, and every now and again I buy it. I love the brown bread and I think (and my mum agrees) that the one in Waitrose actually tastes better than most breads you buy in Russia now. Sadly there is lots of food around in Russia, but the standards are lower.

I remember the time when we had vouchers to buy food in the total deficit sort of era, in the early 90s. That was the lowest of the low, and then you stand (I remember as a kid) and spend time in these queues, to get things like sugar, butter, cheese and sausage, god knows what else, horrendous. My mum looks back now and she has shivers down her spine!

Role of husband

My second husband is more involved in shopping, cooking, childcare, cleaning, that sort of thing. Even by British standards, he's quite good. I don't know what he was like with his first wife. Sometimes I think he runs the house and I just help him.

Would you like to go back to Russia?

Not in the foreseeable future, no. But who knows, I wouldn't be totally adverse to it although I enjoy living here.

What do you miss the most?

The people! I miss my friends. Even though I do have loads of friends here, I had a very good of circle of friends. I miss the fact that the last time I went to Moscow in the autumn, I remember I got on the phone at two o'clock in the afternoon and by 7pm I had ten people around the table in a restaurant in Moscow. At such short notice they didn't think anything of it and said 'Yes, we will come'. They changed their plans, they dropped whatever and they made an effort and as it happens we had a great time. I also really miss going to the theatre because despite all that was going on in my first marriage, we went to the theatre a lot; throughout my university years I would feel hard done by if I hadn't seen anything at least twice a month. There are some other big and small things, like I miss the shops being open until late.

How would you characterize British society?

I would say diverse, extremely fair and I think the UK is more politically evolved than Russia. For example, I would also say that people here are more confident. There is a big question of trust here. I just think sometimes you're so naïve, you don't know what not trusting is and what it means not to trust your government. For example, when I left Russia we didn't trust our government (what's going on) and we shouldn't trust it because we knew. I was still there with Yeltsin but Putin just came to power as well and it was all very euphoric back then. Unfortunately deep down I follow politics, because I worked once in the news and the news sort of bugs you once you get it into your system. I'm all switched on but somewhere you just think, 'Does it help, will it really change my life so much whether we have Labour or Tory next election? Will it change my life as much as a change from Yeltsin to Putin would have?' The answer is no. And I remember I was speaking last year in an interview with an Australian/Russian lady who was a lawyer. She said to me that the day when Russia starts being a stable, in some ways civilize, state is when the personality of the leader would not affect the life of individuals. And I thought she really nailed it for me.

My boys won't be Russian even though they will be able to speak Russian. But they will still be English and have an English mentality.

ADDITIONS:

Death and the cold

I was thinking about *death*. I think there a different attitude to it here and in Russia. Take the whole thing about the open coffin. At Yeltsin's funeral, there is a massive picture in the Russian *Hello* magazine and there is a close up of Yeltsin lying in an open coffin. It's something which every Russian person -- some early on, some later on -- at points in their life go through. A relative dies, friends die, you go to funerals and you look in the face of that person. When both of my grandparents died, they were lying on the table at home. When I first moved here a week later unfortunately my husband's dad died and it was a big thing for his sisters who are all grown up and older than me. They had a big issue with going to see their dad in the undertakers, with going to say goodbye to him. They had never seen a dead body, and they didn't want to see it even though it was their father. I found that deeply shocking. I found that very infantile and there are a lot of other smaller things which I still find pretty infantile with Western people. I think because the [Russian] weather is so bad, the weather makes us tougher; it makes us more ready to face the challenges, it's not just cold outside. We have to live in that cold, go to work, stay in the house. Even when the central heating is on around the clock, you can still feel the cold.

Irina (30)

Life in Russia

I think I will treat them [a son and a daughter] equally and absolutely the same. But I will say to my son, 'be strong, you are a boy, boys sometimes fight and they get scratches or scratched knees and black eyes and it's all right.' For the girl I would say, 'be gentle, you're a girl: you should be a lady one day, mind your nails, why don't you comb your hair in the morning.'

Irina left Russia in 2000 to study in Scotland. She is now teaching Russian at a university in London on a part-time basis while working for her PhD and caring for her 20 month old baby son. She is thirty. Her mother has two higher education degrees, the first in physiology and the second in speech correction and learning difficulties, and her father went to the polytechnic in Leningrad where he studied rocket engineering. They are both living in Smolensk. Her mother grew up in Smolensk whereas her father spent his childhood in Kronstadt, not far from St. Petersburg. He's currently 66 and her mother, his second wife, is 50. She also has two stepbrothers (one is 36, the other 45) from her father's previous marriage. Both are higher educated, both spent their childhood in Smolensk and both are still living there.

Role of grandparents

My maternal grandparents are alive but I've never seen my paternal grandparents. They were teachers all their lives and had higher educations as well. Even my great-grandmother was a teacher and had a higher education, so it's like a dynasty of teaching. My maternal great grandmother played a great role in my childhood; she was my best friend until she died. She did all the sorts of things a housewife should do, but most of the time she was trying to please me. I was the center of her world. She died when I was 12.

Childhood

333

I was a good girl. I was thinking about my education so I was taking a lot of private lessons with a teacher so as I would be up to the level to get into the university. The passing level was very high at the university which I chose; I think it was like twenty one persons applying for one place so if you made one mistake you wouldn't get into university at all. You had a chance to pay a huge sum of money which my parents said they would pay. But I didn't want that: I wanted to do it by myself first of all and to do it free of charge. It was really an opportunity given by the government, by the state, so I wanted that. I had two dogs so that's another hobby I had; they were of pure breed so I had to educate them, to train them properly, to go to different exhibitions, to groom them, and I acquired a degree in expertise of dogs as well.

University

Actually I wanted to go to Moscow or St. Petersburg, but the situation in 1996 when I graduated from school was not very stable in general. My parents were a bit worried about what would happen to me if I went. They thought I should stay close to them, so I decided not to fight them and go to the university where I lived in Smolensk. The university was good, the department was excellent, all my friends were nearby, so I decided to stick with that. I chose the Department of Foreign Languages and a lot of other students who were studying with me didn't think about doing teaching either. We wanted to get a good degree so we went for languages and wanted to learn other disciplines as well.

Marriage

I got married in 2001. My husband is actually Russian. I was doing my diploma work in Scotland. My aunt (who left the USSR in 1988) was living in Scotland so I went to stay with her to do this work. My husband is my aunt's former colleague. He's from St. Petersburg. He has a PhD in biology and pharmacology and he worked here for quite a long time as a scientist as well as doing some teaching at Guy's and St. Thomas's [hospitals]. He is seventeen years older than I am (and remember, my parents are sixteen years apart!) Now he is in business.

Sex, sex education and birth control

I think I learned about sex from my parents. They were quite educated to tell me about such things so I knew about them. Maybe times have changed. We had some lessons at school but it was like a theater or a comedy. Everyone was laughing. Teachers were trying to explain with some words. It was something like a fairy tale -- not meaning everything, trying to conceal a lot of things. So basically the education was absolutely not very good. It was as if, 'Children be careful about sex because it can lead to pregnancy and remember, you will not find small children in a Cabbage Patch.'

Especially in Soviet times, people would try not to say too much about such things because the general ideology was that it was a dirty subject. But everyone wanted them [contraceptives] and I know that every woman was trying to find something or to find a doctor who would help her.

Contraceptives are now not available free of charge as they are here in the UK, but you can buy them at any pharmacy. It actually depends on the person: you can buy pills or whatever you need, all the varieties.

Abortion

They didn't talk about abortions at school but I knew about abortions. I don't think any of my friends had had any abortions. My mother warned me [about pregnancy and abortions] and explained everything, but I must admit I was not active even though I knew everything. Abortions were probably used as a form of contraception because a lot of older women said that they had had a lot of abortions and they felt that it's even better for the body to have an abortion than to take any pills, any chemical substances like that. I can tell you that the situation now is still not very good. My mum (who is bewildered by the situation) told me about some girl, the daughter of a friend, who is turning sixteen in May. She is going to give birth in February, and she is not going to keep the child. Her parents and grandparents are not interested in the baby at all and her mother didn't know about her pregnancy until she was seven months. The girl was

335

good at hiding her pregnancy. So the school does nothing, the parents try to avoid these talks as well. This is just a situation from neighbors, I don't remember who exactly it was, but I was really shocked.

Birth in the Soviet Union and Russia

In my mother's time, the worst thing was that they didn't allow her to feed the baby for three days, saying it would harm the baby. So they were asking the mothers to milk themselves and put the milk in the refrigerator in a big pot, then boiling it. That day they tried to feed the babies with the bottles, but all the mothers were trying to breastfeed the babies, but it was prohibited; if you were caught the baby could be taken to an infectious ward. As my mum indicated, she was taken to a maternity hospital and it was like a prison!

Now you can pay. You have the same care but your husband can stay with you and your mum can be with you. So you have nearly the same conditions as here or even better conditions but you have to pay for it. If you go to a state maternity hospital, then you have to undress before you enter the building because there are bacteria, infections and colds everywhere. They give you some gowns that are yellowish as they sterilize them specially and you have only to bring in slippers. You are left there and after three or five days depending on your condition you will be out. Your husband will see the baby only from the window and he will be in the street waving to you; you will be on the fifth floor or probably on the seventh floor. In Russia the sanitation is really ridiculous.

Were there any problems specific to women?

I think sometimes men probably think that they have more advantages just because they are men. There's a tendency like this everywhere because, when an employer thinks about taking on women for any position, they think about women getting married, getting pregnant, having children and so on. Men are not so family committed so I think this problem comes everywhere and this thought comes to me first of all. Apart from that, I can't imagine anything else.

How do you picture the ideal woman in the Soviet Union?

Actually I don't remember but my personal opinion was that it should be something like my mother, who was working, taking an active part in the family, busy all the time. The other times were quite hard for everyone and for us as well; she was trying to do the best with our free time. We went travelling in Russia a lot. It was not easy to buy clothes or nice things; if there was one factory which produced a line of clothes, everyone had the same thing. My mum went to sewing classes. She bought a sewing machine and she was trying to do something for us. I got a lot of praise from other people, saying someone was abroad or somewhere, but actually it was a dress made from my father' s old shirts; the collar was made maybe a little wavy and the rest was quite nice and the colors were quite nice; she tried to use her imagination. She used patterns from the magazines but at that time especially if you went to the clothes shops you could buy dark blue, red, white and some ugly green cotton, very ugly, nothing else!

Actually now one thing comes to me about an 'ideal woman', namely, the posters which were highly professional -- that was the ideal female person. It's important that that has changed.

What did femininity mean? Would that have meant nicer clothes?

I would say that I was not thinking about that, I thought I was the best. I think femininity should be inside. As for makeup, at that time I was too young, but I always had some cream; my mum bought me some child's cream and I was applying it so I was learning from her. What she had was French mascara. It was important to her that she didn't want me to look like a peasant! Yes, absolutely, you know the point very well.

Balancing work and family

My mum at some point had to change her employment because I couldn't go or rather I wouldn't go to the kindergarten. I was crying, I was holding my shoes, I was not going to the toilet at all and they were just worried about me. So she had to leave and go to collect me and I was so upset. Then my father said to my mother, 'You know that you have a suitable education, so why don't you change your employment.' I could then be at this kindergarten but in a different group and it worked. So for some time she sacrificed herself for my sake.

Prime emphasis on children and the degree of closeness to parents

I'm not sure about every family but I think in my family I was the center of everything and our family was really a family. We were three of us and everyone was supporting each other. We were really a family. Sometimes people live together, they are related but they're not a family. My family was really very close. My eldest stepbrother was already in the army when my parents married and my youngest stepbrother was living with his mum, but he came to us very often. We were going on holiday together so I never thought that he was my stepbrother. He was my brother. We were just living in different places.

Life in London

Why did you leave Russia?

I left because of my husband. I came here to do my diploma, I met my husband, but I thought I was going back because I had my final examinations and I had to get clearance to put all the papers straight then. I came to London to be with my husband.

How difficult was it to adjust to:

Climate

It's really a very surprising question. When people in Russia think about London they think about rain, fog, etc.. But compared to Russian weather, this climate is an absolutely wonderful climate. There is no winter; if you have snow it's a couple of hours of snow! It's absolutely wonderful because you can wear the clothes you want, but in Russia I was wearing tights and jeans. In winter I don't like the cold at all so I tried not to wear skirts at all as it was too cold. Here you are quite flexible: you can have one pair of boots for all the seasons, even in summer. In Russia you would not survive without winter boots with thick natural fur, without any winter fur coat, preferably a natural fur coat.

People

First of all it is very difficult to find authentic British people, that is, English, Scottish, Welsh or Irish. It is very difficult because wherever you are, you see a lot of people from all over the world and I think that people who are not authentically from the British Isles are more open to communication, for meeting and for socializing. **Are most of your friends or acquaintances not British?** *Now* they are all British absolutely, because they have become British; they have become naturalized. They are from other countries, from other backgrounds. I would say that the British/British are more concentrated on themselves; in some respects maybe they think they are better but I don't know. The majority of people we know, even our neighbors, are not originally British.

Language

I studied language at the university in Smolensk and learnt some basics but I would say that the basics are not the real language. We were reading a lot of classic novels and 19th century books, like Jack London and Charles Dickens. When they were trying to make us speak that language and use the structures of that language, they [19c English] are so huge and heavy that a modern language has nothing to do with what is now [current], what is realistic. Sometimes when I started speaking here, people looked very suspiciously at me as they were old fashioned words.

My ideas (about what I wanted to do) have changed a bit since coming here because when I was finishing my education in Russia I thought about acquiring another higher education degree in economics or law or something else at Moscow University or in St Petersburg; then I might move on to commerce, banking, business or economics. But here it would have been a very tight competition for me as I come from another country. I speak English with an accent. I have to think about language [English] because probably if I had spent or would spend a lot of time and money upgrading my language, then it would have been better. I am doing a lot of Russian work, and speaking a lot of Russian at home. At some point I was practically not speaking English at all as I was pregnant with a small baby.

Property

My husband previously was living in north London and we decided to stay somewhere close because he had an office there. Now we have a garden, a tube station not far from the house, and a park nearby. So we have everything that we need. But hunting for the house was quite difficult: we were looking, looking, looking and found nothing that we wanted. We had a budget and then we established a connection with an estate agent who showed us a lot of houses. Some of them were to go to auction. You had to write down your bid, so it could have been the end for us. Then two weeks later we would know whether we had got the house, whether we had the highest bid or too low of a bid. We had twenty minutes to decide whether we wanted this house or not, but when you know all the adjacent roads quite well, you know it's all right! We now have four bedrooms so it is a semi-detached house. I would say we live comfortably here in London as well. I lived quite comfortably in Russia because we had four bedrooms, two reception rooms, kitchen/diner, a spare kitchen, two toilets and two bathrooms.

Schools

If we had enough money I would prefer to send my child to an independent school because really their standard of education is better. My neighbor's youngest daughter is the same age as my son and we meet to play. Her eldest son is seven now and he goes to the [state] school next to ours. Sometimes they have, I think, silly talks: they are imposing some information about Islam. He is not an Islamic boy. Maybe it is the

340

influence in this country but sometimes I think they are not doing the right thing, because a lot of children are from Islamic backgrounds and the school has to make a huge stress on Islam and Islamic culture. But if the children are Christian, give them an equal opportunity or divide them into different groups. But all of them are learning Islam. I think it's not right.

Transport

I must say that it is a bit better than in Russia. It is not as crowded but it is expensive, enormously expensive; it is ridiculously priced. If I had a chance, I'd go by train. I don't use buses, it takes too long and with a child it is really a nightmare, so I drive. But to the university I take the underground. This is the fastest way and we are too greedy to pay £8 congestion charge just to enter the congestion zone.

Shopping

I hate to go shopping Friday, Saturday or Sunday because a lot of people are there and I don't like those women who go shopping as their job. We are members at the David Lloyd [sports] club. Before I had my child I played a lot of tennis. A lot of the women are just dropped off, do nothing, spend money; and a lot of them were going to Brent Cross [shopping mall], buying clothes, trying them on, and then returning them the next week or even within two days, even without wearing them. They were doing it day by day and keeping just a small amount of the purchases because they really don't need much, just some sports equipment, maybe two or three outfits.

Makeup

I think at the moment Western and Russian views coincide absolutely. If you go to Moscow or some other place, you see the same brands or even if you go to smaller shops in St Petersburg or somewhere, the brands are the same. I think that Russian women, compared to British women, spend much more time on their looks even just applying cosmetics and makeup and they spend more money on that as well.

341

Russian food

Some things I do miss, but now it's much easier because a lot of Lithuanian and Baltic markets are opening here. We have a shop nearby so we can buy practically everything there, whatever we previously missed -- *kaffir and tvarog* -- and Russian bread, but you can buy it at Waitrose, so I never missed Russian bread because I could buy it there. But French bread is better!

Has your husband's role(s) changed by being in the UK? [she speaks as a second wife]

I think he is like cognac or wine; he gets better with age. Probably what I got was much better than what his former wife got because he was very young when he was married for the first time. He is still bursting with energy because his character is very strong (if I can put it like that) and sometimes now he's not reacting so much, because he is wiser than previously. He helps with childcare, but not with cleaning. Sometimes he cooks, that is, he cooks when he wants to; it's not his responsibility. I try to cook because I want my family to eat healthily, but if he has the desire and the time, he can cook. Sometimes we shop together, sometimes we do it separately; it depends on the timing. Sometimes in the evening he stays with the child and I can do something, but I have to push it.

What role do your parents and/or your in-laws play?

His parents are still in St Petersburg. We try to go to see them as much as possible and we want them to come as much as possible but my parents are still working. My husband's mum is still working as well at the university; she is a professor who has lots of students and lots of PhD students, so she is busy all the week through. It is quite hard for them to find time to come for a long time but they have tried to come to stay with us. We are on the telephone three or four times a week so they know everything about our lives; we send them photos, videos, so they are really part of our family.

When either my parents or my husband's parents come, it is not a problem for us whether they stay, because they are part of the family every day. Of course, if I had my mum or my husband's mum not far from me, it would be much easier even to go somewhere or to bring a child to them and say okay, I'll be back in two or three hours. So it would be nice if my parents or his parents were around to be of some support. They would be delighted but because we are so far apart, I can't do that unfortunately.

I've got a nanny who comes certain times a week but she couldn't come more times because she has another family to look after as well. We wanted a Russian lady so that she would help my child to learn Russian; she was the only suitable candidate.

If you had another child, a girl, do you think you would treat her differently?

I'm not sure, but I think I will treat them equally and absolutely the same. But I will say to my son, 'Be strong, you are a boy, boys sometimes fight and they get scratches or scratched knees and black eyes and it's alright.' For the girl I would say, 'Be gentle, you're a girl: you should be a lady one day, mind your nails, why don't you comb your hair in the morning.'

So gender would come into this?

Yes, it's a part of the [femininity]process because if a mother or a person close by will not tell a future woman that something about her outfit is not right or probably square (for example, check that the skirt is not right for her hips because it makes her look bigger and her bottom part is already quite big!), I think the advice should come from the family and not from someone outside. If someone outside tells me, 'You know this lipstick or those trousers do not suit your figure', that would just be upsetting. But if my mum or my friends say that to me, then I will be okay. So it would be nice if my parents or his parents were around to be of some support.

Is religion important for you?

I was christened in Russia as a Russian Orthodox and so is my son. When I was in Russia, I did not go to church every week. The belief is in my heart. I can say it like that but I follow good traditions. We celebrate the festive days and we try to do as God tells us.

We still believe. My husband and I belong to the Russian Orthodox Church in London. I wear a cross. We are not going to church here a lot, simply because we have a problem with the church. It's not open when people want to come; it is open only at the time of services and sometimes you can't come between 8am and 10am. I want to come a bit later in the day and they have to close simply because they want to have some rest or something. I know a lot of people who go to church simply because there is a religious weekend school for children; this is an opportunity to talk Russian. They organize a lot of events for children, like New Year, Christmas, Russian Christmas, Father Frost, Easter and so on. So for children the facilities there are quite all right. Probably when my child is a bit older I will go more regularly, as I know some people who go there regularly, believe in God really strong and attend a lot of services.

What other values do you bring from Russia?

My neighbors are Spanish, Japanese, Chinese. What I can say is that we have three children over here [two stepchildren and her baby son] and though they were raised here, still they are Russian inside. Even our eldest [her stepchild] --who is twenty years old now --is Russian inside but British outside. As they are coming from a Russian background, they live here and I think they would love to live in London or the Western world. It would be quite difficult for them to go back to Russia, but they do go back to stay there for a month or two with grandparents or with friends. So they do not lose their connections. They are proud to be Russians! They like it there, they like the food, they like the culture. In other words, the children are still Russians; they are not losing their connections. If let's say someone said, 'Okay, forget everything about Russia, about your past, be only British,' still something would be just blank there where all the Russianness should be. I read stories to my son in Russian; I buy Russian folk books, folk songs and minor things because when he goes to school, he will read English, only English, and this is his only chance to learn about where he is coming from.

Free time

I divide my free time between studying, because I have to do my PhD, and then leisure -- sports, tennis. I would have taken a lot of tennis lessons and I enjoy it. Probably I would play some bridge, the card game, because a lot of friends of ours play bridge in their free time. It's not so bad if you can establish a tradition of playing bridge at home. My husband doesn't play bridge but he plays some other games similar to bridge; bridge is two or four times more complicated than those games but when we play with our friends or even our elder children, it's somehow getting us together. It's really a nice and enjoyable time. With our friends who live in Moscow it's a competition between families of tennis and card games, and studying. But it's children above all; so I'm not talking that if I had free time I would completely forget about my children. They are my priority, so I have to do whatever is necessary for them and then comes our spare time.

What do you miss the most?

My parents, my family actually, because again there's a saying, 'It's not the place that makes people better; it's the people that make the place better'. It's really a Russian saying and we are not a bad people.

Would you like go back to Russia?

I think now it's not a problem where I live. The point is who I live with! Providing I'm with my husband, there's another Russian saying that says, 'You can be happy, even in a tent.' So if we are together we can go many places.

What do you value most about living in London?

Being so close to a lot of nice and beautiful places. A lot of people say now that London is the cultural capital of the world, not Paris anymore.

345

You know that you can take the tube to the center of town and have a walk and enjoy some nice paintings there or go by car. It's a mixture of culture and the city itself -- the image of what it brings and offers. You can go to your right and you will find a lot of interesting places, and you can go to your left and you will find better places!

How would you characterize British society?

It's a difficult question, simply because British society is quite diverse. It comprises a lot of nations, a lot of cultures, a lot of financial backgrounds as well. There are a lot of good spots and bad spots and some no go zones, so I think this is the main problem. Maybe it's not fair to say such things since I came to this country not long ago, but I think that Britain is not made of rubber. They still keep their borders open for a lot of people from very poor countries. I couldn't say that I came here for asylum; I came here because I fell in love and my husband was here. What I was trying to say was if people with no financial problems are coming to the country for a life they want to have, not seeking a better life compared to what they have there, it would make a country better, but if some poor African people are coming here, then they're not earning a lot of money and they are just thinking, how can we become British citizens in order to get some benefits, to get a state flat and then how can they pass it on to their children. Then they think of having three children to get child benefit and calculate that they will live better than how they were living in their African country, even on a very low income. I think this is the main problem of British society. The country will not tolerate a lot of people like this.

I have actually seen a girl like this. She was trying to 'take' our son. The mother was from Sri Lanka. The father was from a Caribbean country. The daughter had twin brothers and one younger brother from different fathers. They all were black fathers, so the Sri Lankan mother is still not white but the mother's dream was to get a flat and her dream came true. She had a three bedroom flat for all the children and she was on benefits; she never worked and there were problems when the mum didn't come home for three days. The girl was phoning the police and looking for her

346

mother. The girl was working, paying rent to her mum for living in the flat and she told us that they were a lot of friends who were living the same as she was and that this was quite normal. I fought like a tiger to break her and my stepson apart. It worked because I was sympathizing with her but when she was telling me these things normally (as if it was an ordinary situation for me) it's an alarming situation. He [my stepson] was [too] young.

ADDITIONS:

Recent times in Russia

You were asking a lot of questions about Soviet times. I was trying to tell you as much as possible about Soviet times, but in recent Russian times it was very hard for everyone. A lot of educated women had to forget their hopes, their desires, their dreams -- everything. They had to fight for their rights and for their living because the government was not paying money to teachers, doctors or nurses and all people in similar occupations. The only place you could earn something was in commerce, so a lot of people with degrees or PhDs or higher education sacrificed that and went into commerce simply because you can earn decent money or just money for living. In the town where my grandmother lives, teachers were not getting any money for nine or ten months; it was very difficult for them to survive and they had to grow some vegetables during summer, then sell them at markets so that they would have something for their families. Of course they were preserving it [food]; it was their food for winter, for everything, but it was extra money in order to buy some clothes and necessary things which they can't produce themselves. I think it was an awful time for teachers and doctors (who were mostly women but there were some, very few, men). You have to be nice to people, you have to educate people. But if you're hungry, for example, or if you don't have a pair of tights or shoes or you're shoes are broken and you can't afford to buy a new pair, that situation was really as bad as war time. Society divided very fast, between poor and rich, and for some people, even the rich people, it was just beyond reach

347

Points of Arrival

How is it for them?

No matter what their original reason for coming here, most of the women who have shared their experiences are very happy to be living in the United Kingdom. Some are still adjusting to a life very different from that that they had in the Soviet Union or Russia and in this process, some have been more successful than others. The need for adjustment and a variable degree of success in achieving it are both major aspects of any process of migration. It is for this reason that the questions in the second section of the interviews above begin with the key question of **how difficult was it to adjust** to a variety of factors. What follows is a brief review and examination of the most universal and frequent responses, as well as the most distinctive and unique. As throughout, the details and interesting bits are in the fine points and specifics of the interviews themselves.

How difficult was it to adjust to life in the UK?

On the question of the **climate** in the UK, many of the respondents rate the climate as very acceptable to excellent. One or two suffered illnesses which they related to climate, that is, they felt they were sick because of the weather and/or until they adjusted to the climate; on the other hand, one woman compared the more acceptable and temperate British weather very favorably with the heat and humidity she experienced in Russia. The only common but significant complaint from some was that they missed the seasonal changes that occur in Russia, especially winter, the lack of snow and all that that entails. Childhood memories of sledding and skiing were noted and pined for with a degree of obvious nostalgia.

The initial problems when moving to a new society concern where to live and how to get about. The process of finding **accommodation or property** can be very difficult and time-consuming, let alone costly. This has been true for many of the women, especially because the women and their husbands knew nothing about the different areas of London or about the whole process of purchasing property in this society. Some who came alone found

348

accommodation with friends of friends or relatives. Some but not all who came with British husbands found accommodation already established for them. Yet others, like Maya and Helena, originally joined their husbands in small towns in Britain and, having come from large cities like Moscow or Leningrad, found adapting to this more constricted life a very difficult process. They frankly admit that they didn't really adjust to life in the UK until they moved to London. Another group of women, those in their 50s whose husbands came as international civil servants, originally found accommodation managed by the Russian trade delegation. After perestroika, when they were entitled to leave this accommodation, they all went out to find private housing and experience the freedom that that entailed. Some of the other women are still living in rented accommodation and are hoping to purchase property when that becomes feasible.

On the question of getting about in their new society, for most of the women the issues involved were those raised by the **transport** system in London. Here, there was a mixed reaction. Many complained about the high cost of transport in the capital. Several remarked that the tube was inefficient and unreliable ['it's a nightmare!'] and compared it unfavorably with the Moscow metro which runs much more frequently, with fewer long breaks of service. In its defense, some noted the fact that the London transport system consists of a very wide ranging network and commended London for this. On the whole the buses were praised without qualification. One woman commented on London's general approach to bicycle riders, something which seems to be changing as more and more bicycle lanes are introduced in the capital and as climate change, the impact of the automobile and other ecological issues gather momentum.

While the importance of both accommodation and transport cannot be underestimated in terms of getting organized, as might be expected, **language** is one of (if not) *the* most important variables enabling someone to fit into, let alone enjoy and experience, a new society. Many of the women had studied English in school in Russia in that they often read the classics which consisted of English (and at times American) literature mainly from the 19th, but also sometimes from the 20th, century. But when they attempted to put this acquired language to use on the streets of Britain using somewhat archaic if not colloquial English, they were instantly recognized as foreigners. Maya puts it like this: 'I was absolutely terrified to discover that nobody could understand me -- no, it's not that. Whenever I opened my mouth, people started speaking very slowly to me. My language was very literary so when I used to go to the little local shop and ask for something, I used to use words I would use in Russian like exaggerate or exacerbate; basically the words were too long or too complicated.... I felt terribly insulted when people started using their hands to explain things to me!' She goes on to explain how embarrassed she was and how the fact that she was spoken to as if she were a child really knocked her confidence. Such experiences were replicated by many of the other women.

Some of the women, however, did not experience these difficulties, mainly because they learned their English from sources other than in the Soviet school system. Although Helena's mother Anna was an English translator, Helena admits she learned her English from listening to American musicals. Masha says she learned English from her own family who were very anglicized. The other side of the coin comes from people like Sophia and Kira, the former blaming her inability to obtain a suitable job in London on her imperfect command of the English language. Kira's way of solving the language problems is to master a new career, a new profession for her as a London guide in which she can utilize her native language by taking groups of Russians around London.

Education has always been very important for Russians. In Soviet times, it was one of the main avenues of social mobility. Most significantly education and culture often went hand-in-hand, with education playing a critical and valuable role within society. This reality has considerably conditioned the behavior of some of the respondents, particularly with regard to their choices about the education of their children. In concrete terms, many opted to send their children to independent [private] schools in the belief that their children would obtain a better, more rounded, more cultured education at these schools rather than at state [public] schools. Some originally sent their children to state schools and transferred to them to the independent sector. See, for example, Helena's reasons for transferring her sons. Others found that state schools were perfectly adequate, even preferable, for their

350

children. Galina sent one child to an independent school while the other child chose to stay at a state school. She also describes how, when she originally came to London, all Russian children had to go to schools provided by the Russian Embassy. When the system changed, she took her children out of Russian schools and placed them in the British school system. Perhaps the worst experience is that of Sophia who wanted her son to obtain a good *English* education. Her judgment was that the state school in which he was placed would make it impossible for him to do so. This started a long process of her keeping him out of school until he could gain admission to a school which she thought would be right for him.

What about the other parents in the schools, did you mix with them easily?

The reaction to this question was varied. Some of the women were able to interact with the parents of their children's school friends, but in many cases this depended on their varying ability to speak English and of course on their ease at socializing. Several felt that they had little in common with the other parents. Natasha qualifies this in terms not only of their different backgrounds but also, for example, of not sharing contemporary interests of importance to the other parents, such as current television programs or political discussions, etc.. Some felt more at ease with other immigrants who confided similar problems of adapting to this educational system. Sophia doesn't really want to mix with other parents because she doesn't want to make new [English] friends: she doesn't want to get totally involved in their lives as is the case, she argues, with Russian friends with whom understanding and therefore ease go deeper.

How did you experience your British neighbors? With whom do you socialize?

For some women this was a difficult question to answer because living in London, a very cosmopolitan city, many of their neighbors were not British by birth but had become British by becoming British citizens. In other words, their neighbors were immigrants just as they were. Many of these women have friends from every different nationality community represented in Britain. But they also socialize a great deal with people (both men and women) who were born in the Soviet Union, who share a common past and a common language. Many are anxious, however, to increase their friendship networks and by no means wish to limit their friendships to other Russians.

Was it a problem being a mother without your own mother or mother-in-law?

There were two distinct responses to this question. The first was given by women who greatly missed their mothers, especially when they themselves had children. They indicated that it was pretty tough in the beginning without their parents. Some of the (grand) mothers came to London when their daughters did have children and helped them out. Vera, for instance, spoke about how she only got a good night's sleep when her mother visited from Russia months after her son was born.

In the first part of the interviews many stressed the role that Russian grandparents play in helping to bring up their grandchildren, a fact which obviously changed once these women emigrated. Several spoke about how their friends in Russia were able to drop their children off with their parents and 'have a good life'. Others mentioned not missing a specific individual in their family but missed not having a family, being lonely; several others felt this wasn't a problem. Only a few spoke about seriously missing their mothers-in-law, although some of the women were very attached to them and have welcomed their mothers-in-law (and fathers-in-law) into their homes, sometimes for extended periods of time. In addition to the fact that these women miss or missed their parents in terms of childcare, etc., the older respondents also indicate that they now worry about their parents as they age, particularly as many of their aged mothers now live alone in Russia.

A second group felt that they didn't have a great relationship with their mothers and therefore didn't miss them to the extent that the first group did. One or two were really quite glad their parent wasn't in this country, a fact which, when they eventually did meet up, allowed the relationship to be more positive than might have otherwise been expected. Larissa, for example, argues for the greater independence of parent and child, noting that distance can certainly be beneficial in a relationship.

Issues about childcare didn't produce very startling answers. Those women who were working had similar difficulties in finding childcare as any other woman in London. Like them, the Russian women either decided to continue working in one capacity or another or some of them decided to stay at home and raise their children, waiting until their children were of school age before returning to some sort of employment. The one different factor, however, was that some definitely want their children to learn Russian and therefore they specify that the nanny or other helper should speak Russian to the child. For some this was very hard to actually accomplish.

Did you make gender distinctions in bringing up your children?

The majority of the women either answered this question in the negative or didn't really respond at all. Others said it wasn't gender that influenced them but different attitudes, such as Victoria who was aware of 'sort of less aggressive behavior [in her parenting] because life is much more comfortable and you are not that stressed. ... it affects your relationship within the family.' Liza admits that the UK probably affected her and her husband's roles as parents – 'here there is a very different concept of parenthood altogether -- more joint, more respectful'. Masha discusses her daughter who was born in Russia and brought up as a typical Russian child by three grandmothers, that is, having their full attention and their full support, in contrast to her son who was brought up in the UK mostly by herself. Maya says that when she had children her values were Western rather than Russian because she didn't have the experience of being a working mother in Russia as she left Russia at an early age. She was also brought up by her grandmother who didn't work, so she didn't have a role model for rearing children.

However, several of the women did say that they differentiated their parenting by gender. Marina says she acted differently in terms of her children's personalities and thinks that her daughter really was more like a

353

boy and her son was more like a girl. Three other women, however, definitely indicated that they would and did bring up their daughters and sons differently. The girls would learn to cook, clean, look after themselves and be family oriented as well as being gentle and feminine, whereas the boys would be taught to be strong and to be the boss, the main provider, in their own respective families. As Galina states, 'I still believe that at some stage the most important thing for my daughter will be her family, however educated she will be by that time.'

Shopping

After living in Russia, was **shopping** in the West every woman's dream? For some the answer was a resounding yes! Two of the youngest women said that they were shopaholics: one 'totally went out of her head' and the other was because she could shop without her mother's guidance. For the women in their 40s, some, like Larissa, found that shopping was her hobby for a long time. For Nadezhda it was a little bit more extreme. '... it [shopping] became like a nightmare almost every day. Shopping, shopping, shopping, buy this, buy that. With the ability to buy if you have money and the amount of goods in the shops, I went crazy. So I said to myself, No, no more, enough. I would say it was like an addiction, like an illness.' For others, shopping was thrilling, but since they couldn't afford it, they just liked to window shop. Marina was shocked when she first arrived because, as she put it, she came from a poor country and found shopping in the West very seductive. Those in their 40s who had travelled a lot weren't shocked by the choices but were rather very pleased. Only Sophia complained about the situation, mentioning the issues of status and money and her great displeasure about being here.

For the women in their 50s many found shopping exciting but also hard work because they had to shop for the whole family or the extended families that they had left behind in Russia. One solution was to go to the sales and to shop very selectively for items to take back to Russia when they next visited. For Liza, shopping was mind boggling and she wondered why she had to expose herself to it. In other words, the choice(s) was exhausting and suffocating, so she would have preferred to have one thing available, let us say a TV set, and that would be that! Victoria agrees that sometimes there was just too much choice. Masha, however, found shopping 'paradise' compared to Russia, especially in terms of food shopping. Maya, on the other hand, was underwhelmed because when she first arrived in the UK she lived in a small provincial town, a place where choice wasn't an option!

The women in their 60s seemed to present diverse answers. Of the two most recent immigrants Anna, who had already travelled in the West, was not overwhelmed by the variety in the stores but merely advocated that one 'couldn't compare two different worlds'. Kira, who finds London to be very expensive, now shops in Paris and the US when her husband travels there for his work. Nadia originally found shopping an enjoyable experience due to better choice, but is now a reluctant shopper, whereas Tamara was 'thirsty and hungry for shopping' and still is. She notes how women in Moscow present themselves as stylish and often go over the top, but this is a phenomenon she understands. Only Vera, who worked in a department store for a few months, muses on how easy it would have been to become a thief. 'I didn't have anything and of course I was pretty poor. I was going through all the departments to the exit and everything was there on display and I thought, Gosh it would be so easy to become a thief…. it was very, very tempting because the things were all there.'

Russian food

One might have expected that food would be one thing that most people leaving their country of origin would certainly miss. In the beginning, many of the Russian women did miss the food they were accustomed to, including caviar which we in the West consider to be a luxury. But many of them now feel that they can buy those same products in Russian stores or in the Lithuanian or East European stores which are now sprouting up over London. Some also mention that these products are available in some supermarket chains.. Helena, for example, observes that not only are there Russian and Lithuanian stores now in London, but in places like Sainsbury's you can buy thousands of ingredients from all over the world, a fact which has changed her outlook on food -- 'It's wonderful', she exclaims.

What did they specifically yearn for? The list, starting from the most mentioned, includes: bread, especially rye bread, tvorok [cottage cheese, curds], other cheeses, kaffir [sour milk], smoked fish, pickled herring, sausages, pelmeni [a kind of ravioli], borsht, gherkins [Larissa now grows her own], mushrooms and berries.

How did some of the women adjust to the different foods they found in the UK? Some had Russian visitors who, for example, brought to London the very same bread mentioned above, although Natasha (in her 40s) claims that bread in Moscow now is not as good as it was when she was a child, so she doesn't miss it. Tanya agrees, saying how she specifically used to miss smoked mackerel but when she went into her local Russian store and bought some, she ate one piece and felt that she couldn't continue because it was much greasier than the fish she now buys here. In other words, she isn't used to this particular [Russian] food anymore. Yevgenia specifically misses her grandmother's cooking and as a young career woman has not been able to find a good Russian restaurant in the capital (an opening in the restaurant market, no doubt!) Others quite naturally cook Russian dishes at home as they remember them.

A negative last view goes to Sophia who says that food shopping here is horrible. 'You are used to these tastes, we are used to different tastes. Everyone likes what he is used to eating from childhood. So maybe here the food is much more healthy, but I miss things such as foods which I used to have.... I cook a lot at home just to prepare food like in Russia. So when we go to Russia we put on weight. We just eat, eat, eat.'

How do you spend your free time?

Like educated and creative women elsewhere, many of these women go to concerts, the theatre, the cinema, museums, art galleries and read in their spare time. Others are involved in sports such as tennis or skiing, while some spend some of their free time guiding their visitors around London. Several complained that their free time depends on money or their lack of money as London is an expensive city. This fact made a few compare 'culture' in London with Soviet times where 'culture' was more affordable 'if you had access to the tickets, if you had *blat*, basically the latter being more essential. If you had these contacts, then 'culture' was quite accessible and there was a lot of it.' [Liza]

Factors relating to husbands

Has the role of your husband changed since he's been in the UK?

Running throughout the answers to this question is the underlying view that Russian husbands, indeed Russian men in general, are not, to say the very least, the most helpful in this respect. Take Vera's answer to how helpful or involved her husband (albeit she is the third wife) is/was in shopping, cooking, cleaning, and childcare: 'Never, good lord, never! Russian men were not brought up to help! The double burden remains in my marriage.' Nadezhda admits that her husband is very Russian and he says, 'I bring the money. So you ....' And Marina acknowledges that her husband is a 'typical Russian husband' who does none of the above. Larissa is quick to distance her husband from the generalization by saying that her husband is totally not a Russian as he grew up in the Caucasus where men were 'very gentlemanly to women.'

Many of the women, however, state clearly that throughout their marriage their husbands have shared in the domestic responsibilities. Victoria says that her husband always helped but surmises that maybe this was a class thing. She also notes that her father played a bigger role in childcare than her mother in Russia. Sophia's second husband continues to clean and shop just as he did when they lived in Russia. Others who say they and their partners did share these domestic roles did adapt to changes in the UK due either to: changes in status (the husband no longer cooks regularly on account of his important demanding job); because the husband's job was less fulfilling and therefore he became more interested in his family/home rather than in his job in Russia; or the husband had a fulltime job and the wife a part-time one. The oldest respondent, Anna, says that her husband's role hasn't changed, rather his life has changed as now he himself takes care of his 100 year old mother. She also says that he was the one to have a double burden as he not only worked but studied at the same time.

Those women married to British men indicated that 'we share our burdens' (Tamara). Put another way, Maya says that compared to her Russian friends, her husband always helped out. 'He couldn't sit and see me without lending a hand.' As Helena puts it, her husband 'helps her run the family.' Tanya's very British husband, her second, is certainly more involved in shopping, cooking, etc., than her first husband, but perhaps the comparison is unfair as her first young husband was fatally ill.

Perhaps the last word on this topic should go to Irina, a second wife, married to a Russian husband: 'Like cognac, he gets better with age.' Now he cooks a bit, takes care of the child, but is not into cleaning! She suspects this help wasn't the case with his first wife.

Whose job would take precedence, yours or your partner's?

While the women in their 30s did not answer this question, two of the women in their 40s said that they work together with their partner so everything was 50-50 or that both jobs were sacred cows! Two others stated that the man's career or job would take precedence over theirs: 'he earns the money'. Natalia explains that normally in Russia a man's job is more important than a woman's and adds, 'it's that Asian thing again.' The women in their 50s had little to add and agreed, except for Galina who said that whereas in Britain her husband would be paid more than she, this wouldn't be the case in Russia.

Of the women in their 60s, Nadia stresses that her husband's career took precedence, but it was her choice because she felt it was her duty and her priority to look after the children. Kira says in her mind her job took precedence because she was responsible for 'our life, our daughter, our holidays, etc......' Vera, on the other hand, humorously adds that her husband's job 'would always take precedence -- here, there or on Mars, anywhere!'

Ties with Russia

Does religion play any role in your life?

This question was asked on the understanding that the Soviet Union, where all of these women were born, strongly promoted atheism. Religion -- all religion -- was anathema to the regime, a position that changed in Gorbachev's time in the late 1980s. So how did these women answer?

The oldest women really said that religion means nothing and plays no real role or certainly not a big role in their lives. Only Tamara says she joined the Russian Orthodox Church in London seven years ago and she felt very much 'at home' in that church. [The troubles experienced within this Russian Orthodox Church in London have deeply affected her.] For the women in their 50s, two go to Russian Orthodox churches from time to time, mostly on special occasions; they do, however, find it easier to go to church when they are in Russia. Two others indicate that religion plays no role in their lives, Liza saying that she is a steadfast nonbeliever who has very little knowledge about religion. Only Maya, who says she's been an atheist all her life, occasionally goes to a Church of England place of worship because of her sons' quite early conversions. She feels that many Russian women go to the Russian Orthodox church mostly for reasons of nostalgia.

Two of the women in their 40s go to a Russian Orthodox church, often with their children but not with their husbands. They also find that it's easier to do this when they are actually in Russia. Two others say that religion plays no role in their lives, whereas Natasha converted to Judaism when she remarried.

It is the youngest women who seem to be the more interested in religion. Thirty-one year old Tanya goes to church every now and then, but says 'I wouldn't call myself an atheist but I wouldn't call myself a deeply religious person.' Another 31 year old, Yevgenia, was drawn very slowly into the Russian Orthodox Church by chats with her mother in Russia who persuaded her to go to church, to try to confess, etc.. Her mother shared some experiences with her, indicating how much she herself was helped spiritually in her own life. Her father, however, remains an atheist. Yevgenia herself is drawn to the warmth and atmosphere of the Russian Orthodox Church in London. Irina was christened in Russia as a Russian Orthodox and so was her young son. As a believer, she and her husband hope the Russian Orthodox Church in London will be open more frequently. She muses that many of the people come to the church because this is an opportunity to speak Russian.

It would appear that the anti-religious campaigns in the former Soviet Union affected the older women whereas the youngest are least affected. On the other hand, the church could be acting as a home away from home, a place to speak one's native language, to socialize with those coming from a similar background.

What do you miss the most?

The first answer to this question is invariably friends and family. But of course there are many variations, including the comments from all of the age groups that emails and reduced telephone prices have made communications with friends and family much easier in the last few years. The youngest women especially miss their family, their grandparents, even their dogs. Irina offers a counter argument to this loss with the following Russian saying: 'it's not the place that makes people better; it's the people that make the place better.' And Yevgenia feels that she can no longer really communicate with her friends from the past as their lives have taken such differing routes.

The women in their 40s also miss the cultural environment that they came from. Some say that even though London does have a fantastic cultural environment, it's not in the Russian language. Sophia was very involved with one particular theater in Moscow and she specifically grieves for that. Helena, on the other hand, cites the loss of St. Petersburg as her beautiful city but also misses the easy camaraderie which exists between Russians. Larissa interestingly notes the loss of her younger self. Nadezhda, on the other hand, says if she wished for anything she would just buy a ticket and go back!

Like Helena, the women in their 50s talk about the loss of their friends and family but specifically mention this loss in terms of the closeness of Russian people. Liza emphasizes this by adding that she misses being surrounded by 'very reliable people'. Galina says 'I miss the life I'm used to' and now sees Moscow sort of as a place to visit on holiday. The only material thing Maya misses is her house in Moscow.

Of the oldest women, two now say they don't really miss anything, adding either that people currently in Russia are 'mad' or that Russians are open, gregarious and sociable. Those close, intimate friendships of the past are what Tamara misses least. She wants her [Russian] neighbors to leave her alone as she has now reached a stage in her life where she wants more space. So she doesn't miss the closeness she experienced in Russia, even though she liked it when she was younger. Now in her 60's she has had enough of taking care of everybody around her! The final response comes from Nadia who says that yes, she misses family and people, but 'I'm here and I'm going to live here. End of story!'

Would you [ever] want to go back to live in Russia?

Some answered emphatically, 'Never, never, never.' Vera even said, 'No, if God is kind enough!' and Larissa indicated, 'Not if I can help it.' Some can't imagine going back to live in Russia unless something drastic happens in the UK. Some reasons for not going back include the difficulties for academics to work in Russia, the more positive response that life in the UK is far more comfortable than life in Russia today, and if comparing Moscow with London, London wins in terms of people and lives being less aggressive. A young Yevgenia offers that 'I love working in Moscow... but I just feel living there is so different. It's not an easy city; it's quite an aggressive city.... It's very dynamic but it's constant pressure, constant stress. I don't like it but I like to get an injection of it from time to time but then come back to London and relax a bit.' An older Victoria (in her fifties) adds 'the more we stay here the less feasible it is. You know it's a completely different country [Russia].... Several things have changed completely and it's not easy to adjust yourself to the way of life there. There are still a lot of difficulties people have to overcome whereas life is much more comfortable here.'

Some say they would not go back in the foreseeable future but maybe would, for example, if the art market in Moscow or the job situation in Russia is better. Others have maintained accommodation in Russia, in Moscow or St Petersburg, either as a stopgap measure, to have a place to visit, to use as a source of income by renting the property, and/or as a place to return if and when their aging parents need their help. Others manage by visiting once or twice a year.

Two replies do stand out. One, from a young mother, offers another pithy Russian saying: 'You can be happy, even in a tent', meaning in her case that it's not a problem where she lives as long as it is with her husband. The other response comes from an older Russian: 'I don't know whether I'm settled here, but I am settled *out of* Russia.'

Equality, femininity and 'strong woman' today

Equality

Discussions with the oldest women about the topic of **equality** often invoked the reply that they never thought about it and they also hadn't changed their views, that is, coming out of the Soviet Union, they felt that equality was a remote 'problem' because 'we are all equal, I've never thought that women had to fight for their rights because their rights are all equal' and they didn't understand the search for femininity. Nadia says 'I never thought [feminism] was really justified because I think men and women are absolutely different beings. The difference is just as important as the similarity, and that's it.'

The women in their 40s conceptualize equality often in terms of men being equal to women, rather than the reverse (!), in that now men also cook, clean, take care of children. They often note that they have the impression that in British families the husbands really do help the wives. Some, like Larissa, think that we in the West have probably gone too far with equality, citing lawsuits by women who are (supposedly, she surmises) harassed by their male colleagues, or like Natasha who feels that it's strange when a woman is or actually chooses to be the main breadwinner. Helena argues

362

that emancipation hasn't necessarily been a fantastic thing for women. And Galina in her 50s notes that although she's never tried to apply for a job, she judges by what her daughter is telling her that women are pretty equal. 'I have never heard of any occasion when my daughter was treated inferior to boys. I have the impression that girls are [now] being treated better than boys.'

The inter-generational responses to the concept of **femininity** are quite one-dimensional. They would all agree that femininity for Russian women is usually related to appearance: image for Russians is very important. As Maya puts it, 'in Russia in terms of makeup and clothing, I always thought I had to make an effort. Russian men expect Russian women to present themselves. They do care about it.' Masha puts it more graphically: 'women shouldn't lose their role of decorating men's lives and I think men should have this attitude as well.' This boils down to looking nice, being presentable, wearing high heels, having a nice haircut, having a manicure. They often comment that the majority of Russian women really do take care of themselves, whereas several women note that British women aren't looking after themselves properly -- not dressing elegantly, not looking after their hair or their makeup. As one put it, she could tell who is Russian and who was not by the way the women dress. So clothing and makeup are very important. But some of the women add that for them femininity means looking after their family, while Natalia criticizes the culture of binge drinking as not being very feminine. Victoria sees women losing their femininity because they have to compete with men. In order to compete, they have to become more masculine, less feminine.

Several women point out changes that they see in Russia which they now conceptualize as a money oriented society, a society which has had effects on the nature of femininity. Marina says that. 'some women are going to the streets to sell themselves, some women are going to university, and some are having a really good job by making a lot of money.' A younger Yevgenia adds that 'Russian women are quite educated and they really have great potential, but many women just decide that the main goal of their life is just to find a man... I often see girls of my age [late 20s early 30s] just try to be cool and make men work, make men pay, make men buy.' So she hints that a new definition of femininity for Moscow girls includes being pampered and spoilt, being rich, going shopping, going on holidays. Natalia suggests that women who can't compete with men as great managers will decide they'll marry quickly, marry very rich men. 'A lot of girls now think not that they'll do something interesting with their lives or have a family, but they all think about lifestyles, just because they will marry quite young, very rich, no matter how old the guys are.... The real ambition is to go to work as a secretary and get married eventually to a rich man.' Galina is somewhat more optimistic that women now have a choice: either to have a proper education and make a career, or, if not good at education or a careerist, she will make a perfect wife. 'Then she will find a rich husband, she will look nice [be feminine], she will be a good mum, she will learn the art of making a beautiful house, designing it. What she wants, she is choosing!'

Thoughts about London and the United Kingdom

What do you value most about living in London?

Almost without exception all of the women have something positive to say about living in London. For some the word freedom was the first thing they noted. This freedom often meant freedom for themselves, that is, personal freedom to make choices, sometimes moral choices. Sometimes freedom meant that nobody would or could meddle in their affairs or it meant one's personal safety in spite of one's political activity or political affiliation. Others mentioned the cultural Life in London, the variety, the diversity, the entertainment, the art exhibits, the theatres, the cinema, etc.. This was often linked with the ability to and the pleasure of walking in the center of the city. Some mentioned the architecture and the environment. Others spoke about their security living here, whereas some mentioned the pleasure of anonymity, independence and privacy that a cosmopolitan city brings. 'If you need something material, you call central London; you see it, you have it all.' [Galina] Put another way, what Liza values is: 'it [London] is relatively relaxed and convenient (I mean the creature comforts) which can't be compared, even now in Russia. You have to go through painstakingly organizing your life in Moscow to get the same standards. Here it comes naturally; you don't have to be anybody to live like that. In Moscow, it's

364

possible but it needs a lot of work to create the infrastructure.' And continuing comparing London to Moscow, some felt London wasn't as stressful a place to live; it was a quieter city, a city where you were not being watched as you were in Moscow. But perhaps the most poignant response comes from Tamara when she says 'What I value most [in London] is my husband and having a home at last!'

What do you value least about living in London?

The largest response to this question has to do with money. London is an expensive city to live in and to take advantage of all it has to offer. This is even more accurate now with the current recession. Another complaint has to do with the transport system (as compared with Moscow) and with traffic jams experienced in the capital. Other negative answers include: food in restaurants [the cuisine], specific situations about crime [see Nadezhda], and Marina's nervousness on the buses. Contrary to some of the other respondents, Victoria misses the closeness of people, whereas Natalia comments on the 'pc ness' in the news, about what's going on politically. Luba, the one respondent who has returned to Russia, comments unfavorably on the behavior of youngsters in her area.

How would you characterize British society?

While some of the responses in the previous section would apply here, there are many others which arose in the interviews. Some may be conditioned by how long the respondent has lived in Britain or by age; perhaps maturity is a factor here. Some mentioned aspects which they found attractive when they first arrived but which have now changed. Others offer more personal responses, arising from specific situations (such as in Irina's case).

Starting with the most common or shared responses, the adjectives which are most used to characterize British society are: positive, tolerant, fair, decent, rational. These are followed by an appreciation of British traditions and values or as Yevgenia puts it, 'it's been here and it will always be here.' As Sophia declares, it is an old conservative society and traditional society;

365

'sometimes I realize that the problems I have are 100 or 200 years of history.'

Several women touch on Britain's democracy and democratic traditions. Larissa states that Britain is one of the best democratic models that exists. Tamara thought it was 'wonderful to feel that you can afford your democracy and your very wide feeling about the world.' Tanya thinks that the UK is more politically evolved than Russia, adding that this is really a question of trust: 'I just think sometimes you're [the British] so naïve, you don't know what not trusting is and what it means not to trust your government.' What Larissa loves about this country is the fact that a politician can't ignore what's written in the papers: 'I think the press is free.' [They don't all agree about this.] Helena argues passionately that Britain is a 'fair meritocracy.'

Another positive characteristic was patience, but this characteristic was also criticized. Take Nadezhda's remarks that 'it's too patient. What's happened in the last 10 years, I think British society is too patient. We came to live in one country and now it's completely different, for example, in the way of crime.' Victoria agrees with Nadezhda when she adds that 'you may see a lot of changes happening in this respect. I think some disintegration is in the process and [since] you ask me what I treasure, I think what I like is the law-abiding part.' Several others mention most positively the fact that the British are law-abiding citizens.

Other responses contradict each other. For example, Anna finds the people she knows to be very friendly and Galina notices a very appealing combination of friendliness and independence. On the other hand, Marina says she meets mostly nice people but 'it takes a long time for people to open up, say 10 years!' and an older Tamara originally thought the people were cold and remote, but now she's glad the sort of closeness she experienced in Russia is no longer happening for her. Natasha feels that the English are much closer to the Russians than to anybody else because, as she says, their inner life is very deep. 'On the surface they are very much uninterested and very [un]excited about what's happening, but actually they feel very, very deeply.'

366

Natalia offers a somewhat different analysis about relationships in Russia. She says Russians are 'very good at empathy but only if you are very down, very sad and very upset and very unsuccessful: everything is wrong in your life. If you bare your soul (*dusha*), then you share it with everyone and you'll get a lot of empathy. If you are confident, successful, strong enough, there will be no good feelings towards you.' This she contrasts with British tolerance. Perhaps this is related to Maya's analysis that the British are very good at gray areas, that is, she finds in Britain that there is always another view, another perspective. She indicates that over the years she herself has changed and finds that Britain exhibits a liberalism, an acceptance, a tolerance which suits her.

The older women also mention that a lot of people of their generation are now quite disturbed, quite dissatisfied. They indicate that many things have disappeared which were social cushions, like social provisions/requisites such as NHS provisions, difficulties with and/or lack of pensions, school system complications. They suggest that these things were available for which you didn't have to have much money, whereas now you need to have money for most things (bear in mind that these comments are all pre-the enormous government cuts of 2010.)

Some other negative comments include a discussion of the role that new immigrants may play in this society. (See Irina) Helena also questions why the working class isn't motivated to improve itself and adds that intellectuals are despised here (it's a dirty word). Yevgenia has noted that British families may not stick together and says that the institution of the family is not strong here. She has noticed that young people may lose the sense of family as a unit. She counterbalances this by saying that this is quite a stable environment.

One final, yet troubling, interjection comes from Liza. 'British society is fine as long as you don't start to pretend to be part of it. That's when you really get slapped on your wrists.... I think it has been proven over time if I or anybody crosses the line. It is a fair enough society if you obey the rules.' So the positive idea and requirement of having law-abiding citizens runs deep in the psyche.

Comments in addition to the formal interview

Sometimes the women added topics which they specifically wanted to be aired, some of which are noted now. Sophia, for example, discusses her **hopes** for the future, namely, that she would get a job in London. This led to a discussion about how *blat* works in Russia where everyone tries to help and where a good word from one person would allow another person to be employed, no matter how qualified on paper one was. Unlike Sophia's disappointments with living here, Masha says 'there have been no **disappointments** about living in a Western society'. Nadezhda adds that her children are happy here and she is pleased to have made the move; she's also changed her occupation.

Others have argued that **education** in the UK should be broader and more intense at the same time. Natasha states that she chose the area she lives in because of the education system and says that *the* value that she instills in her children from Russia is education. Galina notes that education seems to be less important now than it was in her day in Russia, although 'I believe that university is the most important stage not because of the future profession or anything, but just because it's a stage of life. We always believed that you must get educated.'

Some want to stress that we in the West believed that **life in Russia** was quite uniform, that is, that we only think of Russia as a society arranged on one-note rather than a society being a rich tapestry which it actually was. Victoria illustrates at some length that we in the West didn't realize how rich 'the cultural life was in the Soviet Union and how much we read…. The West had no idea how we really lived.' Nadia cogently discusses the role escapist Western [American, British, German] movies played for her. Sophia suggests that ' people were much happier [pre-1991] than now because they were sure about their future. It was not necessary to think about pensions, about money in the future. Everyone was stable more or less, everyone could predict their future. When my son now watches Soviet films, I tell him, "Look, nothing in the shops, no food, just three things …only one type of bread, only one type of sausage, one type of shoes! Look, it's horrible." When he's watching the films he says, "Mum, look, people look much

368

happier. They didn't know what was going on around in this capitalist world, with horrible mafia crimes, etc. There are no tramps, no homeless people!" Our parents' generation regrets so much of this communist time. They were safe, they felt much better, they were happier....I think our generation is suffering because we were brought up, half of our life in Soviet Union with communist/socialist ideology and the second part of our life is completely different, completely money market oriented. Since I am in London, every day I think money, money, I have to get money, I need it for this, to go there. Before I didn't know this word [money]. In the Soviet Union it was a shame to speak about money. Now it's all changed. *Blat* is important. When my dad came here, and we were out, I told him, "Dad, money is everything. Why didn't you tell me, you never told me this!" He said because money was nothing.'

Two other negative views about Russia come from Irina and Luba. Looking back to **post-1991 times in Russia**, Irina describes how 'it was very hard for everyone. A lot of educated women had to forget their hopes, their desires, their dreams -- everything. They had to fight for their rights and for their living because the government was not paying money to teachers, doctors or nurses and all people in similar occupations. The only place you could earn something was in commerce, so a lot of people with degrees or PhDs or higher education sacrificed that and went into commerce simply because you can earn decent money or just money for living. ... You have to be nice to people, you have to educate people. But if you're hungry, for example, or if you don't have a pair of tights or shoes or your shoes are broken and you can't afford to buy a new pair, that situation was really as bad as war time. Society divided very fast, between poor and rich, and for some people, even the rich people, it was just beyond reach.'

Luba was **depressed about going back to Uzbekistan** because of the 'national problems. I am Russian and not an Uzbek. The main language is Uzbek ... and they prefer people who are Uzbek. I think it would be better to go to Russia for my son. I don't see any future there [in Uzbekistan]. **Uzbekistan** is getting worse and worse. When I entered university in the 1990s, many professional teachers who were Jewish tried to go to Israel or America, wherever they could go. Too many really educated people left....So now we don't have any teachers. Therefore students on the last course were teaching arts to students on the first course. What kind of education can they get? You can pay for all of your exams and get good marks. For example, now I don't trust any medical doctors because all of them just pay for their diplomas. Most of the people now go to private clinics; the clinics are more trusted. In the Soviet Union, education was good; health care was good – much stronger than today.'

Yevgenia in contrast is much **more optimistic**. 'Overall, being a 1990s child, I think it has been such a turbulent and exciting time. I feel very privileged to go through this and to catch one life and one set of rules, and then go through this huge change and come to a different country and experience all this. At times I wonder where I belong. I know I'm Russian, I'm proud to be Russian, I always will be. Sometimes it makes me think: I look at my parents and they are quite specific in the way they are. My grandparents are even more specific -- their mindset, their ideals, what they think.... I feel quite European, quite cosmopolitan, but at the same time Russian. ...The fact is I've changed so much, so many degrees.'

The last thoughts -- both positive and thoughtful -- belong to Maya and Liza. Maya says that it 'never occurred to me that I would be a foreigner for the rest of my life.' Liza adds, '...in Russia whatever happens, even now, it is my personal pain and my personal shame, mostly both combined. Here I am **still a foreigner**. I may regret certain things and I may be cross about certain things but it is really not in my backyard. I don't feel like it is my personal problem. So in many ways my feelings and my emotions are spared here rather than in Moscow. At the end of the day, I guess I belong to neither society -- Russia and the UK -- so there is a price to pay. So that is fair enough. But without underestimating the rest of it, I absolutely love London. **I think it is a fantastic place to live!**'

After Thoughts

The twenty-one women who have shared their experiences here have led varied lives, in both their country of birth and their adopted country. Some were well connected: one parent or both belonged to the Communist Party, making at least some parts of their lives somewhat easier. Some conversely suffered because one or other of their parents came into conflict with the Party, requiring the whole family to move from one location to another. For others, their decision to marry a 'foreigner' shaped both their own lives but also affected those of their parents, in some cases deeply.

These differing experiences show vividly the effects of the times in which the women lived. Some endured the very difficult constraints during the time of Stalin whereas others experienced a true loosening of the reins in Gorbachev's perestroika period. Others lived through the difficulties of the chaotic years following the disintegration of the Soviet Union or those marking Putin's rise to power. But the lives of the twenty-one show that lives are shaped by place as well as by historical context. Many experiences were determined by where each woman lived in the Soviet Union, with better facilities and better opportunities in Moscow and Leningrad/St. Petersburg compared to other cities, let alone those found in the rural regions. Parental educational attainment and/or occupation also determined much of their early lives. Gender was a further significant factor, especially in terms of education. Religion played some role in their past, notably for some in terms of anti-Semitism affecting as it did education, future careers, ability to travel, perhaps even limiting whom they could marry. These issues did not apply to those whose parents or grandparents were Russian Orthodox although religious practices of all denominations were frowned upon.

Alongside differences, however, common elements are clearly identifiable. Of particular interest are the shared values from the past which shaped the women's lives in Russia as well as in London. Marrying young, that is, in their early 20s, was generally *de rigour* although some did marry later. The same could be true for the early age at which they started a family. Unlike in the West, the idea of abortion(s) was certainly not discouraged as it was often a -- or the -- means of contraception, given the state of contraceptive methods in the Soviet period. At the same time, very few mothers informed their daughters about anything to do with sex. Schools were also of little use in this area. What was shared was a strong emphasis upon the importance of a good education. If there is any shared element between Soviet and Russian society as far as 'ordinary people' are concerned it is this necessity of having a good education. Education was a deep Russian cultural value, one expressed in the past through in provision of one of the main avenues of social mobility.

Many of the women stressed the significant role their mothers or their mothers-in-law - but mainly their mothers - played in helping to raise their children. (They also noted that their fathers were involved in this task as well.) In practice, this meant that grandmothers, many of whom had had careers of their own, either stopped their jobs in order to help their daughters or, where they had already retired, were expected to help with childcare. This was particularly so in the not infrequent cases where the young couple lived with one or the other in-laws.

What of their migration? The women came to the UK at different times, under different circumstances, arriving either alone or with a husband or a prospective husband. In the beginning, coming to the UK may have meant different things to different women but, with the exception of Luba who unwillingly went back to Russia, they have all really settled here. Only a few of the women in their 50s thought they might in the future return to Russia, mainly to help care for elderly parents. Some of the others' answers about returning could be classified as (more or less) hypothetical, perhaps containing an element of wish fulfilment, along the lines of 'it might be nice to'. The oldest women, however, were emphatically clear that they had no wish to return.

What stands out in all the discussions of the migration experience is the difficulties these immigrants had with the English language. Most had studied English either at school or at university. When they actually came to the UK, however, they found that their spoken English was either archaic, non-colloquial, too accented and so forth. Reading 19th or 20th century English literature had not prepared them for speaking in the $20^{th}/21^{st}$ century. As a consequence many felt they were being spoken to very slowly or even very loudly, as if they were children. Many experienced 'personality changes' which consequently made them question who they were. Some hated being known as 'foreigners' for an indefinite period of time. Some couldn't get employment because of their lack of understandable or current English. Of all the problems the women encountered being immigrants to this society, including adjusting to the climate, to the transport system, to buying or renting property, to choosing schooling for their youngsters, language was perceived as the biggest obstacle. This certainly doesn't mean of course that most of these women have not conquered their initial fears and inability to speak English, something which distinguishes the older women in this study from those in some other migrant communities. After all, the interviews were conducted in English.

Some of the women certainly missed the atmosphere of their youth. They indicated that they missed the place, for example, where they could hear their own language spoken on the street. But in general what they missed most was friends and family, or in some cases family and friends. Several went back to Russia each year to visit. In other instances their parents (and in-laws) made the trip from Russia to the UK, sometimes staying with their daughters for several months during the year. (Here the age of the parent was the determining factor.) These visits made the separation more bearable for some although many said the toughest separation time, both emotionally and practically, was when their children were young and their parents weren't nearby.

While there was some nostalgia for what had been lost and a frequent continuing concern over familial separation, there was a definite and almost total consensus that they are very happy to be living in London. There is a strong awareness of and pleasure in the opportunities that London has to offer in terms of culture, architecture, parks, cuisine. Equally, most have positive things to say about the UK. This doesn't mean that they aren't critical of various aspects of life here and of certain characteristics they see as 'British', but they appreciate the values of a free press, the strong attempts at meritocracy, the form of British democracy, etc..

Ultimately the life experiences of each of these women have been unique. But as these concluding observations demonstrate, there are clearly identifiable patterns of divergence and commonality running through their lives. In an age of ever-increasing social migration, the parallels with the experiences of other groups of women from other cultures and places are many. Here I would emphasise the importance of the fact that this study focuses on the experience of women coping with the particular obstacles and possibilities, both natural and social, that are uniquely experienced by women.

At the beginning of this book, I indicated the circumstances of its inception. It was of interest to me and hopefully to others to chart how the different experiences of several generations had influenced later experience in a very different time and place. That I hope I have done. But I have to confess that as the study progressed something else became of greater importance. To give the intricate detail of this group of women a voice, a voice which hopefully will resonate to the lived experience of many more women in differing times and places.

Glossary

Asood	automated management system
aspirantura	post graduate degree
babushka	grandmother, old woman
beriozka	pre 1989, luxury shops open to foreigners and soviet workers returning to the USSR with foreign currency
blat	use of personal networks, acquiring goods and services and eluding formal channels or procedures
blinchik	pancake, fritter
dacha	house in the country; summer house
dotsent	lecturer; docent; in higher educational establishments
dusha	soul (as in Russian soul)
glubtsy	meatballs in cabbage
GIMO	State Institute of International Relations
GUM	State Universal Store
Izhdivenka	a dependent
kaffir	sour milk
kolkhoz	collective farm
Komsomol	Communist Youth League

Lishniye biletek	spare/extra tickets
MGU	Moscow State University
MTS	Machine Tractor Station
nash	ours; similar to us
nomenklatura	list of appointments reserved for the Party
oblast	region
obshezhitie	dormitory; hostel
Octobrist (Young)	Communist Party youth organization (7-10)
Party	member of the Communist Party of the Soviet Union
pelmeni	kind of ravioli
Pioneer	Communist Party youth organization (10 – 14)
piroshki	pasties, pastries
propiska	residence permit; identification document
raion	district
samizdat	self-published material (previously illegal)
special schools	schools mainly (but not only) for foreign languages
toilet	central public toilets (mainly in Moscow) which had a reputation for selling black market items, especially clothing (sold by speculators, black marketers)

tvorok	cottage cheese, curds
til	military term
uchillishche	school, training or technical college, between A and O levels
vrednost'	unhealthy conditions of work
znakomstvo	circle of acquaintances
8th of March	International Women's Day

Suggested further reading

Bridger,S., Kay, R. And Pinnick, K. (1996)   *No more heroines?: Russia, Women And The Market.* London: Routledge.

(how women are coping in post-Soviet Russia, especially with unemployment)

duPlessix Grey, F. (1990) *Soviet Women: Walking The Tightrope.* London: Doubleday.

(discusses the double burdens of home and career for Soviet women)

Engel, B.A. and Posadskaya-Vanderbeck, A. (1998) *A Revolution Of Their Own: Voices Of Women In Soviet History.* Oxford: Westview Press.

(stories of 8 women's lives, spanning the twentieth century)

Hansson, C. and Liden, K. (1983) *Moscow Women: 13 Interviews.* New York: Random House, Inc.

(13 first-hand accounts of the lives of Soviet women since the 1920s)

Holland, B.(ed.) (1985) *Soviet Sisterhood.* London: Fourth Estate Ltd.

(focuses on the lives of ordinary Soviet women)

Ledeneva, A. (2006) *How Russia Really Works: The Informal Practices That Shaped Post-Soviet Politics And Business.* Ithaca, New York: Cornell University Press.

(from blat in Soviet times to new informal practices in Russia)

Mamonova, T. (ed) (1984) *Women And Russia: Feminist Writings From The Soviet Union.* Oxford: Basil Blackwell.

(a samizdat collection of interviews with a wide-ranging group of women)

Printed in Great Britain
by Amazon